Weighing the Cost of Pin-making

For all of you lovely
friends at the Thayer-stay mad house.
With love and appreciation —

always,

Renni

8/9/12

Weighing the Cost of Pin-making

ULLI BEIER
in Conversations

Edited by Remi Omodele

AFRICA WORLD PRESS

TRENTON | LONDON | CAPE TOWN | NAIROBI | ADDIS ABABA | ASMARA | IBADAN | NEW DELHI

AFRICA WORLD PRESS
541 West Ingham Avenue | Suite B
Trenton, New Jersey 08638

Book and cover design: Saverance Publishing Services

Library of Congress Cataloging-in-Publication Data

Beier, Ulli.
  Weighing the cost of pin-making : Ulli Beier in conversations / edited by
Remi Omodele.
    p. cm.
  Includes bibliographical references and index.
  ISBN 978-1-59221-859-2 (hard cover) -- ISBN 978-1-59221-860-8 (pbk.)
  1. Beier, Ulli. 2. Critics--Germany--Interviews. 3. Authors, German--20th
century--Interviews. 4. Africa--Civilization--20th century. I. Omodele, Remi.
II. Title.
  PT67.B37W45 2011
  809'.896--dc23
                        2011032926

Dedication & Gratitude

To Ulli, with love. The one who is not forgotten lives forever.

And to the brains behind this volume: A special salute—
For want of a just anthem.

To the readers who will find herein
An iota of truth, epiphany, joy, though with its alloy of sadness
Or all of the above.

For vital support and favors too numerous to list:
Professors Akinsola Akiwowo, Lucia Birnbaum, Erckad Breitinger,
Muyiwa Falaye, Duro Oni, Niyi Osundare, Dapo Adelugba, Margaret Wilkerson.
The Adeniyis, Georgina Beier, Yvette Chalom, Ann Einstein, Candace Falk,
Bunmi Fatoye-Matory, Mama Britta, Kacke, Sven, Hideo Ikegami-sensei,
Redmond-Fayiga, Dr. Chidi Achebe, Jumoke, Dr. Robin Gal, Senait Kassahun,
Foluso Omoyeni, Katherine Salahi, Michelle Sutter.

My teachers and mentors—past, present and yet to come.
My family all—near and far
And my friends—the family to whom luck has led me.

EyeDeto, Mama, AbaModele, AbaRifayan , Oba Adegoke Adegboye, Oba
Ogbenuotesoro, Oba Adewumi Aromolaran:
For all the doors you opened.

For showing the kind of interest that makes this work worth my while already:
Aba, Nick, Keinde, Naomi, Ade, the Abioye kids and our growing clan.

To Kassahun Checole, a Publisher with foresight.
For husbanding this project expertly: Damola Ifaturoti

To my own dear Ric:
For being there—always and completely!

And to the ancestors—yours, therefore, mine:

My undying thanks.

Contents

Iwa L'Ewa: A Preface in Verse

by Niyi Osundare

Iwa l'Ewa
(Character is Beauty)

He came
At the dawning of our letters
when an inchoate alphabet challenged our Silence

He came
when old myths dispensed their mysts
And syllables read the dew between the lines

A fame-fraught fog
Played hide-and-seek with the top
Of the trees. Thunder rumbled

In the western sky. He traced its path
And reaped its bolt. He urged the sun's
Chequered journey across day's unsure expanse

He spelt it out in black and white
with chalk from the egret's quarry
And charcoal from the hearth of simmering tales

From his primal chiaroscuro,

A rainbow which counts the blessings
Of liquid colors

The day broke on his brow
Fledgling letters glimmered
Into soaring songs

He did not come to rule
He never came to reign
He only came to learn
And, learning, became a *Tisa*

Osun welcomed him with open waters
Softened his road-hard sole
With her liquid lore

Crabs scrawled his name on clayey banks
Fishes sang his favorite song
The pigeon feathered his fame

To near and distant places
A fire came from the watery depths
And lit him a torch that never flickered

Palaces threw open their gates
For the new and curious guest
Who knew how to eat with elders,

Having washed his hand in Wisdom's bowl
Beaded crowns nodded in assent
From Osogbo to Okuku

From Ede to Ikere Ekiti
Royal drums sounded his name
From the origin common lores

His ears played host to new sounds
He absorbed their syllables
And divined their meaning
 Measuring every inch of their lengthy proverbs.

Ancient shrines offered him a seat
The *Orisa* regarded him as one of their own
Ifa saw his shadow on the divination tray

(His coming came as no surprise
His future feats glowed between the beads)
Ogun knew the metal hint at the tip of his pen

Oya greeted the new comer with a laughter
Quiet as a waterfall
Sango gave him fire to forge his thoughts

Obatala lent him a calabash of clay
In his wall-less house at the Crossroads
Esu cleared all debris from his path

Beloved of Earth and Sky
He rose, re-born

Walk free, Wayfarer,
The roadside grass moves
To the rhythm of your wind

On your right side is Wisdom
On your left Respect
The world has built you a garment of Honour

When you walk

You will not stumble
When you talk

You will not stammer
Walk free
Omoluabi for whom

Character is utmost Beauty

Bible-bled
Quoran-crazed/conquered
We threw out our household gods

Trampled ancestral heads in alien mud
Twisted our tongues to the tantrum of foreign names
Consigned our skin to the blackest hole of hell

Having so obliviously denounced our depths,
How blissfully we floated on the surface
Of foreign fads

You beheld the plague and its cruel contagion
As you pilgrim-ed through the land
Re-assembling scattered godheads

Pristine songs, the drum's broken dialogue
And legs which craved the urgent
Resuscitation of missing steps

At your instance,
Sango set Europe's stage ablaze
With the triumphal virtuosity

Of long-maligned tribes
Oh how so *wholly*
The promise of your pagan campaign!

Mbari o mba jo (If I see this I will dance)
Mbari o mba yo (If I see this I will rejoice)

Memory sprouts, grows,
Fruits, rots to seed;
New roots rise from the ruins

Of old, striving paths,
Spent sweat from the biceps of the gods
Billows into rivers which run through

The toes of shifting mountains.
Murmuring masks, stately statues
Shelves weighted down by the sheer

Cornucopia of artistic harvest,
Stacked floor to roof
In a house of multiple echoes

Mbari o mba jo

Let the season's rain un-do
The children of many fires
Let the old house soften

Into a quarry of new clay:
The past has countless ways
Of addressing the future

Mbari o mba jo o
From the eastern bank of the Great River
The name travelled west
With you as votary and vector

Took on a new accent, a new song
Became the rallying point and fledgling ground
Okigbo's *painted harmonies* saw first light here

As did JP's tide-empowered musings
Soyinka ambled across the stage,
His hands laden with ticking scripts

Nwoko's protean brush populated the canvas
With layered symbols and marvelous structures
Indigo fingers from Ede, Osogbo,

Bata batiks draped the walls
Of Imagination's house
The Mbari smock trumped

The arrogance of chiefly robes

A Black Orpheus had come to song
Lyre in one hand, gong in the other
A seamless future was ripe for rescue

Mbari o mba jo o

Old songs, new voices
Old drums, new accents
Old names, new meanings:

This Renaissance moment
The past re-born

Coming moons pulsing in purple winds
The harvest was almost within our grasp
When the streets ran red with tribal terror
And wardrums silenced the dance of leaping dreams

Our *iron chapter* had just begun. . . .

Akanda, Akanni, *okunrin takuntakun**
Obotunde ore Ijimere
The witty one who knows the hidden

Wisdom in the Monkey's name
Friend of the Rain
Consort of the Rainbow

Sun which rises from every sky
Agbe lent you a sea of indigo
Aloko pampered you with a pot of *osun****

Lekeleke anointed your nails
With the divinity of ivory
From Papua New Guinea

To the hills of Okuku
You wander through the world
In a garment of many colors

---

*   Praise names for the brave and boundless
**   Pseudonym adopted by Beier
***   Camwood
Tisa: Teacher (an iconic figure in old Yoruba society)

Glossary of the Yoruba pantheon in the poem:

Osun is the goddess of River Osun; also goddess of fertility, compassion, and justice

Oya, the fearless goddess of River Niger and Commerce; renowned as the most powerful of Sango's wives

Sango, who reigned as an Alaafin of Old Oyo Kingdom, was deified upon his death as the god of thunder and lightning

Ogun, god of iron and metallic lore; of technology and creativity

Esu, denizen of the crossroads and god of happenstance, is the god who purposely complicates the plot in the drama of human existence to teach tolerance and balance

Obatala is the asexual god of creation and guardian of spiritual and communal ethos

Ifa, Yoruba's supreme medium of divination, is the source of wisdom, knowledge, and the science of being.

(Remi Omodele's assistance with the glossing of the pantheon is gratefully acknowledged)

Niyi Osundare, New Orleans, SC, 2010

Africa's Future and its Ancient Heart: A Preface

by Lucia Chiavola Birnbaum

Full of wisdom that generates the reader's insight, this anthology reminds me, as a feminist cultural historian, that there are many ways of knowing. It also confirms my belief, based on my research findings, that people at the bottom of hierarchies have persisted in keeping ancient ways of knowing and surviving—despite the contradictions that pervade human nature and history. This phenomenon might account for why the fool or the lowly folk—manifested as animals in African folklores—frequently prevail. We may be living today in one of those periodic upwellings of ancient wisdom that have dotted human history, a time typically characterized by the phrase in this anthology, "desperate optimism". The last significant time this upwelling happened all over the world, in my view, was the 1960s. Today, world conditions of life have worsened; it's apt to call our optimism "desperate".

From my perspective, an Africentrist feminist cultural historian, the upwelling comes not only from Africa where contemporary African women are attempting to rescue traditional African values of caring, sharing, and healing—values that hark back to the earliest communities of homo sapiens in south and central Africa after 100,000 BCE. As I have shown in my books, Africans took these beliefs with them when they migrated after 50,000 BCE to every continent (as has been confirmed in the DNA by geneticist L. Luca Cavalli-Sforza). To genetics data, I have added the findings of my on-site research, notably in the Africa-centered regions around the Mediterranean, to support my hypothesis that ultimately African values of caring, sharing, and healing are a part of everyone's unconscious or archaic memory.

This African legacy of beliefs in caring and healing, in my hypothesis, has persisted throughout history and may still be glimpsed today in indigenous cultures. The values, even in distorted forms, also persisted throughout the historical epoch in folklore and the oral traditions of subaltern classes—women and "dark others".

One of the gifts of this anthology is that it reminds the reader of a persistent, non-westernized tradition originating in Africa, a treasure trove of human values existing before and extending beyond the fences of institutionalized religion. Yorubaland, a case in point, confirms the hypothesis that traditional African society may be regarded as the world's source of beliefs in caring, sharing, and healing. This anthology highlights the surviving models rooted in the tendencies among indigenous societies to foster harmony, evenhandedness and consensus by holding land and other resources in common, or loan, to be returned to the community when necessary.

We know from genetics as well as the oral tradition that women were the original gender, whose signs—the pubic V and the color ochre red, connoting blood of childbirth and menstruation—point to women's magical power of giving birth. The significant relationship of African as well as other indigenous traditions is that of mother and child, not male and female. Interestingly, gender relationships in traditional societies are playful and shifting: Oduduwa is sometimes the creator of the earth, a male god who descended from heaven, but sometimes he appears as mother earth herself. Sango is sometimes worshipped as a woman, and whatever the case, devotees always appear in public dressed as women with hairdos to match.

African beliefs are not cast in stone tablets, but fluid, adapting to circumstances. This is in consonance with the belief that Obatala has many manifestations, and like humans, he has weaknesses. He creates humans not once, but continuously. Obatala endows everyone, including those with imperfections—albinos, hunchbacks, and lunatics—with dignity and respect. In this space or mindset, "different" religious beliefs or lifestyles are not *othered*, but considered enriching.

The divine spark is in everyone; the purpose of humans is to discover and be in harmony with the divine spark. Thus, Africans strive for balance between humans and gods, other humans, plants, stones, all of nature. One learns by listening to drummers and chanters at festivals; by listening to the stories and riddles of elders; by participating with one's parents at work and during conversations. In dramatic distinction to modern religions, gods and the world are not separate, but interconnected. The paradoxical god, Esu, by challenging existing ways, creates the possibility of newer, innovative, and more harmonious ways of living. Elders, who are respected for their accumulated wisdom, transmit this wisdom in the oral tradition. Women's power in traditional societies is not power over, but a spiritual power that emanates from her, imparting ancestral values while she nurtures—like all grandmothers—children, grand children, elders, the extended family. Women's particular spiritual power is suggested in the most explosive thing a woman can do—kneeling down holding her breasts. "In that position she speaks to the Orisa and the Orisa listens to her. Anything the woman says while in this position has the possibility of coming to pass." Men live with this power of women, knowing that women may hold nominal political power, but that political power is sustained by women's spiritual power—and checked and balanced by women's actual veto.

Children learn by being, and working, with their parents and the extended family. They learn via experience how to behave morally by acting in harmony with their own "*ori*", and in particular, by learning to be patient, and calm. In ancient African traditions, teachers encourage students to ask large questions: What it is to be human; how we can responsibly use the world's resources; how to foster human creativity. This last point, human creativity, is crucial because the world's resources are finite, but if we respect every human, we have an infinity of human imagination and creativity that enables us to overcome adversity, to endure great natural and human disasters, and create better societies.

Perhaps due to their awareness of this, indigenous societies place great emphasis on liminal times of life, times which were/are often suggested by festivals at which the ancestors are present. These festivals validate the community's resilience by celebrating the past, which is essentially a reminder that every moment has its possibilities, and as such, we need to be sensitive to when it is time to try the new.

So in our own recent era of the 1960s, in the United States as well as across the world, the ancient extended family mindset or psyche returned—even if momentarily—and the lowly people of the world clamored for, and demanded vociferously that we must learn to live, once again, communally. (There was indeed some hope that cooperatives might become the significant economic unit!) We began to see that it was possible to live ethically—without decalogues. We declared that it was possible to spar without ever destroying one another or "the other." We learned that culture could never be separated from economics, politics, or the images in our heads. Ultimately, we saw how ancient wisdoms could connect the world; how imagination could nurture empathy for "others," inspiring us to work for a better world by shifting our focus to *abo*, that tranquil (feminine) realm with its values of caring, sharing, and healing.

Lucia Birnbaum, Berkeley, January 2011

Introduction

The Growing Catastrophe: No Room For Wisdom

by Remi Omodele

Preamble

I never thought I would find myself engaged in a project such as this one, but that was before my fortuitous encounter with Ulli Beier—the man, his work, and his life. As it happens at least once in the life of a typical African, the question of the continent's perennial, endemic, and overwhelming dilemmas had created a few sleepless nights. Beyond the dilemmas themselves, however, the glaring absence of wise and commonsense solutions was confounding.

In response to my questions and ideas, Ulli Beier bombarded me with an impressive array of documents detailing his immeasurable experience and work. For me, the Conversations in this volume stood out, and history might prove them to be some of the most profound and comprehensive commentaries on the issues pertaining to Africa particularly today. In a nutshell, whether implied or intimated, the significance of these Conversations resides in the extent to which they expose today's absence of wisdom in political and private life in a typical modern African community. But it is worth mentioning that the wisdom void in reference is not a uniquely African phenomenon; it is indeed a catastrophe of global proportions, a catastrophe in need of serious, urgent and candid attention.

Speaking of wisdom, outside of appearances in such jocular or derisive expressions as *wise guy*, or *oh, you're so wise* and similar putdowns, the adjective *wise* and its noun, *wisdom*, no longer occupy a pride of place in any modern community or parlance. *Wisecracks* are *cool, emotional intelligence* has had a cameo appearance, and the king of them all—*smart*—is in vogue. Barack Obama is constantly described as smart, and many have called him the smartest President the US has ever had. I have often wondered why the term *wise* does not apply. Is Obama too young to be called wise? But even the elders in the Western hemisphere are rarely described as wise. When was the last time we heard of a wise Senator? I followed the tributes that poured in for the late Senator Byrd, and was surprised to see that wisdom was not listed as the Senator's top attribute. Could it be that our focus on the rather impersonal aspects of science, technology, economics and politics has led to the virtual deletion of this mighty word from our lexicon? It was interesting to hear that "The Committee of Wise Men" had formed to manage the volatile situation in Egypt during the February 2011 uprisings, but that committee was short-lived. As it turned out, not many took it seriously, and perhaps deservedly so. The wise men did not consider the exclusion of women from their committee a serious lapse. So much for wisdom in the 21st century!

Yet even a cursory examination shows that wisdom, at its rudimentary level, is essentially good judgment grounded on intuition, the basic knowledge of right and wrong coupled with the ability to distinguish between the two. When viewed in this manner, we see that knowledge and wisdom are intertwined; that knowledge can further wisdom. But the relationship gets slightly complicated. For one thing, it is possible to be knowledgeable without being wise. But it is impossible to be wise without being knowledgeable. The question then among ancient Africans pertains to the type of knowledge that is most desirable. The definition or the most valued type of knowledge is that which embodies the quintessential ways germane to a society's wellbeing. The mastery of these ways is the cornerstone of a typical citizen's personal accomplishment, and when this mastery is combined with yet another mastery, the judicious management of knowledge, such a citizen is considered to have gained wisdom, and this stage in life is both age- and gender-neutral.

It is quite remarkable that one of the key issues or concerns shared by Ulli Beier, Sophie Oluwole, Roland Abiodun, Chinua Achebe, Richard Olaniyan, Ibrahim El Salahi, Biodun Jeyifo and Wole Soyinka—whether directly or otherwise—is the dearth of wisdom and commonsense that has come to typify the average modern African community, particularly at the intellectual and leadership levels today. In addition to exposing the demarcations and contradictions between today's practices and those of the past, these thinkers also do a brilliant job of illuminating the paths that Africans and the rest of the world must travel to overturn the current state of anomy and bring about meaningful change. To this end, this volume is a clarion call indeed.

Personally, I am grateful that my search for answers led me to these brilliant minds who—rather than simply harp on the ills of the present—speak candidly to the profundity of the simple ways of the past by sharing their personal experiences and exceptional insights. From their early childhood, these notable men and woman were exposed to indigenous culture and influence—even when their parents made concerted efforts, as in the cases of Oluwole and Soyinka, to thwart their interest or exposure. In a typical African community the focal point of childrearing was the integration of the child into the community in such a way as to forestall alienation and the possibility of purposelessness, thus imbuing a solid sense of identity which in turn furthers respect for oneself and one's community. Communicating these types of values, done usually in very subtle ways and forms as described by Abiodun, meant that child rearing occupied a pride of place, and all hands were on the proverbial deck; everyone was a parent—hence the axiom popularized by Hilary Clinton. It literally took a village. In this milieu Oluwole and Abiodun show us how children were encouraged and expected to acquire wisdom even before they were capable of learning practical skills, and we see how seamlessly the seemingly impossible feat was accomplished quite early in the child's development.

When Ulli Beier landed among the Yoruba in the 1950s one of the first things that struck him was the centrality and indispensability of wisdom to the dealings and practice of the elders, whether in the public affairs or religious spheres. He also observed that the people were fervently committed to work, to industry, toiling from dawn to dust—contrary to the wide-spread notion of the lazy African. Interestingly, a firm connection between industry and wisdom has always existed in the psyche of the Yoruba. For the Yoruba, the biggest obstacle to the attainment of wisdom is the type of suffering caused specifically by extreme material deprivation. The Yoruba believe that suffering is sometimes unavoidable, and that like everything in life, it might have a purpose. While it might be useful momentarily however, suffering—if prolonged—creates depravity and warps the sufferer's sensitivity. Therefore, the avoidance of suffering is the goal of the average citizen's daily pursuit, and the Yoruba often devote an inordinate amount of time to activities and ways of life that serve to ward off suffering. Indeed the goal of all religious observance or devotion is to prevent suffering, or in the event that it is evident, eradicate it. So one of the main attributes of a typical god or goddess is his or her ability to overturn misfortune, and redirect the victim. Thus, when one's lot is not aided by one's god or goddess, one shifts allegiance, exploring other viable options. Being able to do this is the prerogative of a healthy, independent mind—evidence that one's personal god and constant companion, *chi* (among the Igbo) or *ori* (among the Yoruba) is still intact. Ultimately, though, the chief antidote to suffering, as specified in the age old axiom, *ise l'oogun ise*, is hard work with its essential elements of discipline and sacrifice; hence the Yoruba's fervent devotion to industry.

It is interesting to note from the foregoing that religion was once one of the tools available to the African to use as a guide, not fatalistically or as the opiate that modern religions, the monotheist ones in particular, have become in Africa today. For the individual as well as the collective, monotheism has created monolithic problems. As is crystal clear throughout this entire volume, pantheism or polytheism provides a variety of answers to a variety of situations and has an adaptability that makes it the perfect antidote for the inflexibility that has trapped the modern world: one ring to rule us all, one solution for the energy crisis, one answer to every conundrum, one party of values versus another party of values. We are stuck; we are not collaborating, we are not connecting, and we are not wise.

That Beier recognized the place and value of wisdom in his new home was a mark of his own wisdom. The man who has come to be styled "German-born Yoruba" had no trouble relating to the ancient African ways for, after all, one of the greatest attributes of wisdom is its power to connect peoples—regardless of the distance that nature and other elements may have put between them. During my stint in Japan my friends and students often characterized my ways as *nihontekina*, (archetypical Japanese). Unbeknown to me at the time, that was a great compliment since *gaijin* (non-Japanese) are typically *not* expected to understand, let alone, exhibit Japanese sensibility. When I explained that many of those ways were actually native to me, my listeners were usually surprised. Apparently, no other peoples or cultural values were supposed to be similar to those of this ancient, polytheistic island nation.

Like many who studied in colonial institutions, I too learnt, and indeed believed, that all peoples were essentially different from one another; that not only were Africans different from Europeans, but Africans themselves were also distinct from one another. There were, after all, hundreds of "tribes" and languages. This type of thinking permeated the consciousness of the typical early scholar and rendered palatable the specious claim that Africans needed the new ways introduced by the colonizer to become civilized and united. The underlying intention, explicitly, the economic ambition of the colonizer, was always well concealed. Indeed today, regardless of how often history has exposed the lie of the colonizer's claim, colonization continues to be trumpeted as essential and good for Africans. Hardly do we ever hear any serious voice suggesting that in the cat and mouse game of colonialism, Africa lost more than it gained or that it continues to lose more than it will ever gain.

To say that the tragedy of the erstwhile civilizing mission is often underplayed is indeed an understatement. First of all, it is often forgotten that to attain and retain the colonial values, the life-affirming ways of a whole race of people—languages, traditions, religion, technical skills, art, and all that identified one as a 'tribe'—had to be jettisoned. Those who resisted the call were summarily dealt with—whether by getting their arms amputated as was the case in the Belgian Congo, or at the very least, they risked being marginalized permanently in their new nation. Whatever the approach, the outcome of the encounter with the colonizer is that Africans have continued to find themselves in a place of limbo between two colliding worlds. Rather than living freely and as the brilliant innovators history and Ulli Beier have shown them to be, Africans have remained, essentially, grotesque imitators, living by the vacuous values long jettisoned indeed by those who ignorantly imposed them. So completely disguised are the ills of the colonial influence that even today, the common tendency on the part of most analysts or experts on Africa is to blame the turmoil in the continent on its elite and series of inept leaders. The rational here is a simple one namely, that African leaders have had enough time to overcome the ills of subjugation, and any way, for how long will the colonizer be held responsible for Africa's woes?

To call this sort of position fallacious is to do it justice, whereas it actually deserves none. The real question is: What has been done in any concrete terms by the United Nations, or any institution for that matter, to undo the ills of colonization and seek alternatives to neo-colonization? How long must Africans wait for the birth of states that are really for them, by them, and of their own making? For how long must Africans continue to live essentially under indirect rule, that is to say, under a scheme whereby the Western world, largely through its corporations, continues to determine African leadership and economic systems? Recently, France, Libya's former colonial master, led NATO to oust Moammar Gadhafi and free the Libyan people from his oppression. Having refused to step down and go into exile when told or advised to do so by the Western powers, the usual alarm was sounded: Gadhafi was "killing his own people." The African Union's diplomatic efforts—led by South Africa's president, Jacob Zuma—were rudely brushed aside. The war to remove Gadhafi has wreaked havoc on a largely defenseless population and killed thousands. But some believe, however, that the uproar is over oil. In "Reports Suggest French Intelligence Encouraged Anti-Gaddafi Protests," a report for California-based *Center for Research on Globalization*, Alex Lantier wrote:

> The French ruling class was intent on boosting its market share in Libya. Before a December 14-17 [2010] visit—by French banks Crédit Agricole and Société Générale, engineering firms Alstom and Thales, and construction firm Lafarge—*Maghreb Confidential* wrote: "French firms are determined to climb higher in the ranks of Libya's trading partners. Italy is currently in number one position, with China second and France a distant sixth."

This story is a reminder, as Ulli Beier recalls, of Britain's main concern on the eve of the chaos that eventually led to the Biafra War: "Nigeria was a big market," and as such, it could not be allowed to split up. Thus, the actions taken by France are in keeping with the proper roles and expectations of a former colonial master, given the main consideration behind the creation of the so-called African nations. Approximately 127 years ago, in a pernicious, if relatively bloodless move, Africa was carved into what now constitutes the continent's nations primarily as gifts, also called protectorates, to the dominant European nations of the time. This singular 1884-5 act at the Berlin Conference effectively ended the people's autonomy. Under the new dominions, Africans got new identities—languages, religions, rulers, boundaries, political systems, ethics, laws and ideologies. The new identities called for a rejection of everything indigenous, except when such could be manipulated to serve the needs and desires of the European overlords. By the mid-1960s, most of the nations were granted autonomy by the colonial masters. On May 25, 1963, the newly formed Organization of African Unity (OAU) hastily recognized the new nations—in spite of obvious and pressing questions about the validity of the so-called nations. Needless to say, none of these nations had the luxury of a debate to determine the bases for the nationhood or the identity of those trapped within the boundaries. There was no time or opportunity to craft either an Article of Confederacy or a Constitution (as was done in the early years of the United States).

Countless books have been written from various perspectives to address the damage this type of trauma can cause to the collective psyche of a people, but to date, any effort to address the artificial boundaries and the incongruous, unworkable nations they demarcate quickly leads to civil wars which invariably lead to a waste of innocent lives without resolving any of the major issues at the heart of the discontent to begin with. After unspeakable devastation and untold profit in the coffers of weapon makers and dealers, a flurry of mediations and peace talks headed by the former colonial master follow and the fractured nation is patched together. In addition to outbreaks of wars, the continent and its people have been undergoing every type of make-over imaginable, but it is obvious from the state of a typical African nation that rarely are the people's lives impacted positively by the endless cycles of make-over.

This calamitous state of affairs is hardly surprising; it is a logical outcome of a faulty foundation. How could the destruction of the ways that had served the people for millennia, their collective humiliation, the brain-drain and the continued rape of their land's resources not lead to a major or indeed irreversible damage to the African psyche? In Western psychology and psychiatry, it is believed that being forced to deny one's identity, values, spiritual heritage and one's very uniqueness or fundamental nature can result in various forms of mental disorder. But when it comes to Africa, this view is discarded in favor of a convenient myth, the myth of the inept African. What is more disturbing is that Africans themselves—due to colonial education which guarantees a lack of awareness of Africa's own traditions of strong leadership—have begun to fall for this myth.

Interestingly, the deficiencies of the education available under colonization—an education basically designed to clone clerks and administrators for colonial work—was already obvious to many 'illiterate' elders who frequently remarked that 'book learning ways were artificial, shallow and inadequate'. Like Ulli Beier, many parents and elders openly questioned the relevance of schools to communal life, but those elders had no way to contribute what they believed would complement the new import. So the schools as well as the churches taught, and still teach with impunity, lessons that guarantee the end of African ways of life. And when or where traditional or tribal ways of governance have managed to persist, they are largely anemic and exploited for ephemeral ends. Under today's political configurations as in the colonial times, even the few elite who might be aware of the efficacy of traditional ways are also persuaded that traditional political systems carry the stigma of *tribalism*—that boogeyman of colonialism. To be an acceptable political player in a typical African nation, a politician must disavow traditional practice, which often necessitates the ritual of name change, to be considered fit for office.

The tragedy here is glaring. While Africans spend the bulk of their energy and time separating the modern from the ancient, the Japanese and the Chinese alike carefully and seamlessly integrate every modern import into their traditional ways of life. In Japan, my children happily joined their friends to worship at the ubiquitous children's Shinto shrines depositing gifts of food, pencil stubs, coins *en route* to their ultra-modern, state-of-the-art schools. At home, they worshipped at the families' conjoined Shinto and Buddhist shrines adorned with the images of primordial ancestors as well as recently deceased infants. Similarly, in the Jewish communities around the world, the children are taught the Torah, and are expected—by ages twelve for the girls, and thirteen for the boys—to understand and comment extensively and intelligently on assigned portions of the book. African children, on the other hand, are introduced to foreign ideas and languages, baptized with European or Arabic names, and persuaded to desecrate or destroy shrines and other icons of the ancestral past. Africans have replaced their own gods and goddesses with the harsh and vengeful male God of the Torah and the saints fabricated by the Roman Catholic Church. So, in a typical home, African children grow up watching their parents set up shrines littered with poor reproductions of European images, thanks to Michelangelo di Lodovico Buonarroti's ubiquitous works—*Pieta, The Last Judgment, Doni Tondo, Tondo Pitti, Crucifix, Madonna of the Stairs* and by far the most popular, *Christ Carrying the Cross*. I have met African Christians who showed me a photo of Michelangelo's *Christ Carrying the Cross* as hard evidence that Jesus died on the cross for them.

These limited or ignorant views and choices invariably distract Africans from appreciating their own deep roots, the very roots that connect them to one another as well as to the global community. The educational institutions, vastly colonial and antiquated, continue to keep the African mind collectively closed. In many cases, Africanist scholars, with their focus on regional studies, add to the problem by creating little niches and irrelevant academic pursuits. Thanks to these experts, we often hear that Africa is too big to be viewed, or claimed, as a unifying experience or identity. Lately, the notion of sub-Sahara has gained currency—though the so-called 'sub-Saharan' nations are located squarely in the Sahara, not below it. According to the architects or propagators of this bogus invention, Egypt, as a relative once bluntly informed me, is not in Africa! The implications are clear: Egypt, having been colonized for so long, and its priceless artifacts all white-washed, even Africans are confused about the real root of ancient, indigenous Egyptians—a confusion which many Egyptologists have since addressed admirably. In Cheikh Anta Diop's seminal study, for example, he provided ample evidence of Egypt's African roots. Diop showed the world that the Africaness of the ancient Egyptians is discernible in works by classical authors of antiquity as well as osteological measurements, blood groups, and melanin found in the mummies. Similarly, according to Josef Ben Jochanna, an Egyptologist who once taught at Cornell, the *Papyrus of Hunefer* enshrines the words of an early Pharaoh's admission that his ancestral home was the land beneath "The Mountain of the Moon", the actual meaning of Kilimanjaro. As Africans migrated from the Upper Nile, they formed settlements known as Nubia, and the Nubian pyramids and tombs have been found to be older than those of the Lower Nile by as much as one millennium. In the 1980s, some artifacts previously discovered in Nubia, and kept in storage at the University of Chicago's Institute of Oriental Studies, were analyzed by Bruce Williams who claimed that the artifacts suggested that the ancient Nubians "may have reached this stage of political development as long ago as 3300 B.C.—several generations before the earliest documented Egyptian king." Paleontologist Louis Leaky devoted much of his life to proving that life, not just the early Egyptians, began in the Upper Nile region.

While we are encouraged to dismiss Africa's cohesiveness—either on the basis of its size or diversity—the world largely regards China as a geographical, cultural, and political entity. One can, therefore, safely speak of "Chinese food" or say "I'm Chinese," but a similar claim regarding Africa invites an interrogation: "Which country?" Also, many so-called Africanists have popularized the idea that no one region or people can present their culture as African because that would be viewed as essentially imposing one's culture on the entire continent. Thus, I have already been forewarned that some will view this volume as too West African to be considered pan-African. To be honest, I was once prone to this way of thinking. A person of West African origin, I was surprised to hear fellow Zulu, Nshona, Luo, Ndebele, Kikuyu, Swahili, Lingala, and Arabic speaking Africans enunciate some of the thoughts that I had been taught were uniquely Yoruba or West African. Thanks to my exposure to the aforementioned fellow Africans and notable scholars such as Hassan El Nouty, Kwabena Nketia, and the Father of Indigenous Sociology, Akinsola Akiwowo, it became evident that my previous lessons derived from the purposeful divisiveness perpetuated by the colonizer who rated the colonized Africans according to his whim or interest. Thus a typical community or protectorate was always bifurcated; the favored group was rated as unique and set up above the other hapless group or groups stigmatized as 'inferior'. This bifurcation, this deliberate pitting of group against the other, is a well-known tactic for exploitation. There were indeed instances in which the colonizers actually succeeded in fabricating new 'tribes'—the Hutus and Tutsis being perhaps the best publicized instance. History has shown that factual as the claims of 'antagonistic tribes' may sometimes seem, such claims were often based on superficial observations, exaggerated, and subsequently codified to be used as a tool to 'divide and conquer'.

These unfortunate tendencies, as Ulli Beier's experience and work in Africa demonstrate, did not have to be the outcome of the Europe-Africa encounter. But the need of an insatiable empire and its allies overrode what had been, or could have blossomed into, peaceful encounters, trades, and mutually beneficial exchanges such as documented in the case of the Bakongo and Portuguese peoples. Greed turned what could have blossomed into a mutually enriching encounter into adversity, exploitation, and eventually, slavery—one of the most heinous crimes in human history. And when the need for slave labor was superseded by the need for raw material for the newfound machines, colonization ensued. Once on the ground, colonial administrators used every power, including their military, to cower African leaders and terrorize the people into submission. In 1863, Adele, the King of Eko (now Lagos) was instructed by the British governor to cede Eko to Queen Victoria, and when he refused (because no king had the right to give away the people's land), the town was shelled by British gunboats, the king publicly humiliated, fined 50 pounds to pay for the cost of the shelling, and then warned "to cease the use of so objectionable an expression which might cause him...trouble." The so-called punitive raid on Benin City by the British in 1897 handed the raiders some of the world's most impressive collection of art work. The king was arrested, removed from his throne and Benin lost not only its king and priceless art collection, but also its monopoly on palm oil and other commodities, thus ending the kingdom's political power and economic freedom forever.

Perhaps the greatest tragedy is that even today, most Africans are unable to see the connection between this unfortunate chapter in their history and today's dilemma. Evidently, this inability is due to centuries of material and spiritual pillage, the relentless erosion of the African's self-confidence and wisdom. In various and complex ways, the erosion of the value systems necessary for direction and coherent existence has led to today's decay and lack of direction. Although it is not altogether unnatural to use the present to gauge the past, it is egregious and ironic, given the evidence at hand, that today's decay and lack of direction should serve as the basis for judging and discrediting African traditions.

But once viewed on their own terms and without prejudice, it is easy to see, as Beier and the speakers in this volume make clear, that the dearth of indigenous wisdom as well as rational values of the past is indeed at the heart of today's anomies. Conversely then, a return to the humane values of the past is the road to real progress. Once asked if Beier "sees the total absence of [Africa's] all-encompassing wisdom in the syllabi of colonial and neocolonial educational systems as the primary factor accounting for the precarious African present," Beier was unequivocal.

> Yes! The Ifa oracle is a great source of wisdom and something that our modern wisdom can be measured against. It could indeed fulfill the same role in Yoruba society that the Bible fulfils in Europe.

Ulli Beier also recalls that some of the positive and rapid progress he observed in the 1950s, his own contributions included, were as a result of the roles played by those who knew how to ground their policies and activities in the ancient traditions and cultures of the people—even when the traditions were not accorded an official space in the new colonial system. This insight informed Beier's approach to his own projects, interests, and development. Now in Australia, Beier continues to advocate and speak to the crucial role of African wisdom in the people's everyday life.

Beier is usually introduced as someone who "needs no introduction." This widely held opinion makes a lengthy biography on the man unnecessary. The same is true for the other exceptional thinkers and artists—the 1986 Nobel Laureate, Wole Soyinka; artist, Ibrahim El Salahi; novelist and professor, Chinua Achebe; historian, Richard Olaniyan; and philosopher and scholar, Sophie Oluwole—whose vital words and experience make this volume possible. What should be of interest is the justification for publishing this two-decade old collection in the year 2011, and there is sadly—as is already discernible from the foregoing—more than enough to write about this question alone.

Since its premise is, bluntly put, that Africans, like most ancient peoples, possess powerful institutions and great wisdom, it is important as a prelude to raise a set of simple questions upon which to predicate our discussion. In the face of the depressing state in which Africa has continued to find itself in the modern era, is it possible to uphold any claim that Africans have indigenous socio-political models that can replace the current unworkable systems, and on which to base an improved future? Although the models are well-documented and evidence of Africa's ancient accomplishment abounds, of what use is the evidence under the present circumstance where Africans have been so effectively turned around that they negate or undermine their traditional areas of strength? The conundrum inherent in these questions reminds one of Lakunle, a charming character in *The Lion and the Jewel*, one of Soyinka's earlier plays. In Lakunle Wole Soyinka treated the world to an articulate, well-read village teacher who is also conversant with traditional values. But as Lakunle no longer believes in traditional values, he must rely solely on his Western ways and skills drawn from his school books. Against the versatile village belle, Sidi, and Baroka, the foxy traditional ruler, however, Lakunle comes off as a caricature, a hollow man, and in spite of his sophisticated modern way, he is a failure.

Ulli Beier tells the story of Reverend Ransome-Kuti, the father of the celebrated musician Fela, who would later turn the real family name, Anikulapo-Kuti, into a household name. According to Beier, Reverend Ransome-Kuti was convinced that his good manners and accomplishments were as a result of his exposure to English customs and sensibility. Beier, who was familiar with both English and Yoruba ways however, believed the Reverend was more Yoruba than English. But the Reverend's attitude was in keeping with the prevalent attitudes and prejudice of Victorian Lagos, Abeokuta, and other colonial enclaves. African inhabitants of those enclaves indeed today still tend to be proud of their colonial heritage, quite as those who would later be styled as *beentos*—those who have been to Europe and returned to Africa believing that they are no longer African. As Sophie Oluwole observed, these Africans—even as they exhibit some of the deepest Africanisms possible—are always convinced that their ways are new and European or rooted in biblical injunctions.

As mentioned earlier, the ignorance exhibited by modern Africans is often the result of inadequate exposure to the indigenous value system as well as a lack of comprehension of the foreign ways they have adopted. I am reminded of a former colleague who used to argue that African women were, prior to colonization, an oppressed group. My ex-colleague argued that the types of freedom I claimed women enjoyed—freedom similar to the types Ulli Beier describes at length in this volume—would be deemed deviant behavior, and any woman who dared to engage in them would be subjected to swift actions to bring her back to her senses. It eventually dawned on me that my colleague and I had two opposing definitions of *freedom*. Additionally, her orientation was bound by a particular type of city life, the colonial life-style rooted in the Victorian. Like many today, my former colleague viewed women's liberation strictly in terms of monogamy versus polygamy and the attainment of Western education versus the lack of it. Nevertheless, she eventually spent some time with her great-grandparents away from the city, and to her credit, she left the village convinced that the women were not the oppressed group she erroneously believed they were. This is a testimony, were any necessary, to El Salahi's view that the dichotomy observable in women who live in the city versus those in the village is easily traceable to the 'stranglehold' which the adoption of foreign values has put on city dwellers, the stranglehold from which village dwellers have, by and large, been spared. But not everyone has the opportunity to have the benefit of the exposure which my colleague in the above story eventually enjoyed, or the capacity to observe, as Beier did, what could sometimes be very subtle forms of independence. Sometimes excessive devotion to the imported ways also renders a typical African convert impervious to the notion that indigenous traditions have any positive values—even when confronted with overwhelming and convincing evidence. Some converts' abhorrence of African traditions invariably leads to the elimination of dietary, aesthetic and practical habits that are of proven benefit. A professor once explained that he got rid of his collection of priceless tribal masks and paintings because they harbored "evil spirits". These spirits often walked out of the wall hangings to attack him, and it was during one of such attacks that he became a born-again Christian.

To the above type of converts must be added yet another type, namely, administrators and technocrats, particularly those whose education and training have conditioned for careers that are usually at odds with indigenous cultures and interests. As such, these people serve their nation as ultra nationalists, and they are convinced that the only valid systems of government and economics are those that are direct imports from, or traceable to, the West. To this group indigenous methods are unacceptable because they are "tribal" ways, and "tribal" ways constitute a threat to national unity. Thus, the solution to every problem is an imported one, a neocolonial one which invariably must involve the IMF, UNESCO, and more recently, the NGOs complete with foreign experts. Unlike Ulli and Georgina Beier's efforts in Osogbo, for example, the problem with these imports is that they are too removed from the people to be of any real and long-lasting consequence. Unlike Ulli Beier's, the altruism of the neocolonial connoisseurs and financiers is questionable, though their goals are obvious. The Africans who serve either as assistants or independent NGOs can be baffling or ambiguous. Recently a well-meaning activist told me that the focus of her activism and organizing was the elimination of Africa's image problem. This activist's plan was to engage an American Public Relations firm to repair the image damage.

An image problem? The Yoruba would liken this approach to that of a doctor who obsesses over ringworm while ignoring the patient's leprosy. It was hard not to point out to the activist that if Titanic ships were to dock at every African harbor today, welcoming aboard everyone willing to leave the continent, the world would witness an exodus of cataclysmic proportions. Though many would evacuate out of sheer ignorance, most would be justified for such is the level of desperation and hopelessness. It was sad to see that her image-makeover agenda had no component that would address the desperation, the continent's perpetual turmoil in spite of its abundance of resources, the backwardness as well as the absence of organic and home-grown approach to social and economic planning; nor had the activist in question taken some time to assess why all the earth-shattering makeovers, books, debates, movements, protestations, discourses—Negritude, Out of Africa, Not out of Africa, The Bell Curve, Black Power or Afro-centricism, to cite but a few—only end up being nothing but a pile of books and purple patches.

I am convinced that anyone who is genuinely interested in finding serious answers to Africa's endemic problems can benefit from many of the alternatives provided in this volume—Ulli Beier's insight, his monumental work in a variety of fields, and his remarkable achievements. What is extraordinary about Ulli Beier's approach to his life's work is that it is informed by commonsense and a truism, namely, that for a society to be truly productive, the people's integrity and dignity must be recognized, given a pride of place, and left intact. Any tampering with the people's integrity and dignity, no matter how well intentioned, is likely to have detrimental consequences. Beier's success is a validation of his own unshakable conviction that every society has something to offer itself; that a typical society has more to offer itself in the long run than any imported or imposed systems—even when fueled by the best intention—can ever hope to achieve. After all, although each society has its own inadequacies or contradictions, it is equally true that the paths or seeds to organic and lasting resolutions are often to be found in the contradictions themselves. Thus, Ulli Beier constantly put the people at the center of his work, and nothing was ever imposed. To this day, he remains of the opinion that he is indeed the beneficiary of his dealings and encounters. Beier's unquestionable accomplishments should serve as a lesson to today's philanthropists, the World Bank, IMF, NGOs, and development economists with a focus on Africa.

To know and understand African traditions the way Ulli Beier does is to be simultaneously in awe of them, but also disappointed that these traditions are on the fringe rather than serving as the basis of public life—moral, religious, political, and economic. In my travels and sojourns in a variety of places around the world, I have come to realize that the further a people are from their cultural traditions psychically, the rockier their road to advancement. Even from a practical standpoint, the exclusion of African traditional models from the array of problem-solving mechanisms available to Africans imposes a serious limitation. In other words, given the endemic nature of Africa's continued failure to find lasting and creative solutions to what are indeed simple problems, a level of flexibility is desirable. An African aphorism comes to mind: "A giant in a proverbial Ekiti town went missing, and the search party turned over everything—including cooking pots." The point is that when seeking solutions, indigenous African wisdom mandates a thorough search, and most importantly, the collective effort of the affected community is enlisted directly. This aphorism also implies that for the search to bear fruit, it must be far-reaching, extending indeed to those areas where *the* answer may not necessarily reside. Such relentlessness coupled with open-mindedness is, after all, the stuff of any serious search. Another aphorism speaks to the need to impose a deadline because time is too precious to waste. So, a community must know when to abandon practices that are provably ineffective or futile. So, for the Yoruba, there is the proverbial trial period of twenty years after which even a devotee ends his or her devotion to an Orisa if no meaningful goals are accomplished: *Orisa ti a ba fi ogun odun sin, ti o ti ba gbe ni, nse ni a ndeyin.* Sadly, this mindset is lost to modern Africans who now view religion as a means of securing a place in heaven—although it is obvious that the religious leaders reap material profit here on earth in direct contradiction of their own teaching. Today, a vast majority of Africans spend more time holding prayer vigils that roll from nights into days, and churches mushroom at an alarming rate. It is in fact fair to say that Christianity is now the fastest growing industry in Africa. The continent has become a fertile ground, once again, for overzealous preachers who exploit the peoples' hopelessness and lack of direction, the seeds of which were sown by the forefathers of the new preachers.

So religion and other forms of entrapment continue to fulfill the purpose for which they were originally designed, namely, to condition the citizens so they can continue to carry out the ultimate purposes for which their so-called nations were created. Happily, no one in their right mind questions the assertion that the purpose of every nation created by the colonizer was to produce and deliver raw material to the colonizer. It follows then that for the colonizer's agenda to succeed, it was necessary to found the nations on a value system that would produce the type of citizens who would govern the nations according to the original design and desire of the founding fathers. In this design, no serious thoughts could be given to the long-term welfare or interest of the colonized. While it is arguable that some Africans have benefitted from the sad, grand design, it is evident that such beneficiaries are simply rewarded for their roles as the enablers of the colonial process. From the earliest stages of this process, the colonizer ensured the perpetuation of the enabler class or beneficiaries, not only through religion and education at the home base, but also, by shipping their young children overseas as if to ensure that such children would have no mitigating benefits that could accrue from exposure to indigenous life. This trend has not only continued to date, but it has now become a fashionable and clean way to launder money and other resources, a trend that further impoverishes the former colonies.

The colonial design has worked splendidly. It is 2011, and it is clear that the legal, political, and economic structures employed in running all African nations remain essentially the same as in the colonial times—only worse on many levels. In a call for papers, Richard Olaniyan, one of our conversationalists, summarizes Africa's dire state.

> Africa is in a state of crisis. What seems obvious is the fact that the issues that are thrown up by the African situation have always recurred: absence of good governance and democracy, political corruption, personalization of state power, widespread diseases, persistent policy failure in education, economy and infrastructural development and dependence on Western expertise.

The color of the leadership has changed, but the systems of government persist, enabling the original intentions to be fulfilled—in some cases more efficiently than under direct colonial rule. For example, nearly all major construction projects, manufacturing, refinery of local materials, military infrastructure, and economic planning decisions continue to be awarded largely to foreign companies or advisers—just as they were in pre-independence times. The slight twist is that the companies now often include Africans either as partners or board members. In one of the most glaring and dastardly business deals of the 1970s, ITT, the international arm of AT&T, secured a contract to overhaul Nigeria's ailing communications system and bring it to internationally acceptable standards. The outcome of that contract is memorialized in *I.T.T.*, the popular release by the outspoken musician, the late Fela Anikulapo-Kuti.

Even in matters concerning life, the reckless disregard on the part of a typical African government is both evident and well-documented. That Africa is a dumping ground for all forms of waste, including toxic waste, continues to be well-documented and publicized. Oil companies pollute the environment wantonly. Typically governments are grossly absent from the life of the community because the only power to which they are answerable is the former colonial master. In a recent *University of Chicago Magazine* article Sola Olopade writes about the correlation between indoor pollution and asthma, a deadly disease that is currently among the "top ten causes of death in the world." The situation could be worse in Africa, but no one really knows because as Olopade says, "in...Africa, we really don't know much...because research never goes there." What is certain is that Olopade's research "shows...levels [of indoor pollution] as high as 14,000 microgram..., [although WHO's recommendation is]...that particulate matter not exceed a daily average of 50 micrograms." In the West this would have warranted an urgent response from the government, but as Olopade states, his team could only embark upon three solutions, namely, work through "village elders...to improve kitchen ventilation; distribute, with the help of grant from CHEST, high heat, low-emission stoves to some of the most polluted homes..., and thirdly, "distribute anti-oxidant supplements, including vitamin E and selenium..." It is incredible that in no part of the article is reference made to a local health ministry or a building department for intervention. The reason for this glaring absence is clear: a typical ministry, when it exists, is grossly inefficient. Very often, it exists in name only. Interestingly two of the three proposed solutions rely completely on aid or purchase from overseas. These are usually short-term solutions, and they rarely work. Given the grotesque absence of a meaningful government, the first solution, namely to work through the village elders, the closest approach to the traditional model, might be the best or the only real solution.

A Yoruba proverb tells us that *idalu ni iselu*: A place is ruled according to the laws that governed its conception and infancy. It is not surprising that decades after their so-called independence, no African nation has succeeded in changing the pre-independence paradigms so that the majority of the people enjoy even the basic needs mandated by the United Nations. Instead, Africans seem condemned to a constant search for solutions to yesteryears' problems—distracting political rancor and endless civil wars, aptly described as "A Colonial Curse" by Jeffrey Gettleman in a recent *New York Times* article. Independence continues to mean nothing more than—to borrow an ancient Chinese curse—"a long stick in a small room."

And with every new effort and invention devised to solve the problems, the small room gets smaller. In "The Dancing Masquerade" Achebe tells a compelling story that speaks to the powerlessness of the continent's leaders today, the core of the insolvability of the perennial problems:

> I was invited to a meeting of the Organization of Economic
> Cooperation which is really a meeting of rich nations—Europe-

ans, Americans, Canadians, Australians—all the people who are doing well in the world. They were celebrating their twenty-fifth anniversary in Paris. And for some reason I was the only one among them who was not an economist or a banker. They were reading their papers, and they were talking about the "structural adjustment programs" which they impose on the Third World. They say to us, "You are not managing your affairs well; you are in debt. So if you need more loans, this is what you will do: You have to remove subsidies on agriculture and this and that. And if you obey our rules, more loans will come your way." So they tell us, "There are a few things that you will have to adjust; it may impose some hardship on you, but we know it's going to work." Then the Chairman of the Central Bank in Kenya said, "A country like Zambia has been practicing this for ten years, but they are no better off after this." But they said to him, "No, you have to give us a little more time... This thing has to work in the end!" Then I got really angry and said, "I am beginning to understand why I am here. I have been wondering what a fiction writer is doing among world bankers and economists. But now I realize that what you are doing here is fiction! You talk about 'structural adjustment' as if Africa was some kind of laboratory! Some intellectual abstraction. You prepare your medicine, you mix this into that; if it doesn't work, you try, out another concoction. But Africa is people, you know? In the last two years, we have seen the minimum wage in Nigeria fall from the equivalent of fifteen pounds a month to five pounds a month! That's not an abstraction. Somebody is earning that money, and he has wife and children, you see?" And it was amazing because the person who had been speaking was shocked! As if he had realized for the first time that Africa was not just a conglomeration of different formulas. ... I said to them, "You are punishing these countries because they are in debt, but America is the biggest debtor of all; and nobody is asking America to adopt politics that would bankrupt their citizens. But Africa, the Third World, they are places where you can try out things. Africans are not really people.... They are expendable!" And that's the mentality that created our problems. "We can go there and straighten them out. Give them the gospel, give them this and that." Then they go and forget us and carry on with their lives.... In the meantime, our own lives have been messed up.

I am aware that some will find fault with my focus on the colonial origins of Africa's problems. Such fault finders will point fingers, justifiably, at the crooks, tyrants and corrupt leaders, and perhaps repeat the flawed view that Africans simply do not know how to govern. But my critics must prove that Africa indeed has a monopoly on corruption, tyranny or that Africans are genetically disposed to produce flawed leaders—more so than people in other parts of the world. My critics will have to explain the virtual disappearance of the basic traditions, for the most part, of safety, order, hospitality and honesty that the early visitors, Europeans and Arabs alike, described so effusively. Additionally, they must explain why—in spite of its enormous human and natural resources—the continent has remained, to quote Walter Rodney, chronically "underdeveloped." The 2010 HDI study shows African nations (except nine) at the very bottom of the Human Development Index. They should explain why the ever-growing critics and think tanks—of which Africa probably has more per capita than any place in the world—cannot offer convincing explanations for why only the corrupt and tyrannical leaders win elections; why the good guys tend to stay away from politics, and perhaps the most puzzling of all, why all the good guys become tainted once in power, and rarely succeed in making any lasting difference. Perhaps more importantly, it will be helpful to explain why there are hardly ever any serious efforts to find and implement home-grown solutions to Africa's problems.

But this work is not intended for the approval or disapproval of critics. It is perhaps necessary to note that neither the harping on corruption nor crucifying the never-ending convoy of crooks who masquerade as leaders has served thus far, or will ever serve, to move the continent forward. Thus, my ultimate goal is to share the tremendous information in this volume with the world's youth upon whom the future depends, and whose frustration is encapsulated in a simple and interrelated pair of questions: "Why does Africa continue to endure poverty, diseases, and turmoil in spite of its natural and human resources? And what are the ways out?" For these youths, this volume can serve as a guide to the many ways in which pre-colonial Africans devised and employed effective tools to fashion a rational and healthy society. And to those who may simply wish to reexamine their preconceived notions, Ulli Beier and his friends provide a fresh perspective on which to base a genuine reexamination as well as meaningful paths to fruitful work. Today the world needs these tools and paths more than ever before, and if we continue to ignore this simple truth, we do so at our own peril.

This work must not be misconstrued as an anti-modern thesis, for there is nothing wrong with modernization *per se*. There are reasons to, however, question the benefit of the current approach to modernization, or any ideology for that matter, that is based solely on the wrong-headed socio-economic and political systems that have become passé and jettisoned indeed by their very inventors. When I have had the opportunity to challenge some 'modernization' partisans, many of whom have built their careers promoting and defending just about any insanity launched by a ruling government, it has become evident that a typical partisan—though versed in his or her field of expertise—knows little or nothing about their own indigenous value systems. Also and very often, these partisans have no real basis for their views but the superficial doctrines and propaganda which colonizing agents once employed to confuse and colonize. This is hardly surprising because, as mentioned earlier, a typical partisan is the product of an education that was designed solely to create Africans whose primary function is to embody colonial interests. Thomas Babington Macaulay provides a rationale for the education designed by the British for colonial India:

> It is impossible for us, with our limited means, to attempt to educate the body of the people. We must at present do our best to form a class who may be interpreters between us and the millions whom we govern; a class of persons, Indian in blood and color, but English in opinions, in morals, and in intellect...

To justify the exclusion of Indian languages and literary material whether in Sanskrit and Arabic, Macaulay argued that they could not be admitted into the curriculum because they were inferior to English, and at any rate, they offered "false taste and false philosophy"—a typical justification for dismissing indigenous literature and languages. In Africa today it is still typical to ban indigenous languages outright or discourage their use by subtle means. The notion that African languages are too inferior to be the media of instruction in schools has persisted while the language of the former colonizer remains the *lingua franca*, even though it is spoken by only 10-15 percent of a typical African population. Perhaps more detrimental to the future of Africa is the reality that even those who are aware of the deficit in the colonial systems of education and government invariably lack the desire or the authority to develop independent options—that is, options that are inspired solely by the needs of the local communities as opposed to those of the former colonial masters.

Among many other oddities, the continued dependence on foreign languages as the official language of education and politics is problematic. We know that language is the source of creativity and spirituality—the most effective and perhaps the only means of preserving cultural traditions intact. This awareness was not lost on the leaders of the nascent nation of Israel, who, as Beier reminds us, successfully created *Ivrit*, Hebrew—out of a largely "fossilized" language—as a lingua franca for the new nation. The idea of adopting Yiddish or German as the nascent nation's lingua franca was considered, but defeated. Beier also reminds us that at least one Yoruba rising politician made a similar effort in the 1950s, but, his hope of making Yoruba a medium of instruction (for all subjects) throughout the Yoruba region was defeated because of the belief that only the colonial language could unify the new nation. In other words, even under a loose "federal" system, the idea of institutionalizing the Yoruba language was a threat to the colonial masters who must have recognized that move as one of the single most important steps toward genuine, as opposed to phony, independence. This sad and detrimental reality continues to manifest itself in the same manner as it did in Beier's times in Yorubaland. Today the truth is that even those who are aware of the deficit of colonial education invariably lack the desire or the authority to develop genuinely independent educational and political systems that are inspired by the needs of the local communities.

The catastrophes that continue to plague modern Africans are the direct results of the holes created by the continuous erosion of the people's own values and traditions. Modern day Africans are some of the few people on earth today who lack the fundamental awareness that honoring one's ancestors is indeed a way of honoring oneself, reinforcing self-worth, and upholding one's dignity. While the Asian and Jewish peoples embrace their ancestral ways as valuable tools indeed in shaping modern life, Africans continue to believe that the only way to technological advancement and other symbols of modernization is by aping the West or Asia. Yet, when we travel to Asia, automobile assemblies and other technological miracles are rarely the attractions—dazzling though they may be. Rather, we happily feed our senses on nature's wonders—beautiful landscapes, flora and fauna; we marvel at the replica or remnants of ancient traditions—the theaters, festivals, castles, and shrines. During my stay in Sweden, summer and other holiday tours took my host family and me to historical sites featuring castle ruins, *lunde*, Vikings' ships, perfectly preserved old barns and farm houses, theaters, and even museums showcasing the remains of sacrificial humans whose death on winter solstice was believed would bring back the sun. The ancient maypole still attracts huge crowds of the young and old joyously feasting. Similarly, in many Yorkshire areas of North England, the visitor is invited to "shop and have coffee," but the real lures are the ancient landmarks from "bygone days that still retain a certain charm and lots of memories."

Africans happily and proudly make frequent pilgrimages to ancient sites in distant places—Europe, Israel, and Saudi Arabia, to name but a few—without seeming to realize that the objects of their trips are the same as those that they have been tricked to discard in their own homelands. When there is any interest in historical sites at all, a typical African nation's investment, as Adam Hochschild once pointed out to me, is in slave ports and animal safaris. A few notable exceptions are the Pyramids in Giza, the mud houses in Djenne and Marrakech, and of recent, Suzanne Wenger's effort in Osogbo where—as a famous devotee of Obatala and priestess of Osun—she brought her artistic acumen to bear on the ancient Osun-Osogbo Sacred Grove, eventually succeeding in turning it to a world-renowned spot. This sacred site was recognized by UNESCO as a World Heritage Site in 2005, about four years before Wenger's death. Properly revered, developed and managed, Africa's ancient sites—many of them of spiritual and natural wonders—can compete favorably with those in any part of the world as tourist destinations. Osun-Osogbo for example is similar in many ways to the Yardenit or Sanctuary of Our Lady of Lourdes.

Another issue of concern is that of travels within the continent. It is clear at the moment that outside of the so-called official visits, Africans do not travel within the continent. One could even go as far as to say that Africans' preference for European destinations is deeper today than ever before. Although the boundaries are largely porous and artificial, crossing them makes travelling by road—where physically possible at all—complicated or at least unpleasant, or both. In addition to bad roads, the red-tape involved in crossing a typical border often makes the choice of destinations out of the continent more palatable. Also traveling by air into a typical African city is still sometimes easier from a European capital than from another African city—a reminder of the way things were in pre-independence times. Sporadic efforts to create regional economic zones such as Ecowas, (economic community of West African states) to encourage cross-border cooperation and interdependence have not been fruitful. Often, they exist practically in name only.

A more unsettling development is the tendency for endless antagonisms as a result of these boundaries, artificial though they are. And thanks to ready access to munitions and disproportionally large armies, Africans are too quick to engage in hostility—even when the Africans on either side of the borders share the same ethnicity and language, which should make peace talks an option. What is even more egregious is that many of the skirmishes that erupt are usually attributable to the discovery of natural resources around the so-called border territories.

Thus trapped within their so-called national boundaries, the traditional African freedom of movement and sharing no longer resonate for today's Africans—although theirs were the ancestors who originated human dispersal by wandering away, as genetic studies demonstrate today, to distant places, and thereby populating the world. Incidentally, prior to the discovery of DNA, genetic mapping and other scientific methods to prove it, the tales of human dispersal were told in many West African oral traditions. Were Africans truly independent today, they would base their institutions on the traditions of hospitality, caring and life-affirming ways, and these values would naturally extend beyond all boundaries. Luckily, one can still experience these ways. In fact, these are the only ways that frequently mitigate the gaps created by Africa's flawed governments, the typical ineffective security apparatus and the resultant lawlessness. Very often, one is left to the mercy of ordinary people who, more often than not, will go out of the way to ensure the comfort and safety of a total stranger. Biodun Jeyifo shares an example of this care, and Beier tells us how indeed in financial dealings, people trust one another more than they do the banks or other official institutions. It is comforting that these tendencies, evidence of traditional honesty and dignity, continue to endure—though they are no longer viewed as Africa's central characteristics.

Yet it is desirable, as an antidote to the current ills, to popularize the traditional value systems of caring and other life-affirming ways as a guiding principle, not by imposition or through some abstract laws or ideology—an impossible feat—but by integrating them into the modern educational systems so that there are no contradictions between one's indigenous values and the so-called modern ways. Viewed in this way, traditional life-affirming customs would translate into care and respect for the environment as it was in traditional society when most towns maintained sacred forests or rivers—or both by merely imposing taboos that were acknowledged by all. Thus, nearly every town and village had forests and rivers which were inviolable. What is interesting is that invariably, the rivers and forests thus protected provided safe haven for wildlife, flora, and fauna. Today, having done away with ancient "taboos" often with nothing to fill the void, modern African landscape, as Beier notes, continues to lose its ancient character and charm. Even in some instances where the government has designated a forest a protected area, and installed guards to enforce its protection, this action has not staved off violators, pollution and other forms of degradation as the ancient taboos did. Ironically, and taboos apart, much of the environmental renewal or preservation that the world is seeking at the moment is enshrined in many of the simple and meaningful ancestral ways detailed in this book. These ways, which the modern world has finally begun to recognize and brand as "environmentally friendly", "sustainable" and lacking "carbon footprint" reflect the levelheaded ways of the ancestral past.

That modern Africans are unable to find their ways back to these simple and reasonable ways constitute the bulk of the continent's tragedy, a tragedy illustrated graphically by the dichotomy which Leo Frobenius once observed between contemporary Africans and their ancestors. After appraising a vast collection of ancient Ife artifacts among other things, Frobenius was compelled to declare that Africans were "Civilized to the marrow of their bones," and concluded that "The idea of the barbaric Negro is a European invention." But Frobenius also remarked that contemporary Africans, on the other hand, were an "assembly of degenerate and feeble-minded posterity" and wondered if there was any relationship between these "degenerates" and the artists who created the works he found to possess "much loveliness". While Soyinka has, in his typical frank manner, dismissed Frobenius's view as "schizophrenic" and "a direct invitation to a free-for-all race for dispossession, justified on the grounds of the keeper's unworthiness," it is not hard to see why Frobenius might have perceived a dichotomy between contemporary Africans and the ancestors whose magnificent works filled him with admiration. It is feasible that the Africans Frobenius encountered were those who had not only become detached from the sensibility and skills of their prodigious forebears, but had become such feeble-minded iconoclasts that but for the likes of Frobenius, ironically, they would have completely destroyed Africa's priceless works of art and more.

Indeed, the situation throughout the continent is not much improved today. It is in fact arguably worse as the rise in the number of iconoclasts continues to outpace that of those who want to see Africa's traditions recognized, honored, and preserved. Hopefully, this volume can help the reader to appreciate the debilitating outcome of these iconoclasts' collective adoption of someone else's *chi* or *ori*. As the Igbo or Yoruba would say, the way forward is blurry once a person—having adopted someone else's *chi/ori*—is reduced to living the life designed for, or by, someone else. This type of life, a cartoonish existence on a collective level, is an apt description of the current state of the majority of the world's former colonies. Having been stripped of their basic human dignity, in some cases gradually and in others suddenly, most of the citizens of these enclaves frequently believe that they have nothing to offer themselves. Apropos this unfortunate tendency, Ulli Beier recalls a corroborating story. Upon arriving at the Ibadan College of London University in the 1950s, Beier often listened to the students as they openly lamented their inferiority, "We can't even make a pin." Those students as well as many generations to follow had been programmed to believe that they were inferior—that their only salvation resided in mastering the colonial ways. Beier often wondered how being stripped of one's cultural legacy could necessarily lead to the attainment of any meaningful skills, lasting values, and rational life style. Even as they bent over backwards to master and acquire the colonialist's ways, the faculty—away from the classrooms and beyond the students' earshot—amused themselves at the expense of the hapless students: "Question: What's the greatest thing about the University?

Answer: Everything. Except the students!"

Of Pin-making and Wisdom: Getting There from Here

> Convinced of their own inferior status, many students at the University College in Ibadan in the 1950s often lamented: "We can't produce even a simple pin." I usually countered by reminding the students that their ancestors lived autonomously for thousands of years before the white man came, and if pins were what they needed now, they could always buy them without losing their identity.
>
> Ulli Beier, Correspondence with Author

> Of course Europeans have long felt that they have to export their culture in order to lift other peoples to a higher level of civilization... They used a formula to justify any absurdity in the curriculum which they imposed on...students. If you asked them why they thought it necessary to teach Anglo-Saxon...at a time when no African language was taught...., the answer was: "We have to maintain British standards... through the notion of having to transcend one culture and having to link up with a "superior" one.
>
> Ulli Beier, "Yoruba Religion," *Ulli Beier in Conversations*

> [Colonial alienation begins] with a deliberate disassociation of the language of conceptualisation, of thinking, of formal education, of mental development, from the language of daily interaction in the home and in the community. It begins by separating

the mind from the body so that they [occupy] two unrelated linguistic spheres in the same person. On a larger social scale it is like producing a society of bodiless heads and headless bodies.

Ngugi wa Thiong'o, *Decolonising the Mind*

The early African intellectuals...enjoyed the "angst" which was created for them through the notion of having to transcend one culture and having to link up with a "superior" one.

Wole Soyinka, "Identity" *Ulli Beier in Conversations*

The in-roads made by the neologism of the neo-colonial era—PROGRESS—in the extreme Western sense of the word, was grafted onto the mind and soul of every African. ... But instead of progress, the African is today immersed in backwardness, and instead of the much needed recognition of his mental and physical prowess in shaping a world that belongs to us all, the African appears destined to continue a contemporary apemanship.

Femi Bodunrin, "Reflections," *Ulli Beier in Conversations*

A Yoruba adage, *ewure sonun Esu l'on a gb'obuko*, speaks to the importance of weighing one's choices to ensure equilibrium in every aspect of one's life. A supplicant who had lost a needle sought Esu's assistance to recover the needle. The literal and metaphorical god of the crossroads weighed the matter and announced that finding the needle was a simple job, but his price would be the supplicant's only he-goat. The supplicant got the message and demurred.

Perhaps the significance of this anthology is the audacity and clarity with which each Conversation lays bare the folly of the thought process and systems that got the Africans to jettison their native intelligence in pursuit of, or continued preference for, largely hollow ways—be those ways religious, philosophical, socio-economic, artistic, or political—regardless of the price. For those who are serious about seeing Africa overcome its predicaments, and attain genuine, sustainable development, the best approach might just reside, as Soyinka says unequivocally, in the traditional approach to life. One of the reasons that Soyinka's view must be taken seriously is that—as illustrated repeatedly in each Conversation—traditional African systems insist on communal living; that is to say, on uniformly developing communities in order to guarantee each person's dignity and well-being. This approach recognizes and mandates sharing as a corner stone, a missing ingredient from today's society where inequality has become an acceptable way of life worldwide; where the wealthiest is allowed to be hundreds of millions of times richer than the poorest. Our tolerance for various forms of institutionalized inequality—homelessness, hunger, wage discrimination and gender discrimination—has reached obscene proportions. In the streets of Egypt during the February 2011 protests, many blue-collar workers spoke of earning the equivalent of $2,200 annually while their boss earns $250,000 or more. Worse than this is the situation in the United States where the nation boastfully celebrates its growing list of billionaires in *Forbes* while as many as 44 million people, one in seven according to the 2009 census, live in poverty. The figure was 36 million in 2007. This volume illustrates how, if we look closely enough at traditional societies before colonialism, we may find meaningful solutions.

Africans were not the only ancient group who attempted to minimize inequality and ensure that each person had enough. Among the ancient Greeks, a hero was someone who cared for the vulnerable by giving away his wealth. There was also a law that forbade the richest person from being more than four times richer than the poorest person. In most of the functioning and rational parts of the world today, this figure appears to be a gauge—as in Germany where the nation's richest are usually not more than four times richer than the poorest. As Beier observes, the traditional Yoruba rulers and religious leaders he met in the 1950s "were not in it for the money." A typical Yoruba community used to dissociate wealth from leadership and religious institutions to ensure transparency and purity of service to the community. Once crowned, a king must not be ambitious, in pursuit of wealth or found to be engaged in any activities that could distract him from his duties. As Achebe tells us, the Igbo people required a would-be king to pay off the debt owed by everyone in the community as a condition for being crowned king. In this way, he would rule over a debt-free population, and as king, he and his leadership would be unencumbered by material wealth or its pursuit. It is fascinating that not only were the Igbo people aware that the mixture of material wealth and leadership would invariably burden the leader and the institution, but also they devised a clever way to circumvent it.

Given the close living arrangements in the olden days, the welfare of one had to be the welfare of all. A Yoruba proverb warns that if one stands by while a neighbor eats a food item that is known to induce coughing, at night when the coughing begins, it will disturb everyone's sleep—including that of the neighbor who watched the ingestion of the food item. President Nelson Mandela and Bishop Desmond Tutu describe the same attitude when they speak of *Ubuntu—Umuntu ngumuntu ngabantu,* "I am because you are"—the traditional philosophy guiding interpersonal relationships among the Xhosa and many other ethnics in Southern Africa. *Ubuntu,* according to Bishop Tutu,

> is a quintessential human moral commitment to other people's well being... A person with Ubuntu is open and available to others, affirming of others... He or she has a proper self-assurance that comes from knowing that he or she belongs in a greater whole and is diminished when others are humiliated or diminished...

In a similar vein, President Nelson Mandela tells us

> A traveler... would stop at a village [and] the people would give him food... [He] didn't have to ask for food or for water... That is one aspect of Ubuntu, but Ubuntu has various aspects. Ubuntu does not mean that people should not enrich themselves. The question is: Are you going to do so in order to enable the community around you to improve?

The Yoruba's answer is *enu kan ki nje ki enun kan maa wo* (No one eats unless we all eat). Another axiom states, *Ajoje ni ndun; ajoje o dun b'eni kan o ni* (Sharing is blissful; but sharing is neither possible nor enjoyable unless everyone contributes). The Yoruba believe that only in togetherness lies human dignity—(*K'arin k'a po ni nye ni*); the lack of dignity for one diminishes everyone's dignity. And, *Oloro kan l'aarin egberun otosi, otosi,* one wealthy person in the city of the poor is a poor person. These axioms all speak to the correlation between equal distribution of a community's wealth and a community's well being.

These ancient sentiments must have inspired Mandela who declared upon his release from jail that "I am not free until we're all free." But Mandela was speaking to a world in which subjugation had become the order of the day; a world in which one powerful constituency could brazenly exploit the other, and justify the exploitation. In the case of many Southern African nations, South Africa, for example, the subjugation and exploitation of Africans was a function of the absurd policy of apartheid. In West Africa, assimilationist or enculturation policies disguised the exploitation and subjugation, but the erosion of traditional values had begun in earnest.

Thanks to his interest and commitment, Ulli Beier was able to discern many aspects of the traditions of sharing and caring when he arrived in Yorubaland in 1950. The kings and the elders were still keenly aware of their responsibility, particularly as it pertained to the welfare of the community and the vulnerable within it. A vestige of the ancestral past when the king was held responsible even for events beyond his control, and when even a natural phenomenon such as a drought or a plague could cost him his throne or his head, the king and all those in leadership positions were intensely aware that their own well-being and success depended squarely on their subject. As such, the palace or the abode of a typical leader was a veritable welfare center, a *gateless* space accessible to everyone, including the lowliest in the community. In the Ikere palace, for example, *owa ase*, the kitchen quarters never closed, and the cooks could only estimate how many ate breakfast by the number of *akara* (bean cakes) that were served—hence the Ikere invocation: *wa m'akara ka'mo*, (may your offspring be numberless). Most days, the cooks lost count of how many *akara* were cooked since anyone and at any time could find shelter as well as a means of livelihood within the palace. This generosity explains why most of Africa's valuable artifacts used to be found at the palaces. Where else could artists live, eat, and work virtually free from the vicissitudes of day to day life? Thus the palace was always teeming with life, and hence the Edo saying that "In the palace, there is never quiet."

Behind this seemingly elaborate system was a simple equation, namely, the leaders' awareness that they were relevant only as long as the entire town enjoyed harmony and contentment. As leaders, therefore, they were directly answerable to the people whom they ruled, and although the people actively helped the leaders to remain aware of their responsibilities the leaders were ultimately held accountable for everything that happened under their rule—including natural disasters. Consequently, traditional rulers took every measure possible to be transparent—though they could often seem aloof to the foreign eye. Due to the transparency and accessibility, displeasures were often resolved before they could escalate. The provision of goods, particularly food, was high on the list of a typical leader. In this regard, a ruler in a typical agrarian society had to be very industrious, often diligently competing with his or her subject to demonstrate that he or she could produce as many, or more, crops as any other farmer. As Beier tells us, that was a prudent choice because a typical ruler was responsible for caring for the needy, unexpected guests, and the catering of important festivals was also oftentimes his responsibility. Easy access to the palace meant that the King was approachable, which surprised Ulli Beier when he first visited some West African towns he would later call home. Generally the king had no personal security forces to shield him from the wrath of his people; only the people themselves could guarantee his protection. (The recent uprising in Egypt is a reminder of what was possible in the olden days. In fact, similar uprisings against the Ogoga of Ikere have been witnessed in the past three years—in spite of being guaranteed protection by the Federal and State anti-riot police and the military). To this day, a typical, traditional ruler still prides him or herself on the level of the rapport that he or she enjoys with the townspeople. In this context, Soyinka's public criticism or his private visit to the powerful Ooni to voice his objection to what he deemed to be unbecoming photographs of the King is not as out of place or unique as some might wish to view it.

Beyond the harvest cycles and other periods of abundant food supply, ancient African leaders must also ensure the availability of food, a necessity which led to the invention of elaborate food preservation systems. For societies that were not exactly revered for their sophisticated technological accomplishments, the extant granaries, yam hangers, and smoked fish baskets are a testament to the fact that traditional African societies devoted a remarkable amount of time, resource and energy to food preservation. Naturally, a typical population often enjoyed bumper harvests the preservation of which made dry seasons or poor harvests survivable. With food generally in ample supply, society could focus on other basic necessities by organizing itself into guilds such as weavers, dyers, basket makers, mat weavers, hunters, and for those in the riverside areas, fishermen. Training was accomplished through apprenticeship, and both goods and services were bartered to ensure even distribution of both.

Comparable to the sense of responsibility displayed by the leadership element was the communal devotion to the care of the children. Regardless of the parents' station in life, the child—as we see in the Conversations with Abiodun and Oluwole—was placed at the center of the community's loyalty and priority. This might sometimes mean that a community was overindulgent or overbearing, but the children were always aware that they were the center of everyone's attention. Conversely, the child was never a passive receiver; there were appropriate responsibilities which included household chores and errands as described by Abiodun. As a result, the child grew up being well aware of the reciprocal nature of what growing up in the proverbial village meant. Children were trained to believe that they had something to learn from every circumstance and member of society. In other words, the attention enjoyed by the child also came with a uniquely high level of expectation. While allowance was made for youthful exuberance believing "that a child will be a child", being young was not accepted as an excuse for deviancy. In fact, there was also the notion that children could be so mature and wise that they were accorded, as Soyinka describes, a legendary status. The general belief indeed today is illustrated in the axiom, *a n ri omode agba, a sin n ri agba omode* (there are undeveloped adults just as there are wise and mature children). A child was expected to exhibit the same level of self-control, listening ability, and thoughtfulness as a typical adult. Being calm and attentive were key indicators that a child who exhibited such traits would grow to be capable of critical thinking, and be able to make rational decisions. This type of preparation was also viewed as essential for navigating the treacherous road to old age, for much as they valued old age, the Yoruba were equally aware of its challenges, hence the aphorism: *asorooda bi agba* (aging is the challenge by which all of life's challenges are measured). But the challenge of aging was mitigated by the reverence and care which elders typically enjoyed.

The prominence of women is another characteristic of traditional African society about which the interviewees are unambiguous in their representation. It is a striking irony that only one female is featured in this volume, but this irony is another mark of the rift between the ancient and the modern. As Ulli Beier's numerous encounters and relationships with the Iyalorisa and women traders show, indigenous institutions did not discriminate against women. In the modern world, particularly in the United States, the epitome of democracy and equality, on the other hand, women were denied voting rights until the 1920s, and it took 200 years for Americans to see a female in the Supreme Court. Although various forms of institutionalized discrimination or disenfranchisement are rampant in modern Africa, modern African women would do well to realize that the answer to their current predicament lurks in the ancestral past, and not in the Christian, Victorian, and Islamic systems which were once believed to be the beacon of liberation. It is useful to recall that the first institutions to face annihilation as a result of the encounter with the Arab and the West were those where women held significant sway—be those institutions political or religious. Whether or not the colonial powers intended to undermine women exclusively, the outcome of their policies is incontestable. For one thing, it is evident that the presence of women in official spaces—whether political or religious—diminished drastically under colonization. Even in those areas where women could not be easily dislodged, the colonialist embarked upon various strategies of intimidation and control. In Abeokuta, for example, the colonial government imposed unbearable taxation—the intention of which was, as it was generally the case across Africa—to subjugate the powerful women traders. There were other coercive methods through which women as a group invariably lost their religious, political, and to an extent, their economic powers. One of the most effective means was marriage which, in the Christian and Islamic traditions, required complete submission to the husband's domination. Contrary to the traditional society where the woman enjoyed tremendous flexibility in marital matters, life in Victorian and

Islamized Africa was such that the control of the woman and her body was complete and total. Viewed and treated as an institution, the laws guiding marriage were often rigid and weighted heavily against women. To begin with, the stigma of being unmarried came to be dreaded above all else, and being married became the primary goal of the woman. And once married under the new penal and religious codes, she could no longer divorce without a legal proceeding run by an all-male court. Under colonial rule, a woman seeking divorce must be ready to remarry immediately after being granted divorce. In fact, to have her case heard, a new husband must be referenced in her petition, and he or his representative must appear in court to guarantee that upon the conclusion of the legal proceedings on the court date, the new divorcee would leave the court for the home of her new husband. Akinsola Akiwowo, the renowned Father of Indigenous Sociology, believes that the new way was a deliberate invention to discourage women from making independent decisions regarding marital as well as other personal issues. In my interview with him, he narrates several stories of women who found ways to thwart the colonial imposition. Among the stories was that of a school teacher in Egbaland. As expected, she showed up with a man for her divorce proceedings, and once she was granted divorce, she hired a band and danced around the town singing about her exploits: "The court proceeding is over, and I am a free woman." Apparently she had no intention to remarry right away, and her jubilation was intended perhaps to signify to her fellow women that the system could be manipulated.

Although it could be manipulated, the colonial system was inconvenient and demeaning to women in that it brought far-reaching limitations including those that could not have been imagined in traditional settings where the flexibility enjoyed by women in marriage extended to widowhood and old age. When a woman became a widow among the Yoruba for example, she, and only she, could choose her next life style, and the choices available were numerous. In Ikere, a widow could elect to marry her deceased husband's relative, retire to her place of birth, take up residence in the palace, or move in with any of her children. The code word for the latter choice is *iyan'mo*—choosing the child or children, that is, over marriage. A clear declaration of independence, the woman who chose "her children" would remain single, although she could always change her mind. These choices made sense in a society where marriage was largely for procreation. A widow would usually remarry if she wished to have more children. If convinced that she was barren or could not bear a child for whatever reason, a woman could set up her own household, take a wife, and in this way, she would create her own offspring. Typically she would pick her favorite relative or godchild to father the child or children. A woman who elected to take a wife was fully recognized both as husband and father. Her children would be recognized and welcome in the paternal clan as 'omookunrin', that is, in the same capacity as those of her brother's—the descendants of a male—whereas as a mother, her children would be recognized and welcome in her paternal clan as 'omoobinrin', the descendants of a female.

The life-style choices and flexibility described in the foregoing are not limited to the Yoruba. The Akan is a matrilineal society, and among the Lele, another matrilineal group, polyandry is not only acceptable, but it is sometimes pushed to what might seem an extreme form to the foreign or modern observer. For example, a woman who is deemed too beautiful to choose only one of her many suitors may marry all of them. The suitors—who are often members of the same peer or trade group—understand that their bride is the one who must come to a decision regarding the types of relationship she will have with each man.

One of the many bases for female empowerment in the foregoing was that the women had their own institutions which were run exclusively by them. Under the female jurisdiction, a female offender could only be brought to the court of her peers, or to a court of any of the female chiefs or both. In Ikere, for example, nine of the quarters in the palace were occupied by women leaders who had their own protocol and entourage. In the palace as well as throughout the town, the power of women was palpable. When they felt violated, women, particularly the affected group, could strike, Lysistrata-style or indeed leave their town en mass—taking refuge in a neighboring town where the female leadership in the host town would organize a welcome. The palace was a typical place of refuge for such occasions. The writer's mother once led the women of Ikere in hosting women from the neighboring town of Ise, who took refuge in the palace of Ikere to protest a policy that they deemed inimical to their well being. As recently as the 1960s, I witnessed a case in which a female group took the pastor of a church to task after he gave a sermon chastising them for being too brazen and disrespectful to men, particularly, their husbands. News had reached the pastor that the women, whom he nicknamed *Egbe kiloko nse?* (Who needs a husband Society), had engaged in unchristian acts. The specific charges were that they were too independent; they acted without their husbands' permission, and since they were away too often from their households, they were also found guilty of neglecting their husbands. On the following Sunday, the women submitted a "cease and desist" letter addressed to the pastor and the congregation. They argued that they were breaking no rules by creating their own wealth and attending to personal matters as free citizens should.

This story finds resonance in the incidents or experiences described by Ulli Beier and Roland Abiodun. Even today, many of the so-called "illiterate" women in Africa find it amusing and incredulous whenever I tell them that "equal pay for equal work" is still subject to debate in the Western world; that it took approximately 200 years for a woman to be appointed Supreme Court Judge in America, and that women did not gain the right to vote until 1920. For one thing, according to the traditional market, and prior to the advent of the colonizer, women were firmly in charge of commerce. Women were at home in the market, and much of what was sold was also often their handiwork. They were the weavers, dyers, spinners, cooks/caterers, and when they chose to do so, they farmed the land and fished just as successfully as men. Where and when men dominated the agricultural scene, women were relied upon for marketing the produce—cotton, yams, meat, and vegetables. In the communities where hunting was the confine of men, as among the Yoruba where the league of hunters whose patron god is Ogun, the god of creativity and technology, the hunters depended upon their fellow female devotees to market the game. The source of the women's income was the commission that they deducted from such sales. Thus, in Soyinka's *Death and the King's Horseman*, the young girls explain to the intruding policemen that the marketplace "is the home of our mothers."

The failure of imposed and artificial ideologies is evident in the decay and backwardness that continue to plague particularly the so-called third world peoples who lack the independence to use their own wisdom to chart their own waters or create their own destiny. For the world in general, the unending wars, hunger, and diseases as well as economic arrangements which permit 10 percent of the people to brazenly hoard 90 percent of a society's resources, constitute a clear clarion call to all of us that unless humanity evolves, the world, not just the third world, is endangered. We must wake up and realize that we have replaced Victorian colonization practices with global corporate colonization, and that our Western "democratic" governments and "free-market" economic practices are inadequate to deal with the power that these corporations, and the 10 percent of the population they represent, wield over the governments, economies, and lives of the masses. There is little that is democratic about most global corporations or the political systems that they invariably and of necessity must prop up.

This is one of the many reasons why the nuanced approach of traditional African values found in these Conversations is exceedingly critical at this time. When Westerners read about the African palace system, they think of European palaces and royalty, but as these Conversations and this introduction make clear, the African palace system was not merely a place for a king. It was an entire social welfare system that supported the well being of the community. The leaders served at the behest of the people, and worked hard and consistently to maintain the people's trust. Further, the local markets were free, and the exchange unfettered by unnecessary regulation. The same practices that held the interest of the community in light with the interest of the individual can be seen in the rights of both men and women, which were held in light of each other. The balanced understanding of communal values and individual liberty allowed Africa to develop a rich cultural heritage that Victorian and now corporate colonization have obscured but thankfully, as these Conversations make plain, not obliterated. These customs, distilled from the ancient wisdom that comes to life in these Conversations, are the one resource that could not be extracted entirely from the African landscape, and because of their adaptability, these customs have unified the continent—whether we look at the culture, the language, the palace systems and more as practiced along the Nile or in Qunu.

The changes we must make to repair the damage to human dignity in Africa in particular, as well as to the world in general have been brought to the fore by the economic collapse and the ensuing chaos and despondency that have jolted the world in the past three years. In addition to the protests and yearning for change, a host of organizations and individuals who have become disillusioned with the governments or the status quo have set up shop to work as Non-governmental Organization (NGOs) or philanthropists. But oftentimes, their approach to solving the monumental and multi-pronged problems facing a typical African community is often based on defunct and ineffectual programs designed by unaware, though well-meaning, experts. Ironically, here again we have somewhat a throw-back to many of the events witnessed by Beier in the 1950s. Like the foreign experts of those bygone years, those of today—armed with an impressive array of degrees and technical experience, accompanied by a sprinkle of Africans—suffer from a massive disconnect or inability to see that imposed solutions are wasted solutions; that any solution, even when germane to a problem, must be organic, and implemented in such a way that the people concerned can take proper ownership of both the problem and its solution.

For instance, today's campaign in favor of sustainable life style should find resonance in the meaningful ways of the ancestral past, but presented in Africa through the filters of foreign language and expertise, Africans are either skeptical or unable to grasp the larger message behind the sound bites. Recently, I spoke to a former colleague, now in a position to effect changes. His attitude was that the renewable energy campaign was relevant only to the none-oil producing regions of the world. He also viewed the attempt to spread the campaign to Africa, particularly the oil producing regions, as a smokescreen—an attempt to thwart development by crippling Africa's largest source of revenue.

Belief that traditional African institutions can play a role in addressing African problems or furthering development has led me to found My Palace Initiative (MPI), but thus far, I have been amazed by the level of resistance that I have encountered. The goal of MPI as an organization is the restoration of African palaces with a view, among a myriad of possibilities, to returning them to their genuine and principal traditional use as hospitality and welfare centers, grassroots organizing, incubators for innovation and self-help, hospice or retirement homes for the needy, artists' workshops, a center for education where matters of global importance can be broken down to readily digestible and actionable bits. I have encountered skepticism and admonition indeed from individuals whom I had expected to be more aware. One critic expressed the opinion that I should be working in Darfur because philanthropists and humanitarian workers would support my work. I tried to convince my adviser that the failure to strengthen and utilize African institutions is what often leads to strife and other social problems. Another critic believed erroneously—no matter what I said about the real function and place of a palace in African tradition—that my time and effort should be directed to education, not to kings who, by their very nature, represent the opposite of progress. Asked to elaborate, this critic told a story of a recent event where the retinues of a well-known monarch were seen hunting for a human to sacrifice, a credible story as it was told to him by an African eyewitness. For this critic, that story was sufficient to discredit the traditional system of government altogether.

It goes without saying that a major challenge awaits those who wish to effect any profound, as opposed to superficial, change in a typical former colony, and the challenge is made doubly daunting, as demonstrated through-out this volume, by the firm grip of colonial-neocolonial values codified via dreadfully anemic educational systems and religious indoctrination that make it offensive to accept or practice any aspects of the ancestral ways—even when the ways are efficacious. Added to all these is the indomitable coffin nail, a government that is run essentially and typically by about 10 percent of a vastly dispossessed population, largely ignorant of what their so-called nation actually represents, and uncertain of their actual place either in it or in the world.

Still there is reason to hope that the world will wake up and start a process of self-regeneration. My recent visit to Global Funds for Women (on behalf of MPI) afforded me a chance to speak with group's Executive Director, the brilliant Kavita Ramdas. Among the many things Kavita and I discussed was the world's shifting trends particularly as they pertain to women. Kavita pointed out an interesting irony, namely, that people in America have started living like the people in traditional societies; Americans are turning away from frozen, TV dinners, and buying organic and locally grown produce. But in much of the so-called third world, ironically, the reverse is the trend because colonial legacy remains the model. A huge part of the colonial legacy is the ever-growing power and influence of corporations. In a typical third-world community today, corporations push consumerism and other economic externalities not only as the ideal life style, but also as the biggest indicator of progress. So it has remained fashionable to date to import packaged food items—potato salad, tomato sauce, Uncle Ben's rice, powdered and tin milk, to list but a few—into indeed the most fertile regions of Africa.

David Korten, the world famous co-founder of Positive Futures Network, sheds light on the global trends that keep Africa entrapped and dysfunctional. His first warning to me during our brief conversation at a conference in Washington DC—and I promised to quote him—was "If you want real solutions to your people's problems, stay away from economists." The whole world, and not just the former colonies, Korten argues, is operating an unbalanced economy. A Stanford graduate and Harvard Professor who spent his earlier career setting up business schools in the developing world, Korten became disillusioned with development economics after, as he told me, thirty years of service as a development economist dealing with development failure and social disintegration in the third world. He eventually realized that a huge part of the problem was that the world was increasingly being run by corporations which he contends are modern versions of Empires. His analogy is apt. Developed about 5000 years ago, Empires engaged in the practice of unequal distribution of power and social benefits to a small segment of the population they controlled. Corporation and empires are thus similar in that both organizations are based on hierarchies, chauvinism, and subjugation indeed through violent means. In our era technological advancement has only made corporate control and profit more readily achievable while the resultant damage to the environment and human communities continues unabated. In *The Great Turning: From Empire to Earth Community,* a book he published in 2006, Korten predicted that the world was about to face a meltdown in which climate change and financial crises would combine to create a global calamity. But he also believed that the calamity would lead to significant changes that will end the paradigm of corporate rule, replacing it with "Earth Community", a sustainable, just, and caring community—exactly the type of paradigm Beier and virtually everyone in this volume claim to be a way of life in traditional societies.

Weighing the Cost of Pin-making: Ulli Beier in Conversations contains strong statements similar to Korten's, and in addition to the indictment of the unfortunate events of the past, provides direction for the way forward and out of the current quagmires. Luckily, many of the unfortunate circumstances and factors that made the subjugation of Africans not only possible, but easy, have been exposed and discredited scientifically. The notion of the inferiority of the African both at home and in the diaspora used to enjoy universal acceptance, and people of African descent were automatically placed at the base of the social ladder. As late as 1969 *Harvard Educational Review* published an article in which Arthur Jensen—a professor of UC at Berkeley's School of Education—claimed that African Americans were genetically disposed to have a lower IQ, about 15 points lower than that of the whites. According to Francesca Cavalli-Sforza and Luigi Cavalli-Sforza, Jensen's view also enjoyed the backing of William Shockley—a Nobel Laureate, a physicist, a Stanford professor and a co-inventor of the transistor—who "staged a series of conferences to promote Jensen's convictions, to which he added his own proposal for "social engineering": A monetary reward for black women willing to be sterilized." But Jensen's theory of biological hereditary fell apart in time, giving way to the idea that the type of difference he observed was as a result of "social class rather than ethnic origins."

What is interesting is that as the foregoing battle was going on in the science world, and many Africans even in the continent were persuaded as to their own inferiority, Ulli Beier was waging his own battle in the streets of West African towns learning from kings and outstanding Olorisa, arguing with his university colleagues as well as the new if misguided African elite, founding magazines to publish the works of budding authors, attending conferences to promote his findings, and saving ancient treasure from awaiting ruin. (Ulli has since returned his collection to Osogbo to fill a new museum built for this purpose by one of the children of a King who entrusted the palace collection to Beier.) Interestingly, many of the projects launched or inspired by Ulli Beier decades ago—pioneering literary and artistic endeavors, the Osogbo School of Art made possible by Georgina Beier's unique approach to the arts—are not only thriving, but are also held in high esteem globally.

So this volume gives one hope and optimism—not the usual "feel-good" and hollow type, but real reasons to believe that when problems are sliced down to manageable sizes, and the people are entrusted directly with the search for, as well as generating vital solutions, meaningful and lasting results ensue. In other words, with direct and persistent action genuinely aimed at real problems in every deprived community, the world can rid itself of the prevailing cycle of wretchedness. This optimism, like Biodun Jeyifo's "desperate optimism", must be given wings by our collective insistence that all the world's peoples deserve the freedom to develop and engage in practices commensurate with their core value systems, interests, and basic needs. This is to say that our focus and approach to development must shift from the wasteful, grandiose and frequently useless projects to small, relevant and sustainable ones, and the measurement of the success of the new projects and programs that they harbor must reside completely in the degree to which they bring dignity to every vulnerable person in the community.

For this to happen on a consistent basis, the political and economic systems as well as the qualifications, roles, values, and responsibilities of those in leadership positions must be reassessed and realigned to reflect the people's interest. It is in bad taste; it lacks simple good judgment, and it reflects poorly on the world community when leaders of the world's poorest communities are found to be not only inordinately wealthy—as was the case with Mobutu Sese Seko or recently with Hosni Mubarak whose overseas assets are believed to be worth $70 billion—but readily find safe overseas haven for what often turns out to be unearned wealth. Obviously one of the urgent and most helpful measures would the cessation of the financial policies that make the transfer of these funds and other resources possible and legal. Ordinarily most nations of the world have stringent laws, as was the case in most African traditions, prohibiting the harboring of stolen goods. In the mean time, and more urgently, retrieving Mubarak's 70 billion and similar assets, and putting them to better use at home would be a good first step. In the words of an ancient Buddhist sentiment encapsulated in the Japanese axiom, *Senri no michi, ippo kara*, (the journey of a thousand miles begins with a step).

An African axiom, *ogbon ki n tan l'aye ki a waa lo s'orun*, characterizes as fallacious the notion that the world can be so bereft of wisdom as to warrant a heavenly search. In other words, commonsense tells us that within a typical community reside the robust opportunity, mores and, in the final analysis, the awareness and wisdom that are essential for the community's survival. And when not grounded on the intrinsic values of a society, even the highest technological accomplishments can prove hollow, leaving the members of such society terribly flawed or indeed vacuous. The dismal state of the African continent today should serve as a serious indication to the world community that we cannot—to borrow Albert Einstein's words of wisdom—"solve our problems with the same thinking we used when we created them." It is crystal clear that supplanting colonialism with neocolonialism has worked out in Africa just as perfectly as share-cropping did in post-slavery America!

The adjustments that all of us must make—and why—are encapsulated in the wise saying of the indigenous people of central Africa which cautions, "If your cornfield is far from your house, the birds will harvest your corn."

REMI OMODELE, Berkeley, California, 2011

Ibrahim El Salahi
"IDENTITY"

U: Some time ago you told me that a Sudanese has a double identity, an Arab identity and an African identity. Can you elaborate on this? And above all, at what stage in your life do you become aware of this because presumably a Sudanese child is not conscious of a conflict of identity?

I: When we talk of identity we must take many factors into consideration. These are the individual, the communal, the cultural, and the geographical aspects. In the Sudan we have this duality in our nature because our fathers came from Arabia, a long time ago, but our mothers are African. If you look at our features—our hair, the color of our skin, the shape of our lips, we are African. Yet on the cultural side, our language is Arabic, our religion is Islam, and our reflection on life is a mixture of the two. Sometimes, when we meet people from other Arab countries, they don't accept us as Arabs; they regard us as Africans. Strangely, when we meet people from West Africa, they don't regard us as Arabs; they regard us as Africans. Only the people in our own country—say the people in the Western Sudan, they refuse to accept that we are Africans. They think of us as Arabs! And many times I tell them, "Look at me, look at my hair, my skin, my features, I am one of you. Why don't you accept me as such?" But they reject us. Yet in many ways our outlook on life is very much African.

U: Can you give examples of that?

I: Think of our sense of community. Think of music, of the way we respond to dance! We use the pentatonic scale which is common in Africa; we don't know the Arabic quarter tones. In fact, we don't find Arab music all that interesting. People who have spent a lot of time in Egypt may

Photo by Osman Salahi, courtesy of Katherine Salahi

acquire a taste for it, but spontaneously we can relate better to music from Ethiopia or Senegal.

U: What about purdah. Isn't that something that separates you rather from other Africans?

I: Well, that is the Islamic part of our heritage. Our women started to cover their faces in the Turkish period, but only in the towns, not in the villages. In the villages the women are quite free, and when their men are not around, they can fulfill the functions of a man. We have no separation of the sexes in the villages at all.

U: What about the visual arts. What kind of imagery did you grow up with?

I: Let's go back to the ancient culture of the Sudan. Though the Sudan was part of the Nile valley, and though it was often politically dominated by Egypt, the culture of the lands of Kush and of Meroe was basically African. Strangely, after the destruction of Meroe by the Axumites in the third century AD, the priests who fled from the invaders carried the secret of iron and bronze smelting with them. And some people believe that they carried these arts into West Africa, stimulating, maybe, the growth of the arts in Ife and Benin. There is an ancient Meroic town which is famous for what we call the "yellow pictures," meaning reliefs on the houses. They are very well preserved, and strangely, on many of these faces, I found typical Nigerian tribal marks—the three vertical lines, the one that cuts diagonally across and so on. But whether it is through diffusion or contact, or whether it is simply our basic human nature, I have found that we are very much African.

U: During your childhood in Omdurman, were you aware of such things? Was this something people talked about or did this enter your consciousness much later?

I: Strangely, as children, we were brought up as Arabs. The only history given to us was always related to Arabia. Yet the bed time stories we were told were very much African stories. We had the typical trickster stories, for example. Only that with us, it was the fox who always outwitted the other animals—rather than the tortoise or the spider as you have in West Africa.

U: Who told you those stories?

I: Actually in the house we had an old lady whom we called Hukmuruda, a term which means, "Her judgment is acceptable to us." She had been my father's nanny, but we thought of her as our grandmother. She was very old, but still very alert, and she was both humorous and kind. But she was actually not my grandmother; she was the slave who to looked after my father whom she came to regard as her son. I was most confused about this as a child, and I kept asking, "Where does she come from?" I was told that my grandfather belonged to the Hawara tribe that was half Arab, half African; but my grandmother came from Chad. She was the daughter of a chief, and she brought the slave woman with her. Strangely enough, Hukmuruda spoke Arabic, just like us.

U: Let's get back the visual arts. You talked about the art of Meroe, but you haven't told me yet what kind of art you were surrounded with in your daily life in Omdurman.

I: ... When I began to study art, I quickly became aware of, and interested in, local pattern and decoration. I found that the sense of decoration we have in the Sudan relates mainly to Africa—the baskets, the woodwork, the leatherwork; many of the shapes we use are not used in Arabic art at all. But I found many similar examples in the rest of Africa. ... So from there I began to wonder. "Where do I belong?" It didn't worry me because as an individual, I have always felt I can belong anywhere in the world. But something inside you calls for identity, particularly when you come into contact with the group of people you have always been told you belong to, but they don't think you belong to them...

U: When did this first happen to you?

I: I think it happened mainly when I went to England. I was the secretary of the Sudanese Students Union, and I was supposed to attend the general meetings of the Arab Students Union. I began to realize that what made sense to them didn't always make sense to me; and they too thought of me as being different...

U: Did you feel they were displaying an attitude of superiority?

I: Definitely. One has to admit it. We tend to ignore it or pretend it's not important. But it is there. They are polite enough, and when you show that you speak the language—sometimes better than they do!—there is a bit of respect. But usually, they are not so subtle. Let me give you an example. There is a Palestinian in Qatar. He is a very nice man; a good friend of mine, in fact. But once I felt strongly about an issue. I thought that some of us expatriates in Qatar were taking life too easy. I said we were there to help the country; that they accepted us; that they were generous to us and that we had no right to waste our time. I blew my top.

Then my Palestinian friend said, "This must be the Negro element in you; you have the 'stubbornness' of the Black!" This notion of "black stubbornness" goes back many centuries when there was a revolt mounted by the black slaves in Iraq.

U: When a student from Khartoum or Omdurman describes himself as Sudanese in London, does this identity include the people of the Southern Sudan?

I: This Sudanese identity is probably our attempt to mend our home. As you know, there has been this strong political movement in the South because they believe that they have been dominated by the North. But while John Garang, the leader of the liberation movement, is fighting for an African state in which all minorities will be fully respected by whomever forms the majority government, there's no question about the Sudanese identity. Now to come back to your question, when I met Sudanese students who were from the South in London, all the differences dropped, and I was left with one thing: the feeling of affinity. There were shades of color, yes, but most of us from the North did not perceive any difference. It was the Southerners who felt that there was a rift, and they would sometimes say, "Aahaa, you say we are equal, but would you let one of us marry your sister?" Now some of us feel that many Southerners have moved to the North and they have found employment in the big cities, and they are living in harmony with the people in the North. Many have become doctors and lawyers, even ministers in the government, and some have married Northern women. I think I can say that the best Minister of Information the Sudan has ever had was a Southerner.

U: If Southerners are highly sensitive to this question of common identity, maybe one should remember the history of the conflict. For centuries Arabs had carried on a slave trade in the Sudan...

I: The slave trade had definitely something to do with it. For example, my mother's father was a slave trader. He was known for it, and I still remember seeing the wooden stocks and the chains lying in my uncle's room. I remember when I saw them in that room and I said: "What are these things for?", and my uncle said: "That's how they brought the slaves". And I said: "What slaves?" And I realized that the one who was telling me about it was one of the slaves! He said that was how people from the

Nuba, the Dinka and so many other places were carried away. I am glad that the white ants have since eaten those stocks, but the fact remains that my grandfather was a slave trader. He had many wives some of whom came from the Arab tribes, and many were African slaves whom he took as concubines. But with such a history how can we ever attempt to create separate identities in the Sudan?

U: Now you have been in political exile since 1976. You have lived and worked outside your country for fourteen years and it would clearly be unwise for you to return. What does this do to your identity? You have explained how you have built up a Sudanese identity over the years; how your concept of what is a Sudanese became more complex over the years. Then suddenly you had this traumatic experience in the Sudan, and you are forced now to spend your time between Britain and Qatar—two countries that have been kinder to you than your actual home.

I: I feel terribly frustrated. Naturally you feel relaxed in your own country. There you really know the people; you understand their ways. That is the place from which your artistic inspiration comes. In exile, I feel split within myself. Yet where I work now, in the Gulf, I am respected as a person; I am trusted. I have been given a job that is not usually offered to a foreigner. I feel quite relaxed, but it is not home. My other "home" is England where I've never had a job, but where I could work freely as an artist. Still you feel pushed into a corner in that country because though you have all the necessary papers and a residence permit, you are not likely to get a job.

U: How much time do you spend in London these days...?

I: I only go visiting London nowadays for about two months a year. The longest time I ever spent there was four years, from 1982 to 1986.

U: England has now become a multiracial country, with many different communities living side by side. Do you live in an English community or amongst other exiles?

I: I live with my family. I began to take roots in England a long time ago. I married my first wife there and I had four children from her. My children are now beginning to have children, so I have become a grandfather. I have three boys and a girl from Eve. The oldest is married and has two children. The youngest has a girlfriend, and they are expecting a child. Now I am married to Katherine who has had two boys and two girls. All are British subjects. So in Britain I am an unemployed father and grandfather who must go abroad to feed his children. In London, my neighborhood is mostly English, but we keep in close contact with the Sudanese community and other Africans. But basically I would say I live with my family.

U: Did Eve's children start school in the Sudan?

I: Yes, but they completed their education in England. My eldest son is a musician, and he is now trying to set up a recording studio with a friend. My daughter took a degree in psychology. Of the other two boys, one studied printing and the other, photography. They both work in Eve's printing business.

U: Well, what is their identity? They grew up in the Sudan, but they are now British citizens and appear to have settled down there.

I: Strangely enough, they see themselves as Sudanese! How? I don't know. Part of it is maybe that Eve keeps an open house like a Sudanese. People drop in all the time; there are no British formalities. So they have retained some element of their early lives in Khartoum. Secondly, members of my extended family visit them quite regularly. My mother, my sisters and my uncle all come from the Sudan to see them regularly. The children in turn visit the Sudan. Eve goes there once a year. She simply appreciates the life she had in the Sudan much more than her own environment in England. My second son feels himself very much a Sudanese. He doesn't want to live in England. He plans to open a photo studio in Khartoum. Unlike my other children, he refused to be naturalized in Britain, and he carries a Sudanese passport. He wants to marry a Sudanese girl and live there. Of course, they all speak Arabic. They speak Arabic amongst themselves and with their mother.

U: And are they Muslims?

I: Well, they call themselves so, but they are not practicing Muslims. When my eldest son's wife, who is a Christian, wanted to baptize their children, my son said: "No, no, no, they are Sudanese!" He completely refused. But he does not practice the religion; he doesn't pray. He only goes to the Islamic Centre for the big festivals like Ramadan; it's a social festivity for him. All my children drink, and they lead exactly the same lives as other young people in England.

U: Now Katherine's children are still quite small and they are growing up in an Arab environment in Qatar.

I: But strangely enough, they are very English, which worries me a bit. They go to an English speaking school because we know that our time in Qatar is limited, and they will have to fit into a British school system sooner or later. We can't take them to the Sudan because there are so many problems there. It is not safe, and the school system now is very poor. So England seems the only place left for them to go. But in the English speaking school in Qatar, most of the children are British, though there are a few Pakistanis and Indians. There are very few Arab children indeed. I've been sending them to an Egyptian teacher to learn Arabic, but I don't know how it happened, they seem to have an inbuilt resistance to Arab language and culture. Katherine herself is very keen on learning the language, but somehow it doesn't seem to work with the children. It's very strange.

U: I can see how it happens. In London your children would grow up amongst an English majority, but physically they would stick out as non-English. Rejection from English children would naturally push them into a Sudanese identity. But growing up in Qatar, they grow up as part of an expatriate community...

I: And strangely, they always want to go back to England. I ask them: "What is there in England that is not in Qatar?" I mean there really are far better facilities in Qatar, and they attend a much better school! Ironically, what they look for in England is Eve's household, their older brothers and sister and the whole relaxed atmosphere of the place. So, what they look for in England is really a Sudanese kind of atmosphere...

U: Are you bringing them up as Muslims?

I: Sure. I am a practicing Muslim, and for me, it is something fundamental. As a Muslim it is my responsibility to teach my children the religion because it gives them an Islamic identity and a set of values. To me, the set of values is far more important than anything else. As human beings they must have some moral values which are stable; values that can help a person to deal with other human beings in a fair way. So I agreed with Katherine that they go with me to the mosque. Even my young daughter comes with me sometimes though I dress her up as a boy. Because when she asks me—"Why don't you take me along with the boys?"—I feel I cannot fail her in this.

U: I suppose they don't necessarily need formal teaching since the essence of the religion can be transmitted at home.

I: Yes, actually I've been very careful about this. The formalities of the religion are so rigid, and because they are usually taught, or we are constantly learning them through certain interpretations—and I disagree with a lot of these interpretations—I worry that my children might object to these because they become so rigid.

U: I suppose most religions become overlaid with interpretations over the centuries, and often, the original meaning of the religion can get completely lost...

I: And I keep far away from it because I find that most of the time the ritual of religion is far away from the spirit and it becomes rather hard, petrified.

U: I think tomorrow we should talk about the values that you see in Islam, and above all we should talk about the values that you want to pass on to your children. Because whatever it is a man wants to pass on to his children that is what matters most to him in life, and that is the real essence of his identity.

I: Let me just make a link here. Apart from the cultural and ethnic identity I find myself much more a Muslim than an Arab. Because the Arab thing can have all kinds of racial overtones, it's from Islam that I get my values.

Ibrahim El Salahi

"ISLAMIC VALUES"

U: You mentioned yesterday that you distinguish between your Arab identity and your Islamic identity. Can you elaborate on this?

I: The Arab identity refers to my origin, but I do not usually attach much importance to that at all. It's values that make a person; they guide you, they make you a better person and they help you to create a better society. The values that have formed me are the values of Islam: the faith, duties and social network. Maybe I should say a little bit first about the faith. We believe that Islam is the last word of God; that there is one God, a God who is just, and who delivers guidance and revelation through a series of prophets to bring the good word to the people, and help them to realize their own value. God is the Creator. He is the provider and he is the sustainer of the two worlds—the here and hereafter. We attribute 99 names to him, and these names denote his perfection. In the Prophet we have the one who interprets all the messages, and he is our guide. He is the leader; if you follow what him you will be saved. In Islam every person is for himself because there is no priesthood. It's a very personal experience. The Imam is not a priest; just a learned man. That's what makes Islam different from Christianity. Islam is appeals to your intellect. You must understand what you practice. Once you understand, you follow. If you don't, that's up to you. The decision is left to the individual. The Moslem is very clear in his mind as to what the 99 names of Allah mean. When we say "Allahu Akbar", God is great, we mean that he is greater than myself, greater than my father, greater than the ruler, greater than my greed, and greater than my aspirations. He is unique and complete, hence the adjectives of perfection. He is the absolute example of goodness and the creator of goodness itself. Another important point is that we believe that Islam is the final word of God, though Islam recognizes all the previous messages, starting from Abraham and going down to Mohammed. A Moslem has to believe in all of these. So we are partly Jewish, partly Christian and mostly Moslem. We believe in all the messages that came before, but Mohammed is "The Seal". His is the final message. So this is the faith. After that comes the practice—which is partly personal and partly social.

The personal aspect concerns the duties. We have the same ten commandments as the Jews, but they are explained in detail—what we should do and what we should not do, and with reference to the history of mankind. We speak of "The Five Pillars of Islam." The first is the Announcement, a declaration of faith in One God and in Mohammed, his prophet. That is the first thing a Moslem must do. The next is Prayer, the link between the Creator and the created. The third pillar is Almsgiving, an absolute obligation in Islam. It is made very clear to us that any wealth we may possess is only lent to us by the ultimate owner, God. It is our duty to look after it well and to distribute it well. The Prophet says, "He who sleeps with the stomach full, knowing that his neighbor is hungry, is not a proper Moslem." You have a commitment to your neighbor, regardless of whether he is a Moslem or not. Then there is the Fasting during Ramadan. This has many values, but mostly, as we say, it is an act of obedience. Secondly fasting makes you really think about the poor because for one month in the year you become aware of what it means to be hungry. The fifth pillar of Islam is the Hajj, the pilgrimage, which is another social aspect of Islam. It is not only that you perform a very ancient ritual, but the Hajj also gives you a very strong sense of the unity of mankind. In the Hajj people come from East and West and from all parts of the world, and there is no difference between them whether they are black, white or yellow. They all join in performing the same ritual. Equality is essential in Islam. The Koran says it quite clearly: "We have created you from a male and a female and we have made you into tribes and nations so that you may know that the best among you is the most pious." And the Prophet also said very clearly: "There is no difference between Arab and non-Arab, except piety." This basic sense of human equality dictates the actions of a pious Moslem. You have to take care of those you are responsible for, like members of your family as well as those you are not responsible for. The Moslem is advised to take care of his neighbor, even the seventh neighbor away! If something happens to any neighbor he becomes your responsibility. The person who has best personified the Islamic way of life was Omar, the second Khalif. With all the power he wielded he remained a completely modest man, caring for peoples and remaining at one with them. He once said: "If a mule trips over anywhere in Iraq and breaks its leg, I am responsible." That is the true spirit of Islam. There is a famous anecdote about an emissary from the court of Persia who was sent by the emperor with a message for Omar. When he arrived, he asked the people in Bagdad: "Where is your ruler?" They pointed to a man in a simple gown, lying under a tree, and said: "That is he." And the emissary said: "That one? Is he not living in a palace? And where are his body guards?" But later, after he had met the ruler and when he understood how Omar conducted his government, he said: "He ruled, he became just, he became safe, and he slept." Omar could live in the utmost simplicity because he knew that the wealth a man has acquired is only a test for him. Will he be able to make the right use of it? My own father also regarded himself as the administrator of his wealth, not its owner. He was a teacher of religion, and he was very well paid because he was highly respected as a member of staff in the Religious Institute in Omdurman. He had students coming from as far as Mauretania and Pakistan, and some of them were quite poor. I remember that they always visited us on payday, and my father would distribute money to them, and what he kept was just enough for us. We had just one garb each, and until it was really worn out, we would not get another one. My father had very little, but it was not until I grew up that I understood the wisdom, the real value behind it. I realize that these values with which I was brought up are really human values. A good Christian or a good Jew could say exactly the same. The Jews have a custom of always laying a spare plate on the table for the unexpected visitor. I have Jewish friends in the Sudan and they welcomed me to their house—even to the events that are only for Jews. I also have Christian friends who prayed for me. So the values are also universal. My experience of Islam has made me what I am today. From Islam I have my love of mankind, a sense of equality and a sense of pride. When I say 'pride', I don't mean vanity; I am proud to be a valuable creation of God. The values in me are a sign of Godliness, and this is sacred. Also I have to function as an individual because in Islam everyone stands for himself. There is no lamb to save you. But Islam is a fair deal: God gave you your mind, your brain, to discriminate between good and evil; you can go this way or that way. You are committed to society, to human society on a large scale. Whatever you love for yourself you must love also for your fellow human beings. Whatever you love in the world—the smell of it, the taste of it—you must help your fellow human beings to share it. In the end, it is not your attendance at the mosque or the performance of rituals that really matter; what really matters is the way you deal with other human beings. You will not be judged by your actions alone, but also by your intention to do good. If a man goes to Mecca three times, but at the back of his mind he thinks he may find a woman there to marry, or a business partner, then the Hajj has no value because he did not have the right intention. So these things are the real values to me in life and they are far more important than tribal, historical or geographical roots.

U: When you explain it to me like this it seems very simple. It seems like something that is within the capacity of every human being to accomplish, given the fact that he has the good intentions. But at the same time, if you look at mankind, if you look at the Islamic community, how many people do you see living by these values?

I: Very few! Many people who consider themselves Moslems are not Moslems. This has been a problem for a long time; people are easily tempted to make do with the *Dunya*, the earthly, lower form of living. People are too much attracted to pleasures, comfort and the excitement of the *Dunya*. Most people are preoccupied with accumulating wealth, wives, children, homes, pleasures..., with the result that they cannot respond to the world like a Moslem. A Moslem has to have PEACE within himself and he has to preserve peace for other people. That is why we greet each other "Peace be with you", and shake hands to show that we are not hiding anything from the other person. Islam tells us: "If someone greets you, answer him with a better greeting!"

U: Now to the crucial question. To what extent can you transmit these values to your children—since they're growing up in a world that is very different from your own childhood? You had the good fortune to grow up in real modesty and simplicity. But where can you find that in the competitive consumer society of today? How will the wisdom you transmit to your children not get drowned by the distractions and the temptations of the mass media culture and the entertainment industry? The innocence of your father, would it not be trampled upon by our modern materialistic world?

I: In Qatar we had a problem finding the poor! You know that when we sacrifice a ram it has to be divided into three. One part is for the family, one third is for friends and neighbors whether they are Muslims or not, and the third part is for the poor. I remember once going from place to place, and nobody would take it! I found a beggar sitting in front of the mosque, and I brought this meat to him and he said: "What is that?" and when I said: "Meat", he shouted: "I don't want it!" So I roamed about again to look for another poor person. When I finally found another beggar he also said: "I don't want it!" So I just left it there and ran away! How can you find a poor person in such a welfare state? Yet I think that the practice of all these rituals is important given all the tension and torment in modern society. We have to demonstrate in public that we believe in these things. I remember that once we were discussing the issue of whether to stay in Qatar or return to England, and my eldest son, who was then eight years old, said: "Here in Qatar we have everything we need, but I'd rather go back to England and be poor. I'd rather do what I want to do and be happy. I never want to be rich. If I had money, I'd give it away to the poor." So I felt that I had installed some ideas in his mind. In Islam you have to be an example to your child. You have to practice, and you have to let them see how you practice. When they are small, you take them to the Mosque; you let them participate though they understand very much. After the mosque, you take them to the chocolate shop to add sweetness to the Friday prayer. Then at the age of seven, you begin to tell them directly. You tell them what should be done. You begin to teach them that a good Moslem will always be where God wants him to be, and he will never be where God does not want him to be. At the age of ten, you have to become a bit firmer. But then, when they reach adulthood, it's up to them. I have the same worries as you. The world no longer has the same values it once did. It has become more and more difficult to impart your own values to your children.

But I have learnt from history that people go through certain phases. Like a spiral that curves behind and gets out of sight, it will twist forward again and reappear, but higher up. I am not all that pessimistic. We are going through a certain period in history. Well, let my children move through it. Let them discover the world. We for our part must preserve the values we believe in until the spiral turns round. In the world of politics, in the world of "progress" and "development" people are trying this and that, and when they realize it doesn't work, they try something else. Maybe people will come back to the values which the Jew found, which the Christian found, and which the Moslem found. And maybe they will come to understand that we are all worshipping the same God, only from a different point of view.

U: This interpretation of the world has given you a very stable identity because these basic values you are talking about are not really affected by new developments in high technology or by traumatic political events that may upset your country. But your children, who are partly English, do they not find it difficult to practice these beliefs in an environment like England?

I: Well, there is really nothing to stop them from practicing because there is a large Islamic community in England, and Moslems are allowed to observe their Friday prayers. But the environment at large militates against it. The consumer society with its liberal attitude allows you to do almost anything you want without the need to adhere to any creed whatsoever... Luckily, my children spent part of their childhood in the Sudan and with the family. So they had a good foundation in that kind of living and in ethics. Deep down they are still very close to it and when they visit the Sudan, they try to keep that side of them alive... I realize that the next generation may have different ideas. My children have a foot in both worlds, but their children may end up as Europeans, and the Sudan may be little more than a memory. But still, we must remember the saying we have: "You cannot bring to the light those whom you love. God will lead those whom he wishes to the light!" So we do what we can as much as possible, and leave the rest to God. When I come to London, I conduct myself as a Moslem. I celebrate Ramadan, I sacrifice a ram, and invite people to let them know what it is all about. But I realize that I'm fighting something big; I'm fighting a society that does not believe in anything.

U: What about Eve and Katherine. Did they become Moslems?

I: Katherine became a Moslem, but I didn't ask her to. You know in Islam a man is allowed to marry a non Moslem as long as she belongs to the people of the book, the people who have a sacred book, i.e. Jews, Christians and Moslems. She saw how I functioned; she saw that my life was governed by these values, and so she accepted the idea. She does not practice, though. We agreed that I bring up the children to the best of my knowledge. She had no religion; she's from a liberal family. They live their lives like civilized human beings, but faith does not come into it. Eve never became a Moslem, but my father accepted her fully. Other people complained and said: "Why do you have to marry her; why don't you marry your cousin or so-and-so?" But my father had no problem; he knew that the religion allows it, and he fully accepted her as a Christian and the mother of his grandchildren. Eve understood the Moslem way of life very well. When it came to the fasting month she would fast with us for social reasons. She would celebrate all the Moslem feasts, but at the same time we always had a Christmas celebration and even my father attended. He enjoyed himself and quoted verses from the Koran about Jesus. Sometimes the children felt lucky because they had the Moslem feasts from their father and the Christian ones from their mother. Now that they are a little older, they begin to realize that there is no harm in being heirs to ideas from Africa, the Arab world, Europe and from Judaism; that two parents could come together and create a family like ours. We all appreciate our accumulation of cultures and that this has enriched us very much indeed.

Ibrahim El Salahi:
"THE ARTIST IN EXILE"

U: Yesterday, reflecting on your life, you said: "I am a Sudanese, but I have
    made my home in Qatar and I keep a second home in England, so I had
    to become a little bit of an Englishman; and right now I am in Bayreuth,
    so I have to be a tiny bit of a German, too." You are touching on a point
    here that concerns many of us. Artists and writers from all over the globe
    are forced to leave their countries and work in exile. In the process of
    putting down new roots, of adapting to new conditions, they are also
    anxious to preserve their old identity. How has your own exile affected
    your concept of nationhood? In what way has it shifted your loyalties
    and in what manner has it modified or extended your sense of identity?

I: I think it has affected me a great deal—almost to the extent that the local-
    ity of your own home becomes almost a past dream; very, very dear, but
    more like a distant dream. You have a longing for it; nostalgia as it were.
    ... But this is a common human experience because throughout history
    people have migrated across the globe—the Huns pouring into Europe;
    the Indonesians crossing the Indian ocean to settle in Madagascar; the
    Jews scattered all over the world. Man must have an inborn capacity to
    adapt. As a child one feels that one's home is the centre of the universe. As
    a child in the Sudan I thought that England, France, the Philippines were
    on some remote periphery of Khartoum which to me then was the centre
    of everything! But as I moved out to London, my new home became
    the centre of the world. There is an instinct that makes you try to adjust;
    to put down new roots; to search for the common human elements in
    the new surroundings. Yet you feel torn inside, particularly when you are
    confronted with a set of values that is completely contrary, not only to
    what you believe, but what you know. Then you find yourself a complete

stranger and you go through emotions like: "I left my paradise to come to this hell? It doesn't make sense." You begin to worry: "Will they accept you? Will they care about you? Will they allow you to function? Will they believe that it is your right to be there?"

U: You referred to exile as "Hell"... How is that manifested?

I: When people denounce your humanity; when they deny that you are a human being who has a brain, who has feelings, and is sensitive enough to absorb, to understand, to respond; when they judge you by your exterior...

U: To bring it down to concrete terms, did you experience racialism in England?

I: Oh yes, quite a lot. Let me give you an example. I was looking for a room because I needed a place big enough for me to paint in. One day I saw a card on the notice board from a lady who said that she wanted to rent a room particularly to a student from the Slade. So I phoned, and she asked me to come. But as soon as she saw that I was black, she said she was sorry, but the room had been taken. You know what I did? I practically put my foot in the door and I said: "Please, I have been running around to look for a room and I feel very tired. I accept the fact that your room has been taken, but just let me come in for a while and rest a bit." She became embarrassed and allowed me in. And I didn't touch on the subject at all. I just told her where I came from, what I was doing. I told her that I had come to learn, to know more about people and their art, and to go back home. Then suddenly she got her raincoat and her umbrella, and she said: "Look, come here, I'll show you a place with a big room which is far less expensive than mine." So I went with her. There was a teacher and his wife who, both English, had decided that they were going to rent a big flat to help foreign students, particularly Africans, who had a lot of trouble finding accommodation. I remember the room was £2.75s with full board! And the lady who took me there? We became good friends, and later on we would often remember that first incident and joke about it. And when she became embarrassed, I comforted her saying: "I understand your feelings, but try also to understand my feelings. I am from a society where I feel no difference between others and me; no one is better than me and I am not better than any other person.

U: Well, this is rather typical of you. You are setting out to give an example of racialism, and you end up telling a story of unusual kindness.

I: Yes, but the racialism existed all the same, even among some of the young artists at the Slade. Those were the days of the Jive, and we all went dancing a lot. And one New Zealand student, in particularly, maybe he was jealous because a lot of the girls liked dancing with me, turned around one day on the dance floor, and said to me with such hatred in his eyes: "You bloody nigger!" I had to laugh, and my laughter made him even angrier. At first I didn't even know what the word meant. But later when I became aware of the insult, it didn't worry me either because I thought: "I'm not a nigger; I am Ibrahim Mohammed el Salahi who happened to be born on September 5th, 1930. I came to London to study and work and know people and return home! So if that's what he says, that is his problem."

U: Okay, well in your student days, you could laugh it off. But what about the time you had to go into exile; the time when you knew you could not return to the Sudan, and that you would simply have to live with such attitudes? Isn't there a danger then of closing up within oneself, of isolating oneself with a vision of one's culture that gradually becomes more and more removed from reality? Isn't that what happened to the Jews in the diaspora, that the religion became more and more closed up, formal and rigid? Under this kind of pressure a human being can react in two opposite ways: you either withdraw from your surroundings—isolate yourself and protect your own values in some kind of "pure" form—or you respond to the foreign culture by extending your horizon, your personality and your identity. What happened to you when you were forced to leave the Sudan, when it was impossible, even dangerous, for you to return home? Because I know from my own experience that the foreign society appears much more menacing then, and is much harder to cope with.

I: I may have mentioned to you some time ago that some years ago we returned to London from the Gulf. I had had enough of my job, and I thought I'd go back to the family in London. But once there we were quickly running short of money, and I thought I'd better get a job, any job. I went to the employment office and went through lots of cards that were all pinned up in neat rows on the wall. The official sitting at her desk was staring at me all the time, and whenever I took a card over to her, she said, "Oh sorry, it's just been taken." At last I found this job, a sausage packing job. The salary was £46 a week—just about the lowest pay you could get. But I thought I might just as well start with anything until something better turned up. The lady asked me for my qualifications! I told her that I had a degree in Fine Art, but she thought that was irrelevant. She wanted to know what else I had done. I said I'd been working in the Ministry of Information in Qatar, but she was unimpressed. So I told her that I really needed the job and I wanted to do it! Then she phoned the firm and talked to somebody there, and then she turned around to me and said: "Look here. This is quite a difficult job. It needs a very efficient person, and above all they require someone with the highest standards of cleanliness and hygiene." And I said: "But I am probably cleaner than most people. Just give me the chance." Then she said: "How old are you?" I said: "I am fifty." "Maybe you are a little bit old," she said. But I told her: "My hands are not old, and my eyes are not old. I can work and I need the job!" Then the last thing she said was: "Do you have any previous experience in sausage packing?" That was the last straw!!! I said to her: "Thank you very much, I don't have any experience in sausage packing, and I don't think I ever want to!" This experience made me curl up inside, and I retired into that attic room in our house to paint. But even in moments like that one, I carry my values within me, partly Moslem and partly artistic, and under pressure from the outside world I closed up to protect those values. But I suppose you can close up either destructively or constructively.

U: But nevertheless at some stage something else happens to you as well because now you do feel part of a bigger world and you are virtually running three parallel homes...

I: Let me go back to the Sudan for a moment. You know how we deal with one another in our social activities—eating together during big and small occasions. When a guest comes to your house or when someone moves into a new house or during one of the big festivals like Ramadan, everyone brings whatever little food he has from his own house, and whether it's a lot or just a little bit, they all put it together, sit around and eat together. What you have you share with others, and this brings about a feeling of kinship, togetherness and closeness. When I came to England as a refugee—after I had been jailed in the Sudan—I brought this way of life with me, and I was willing to share them with others. I was willing to share with my hosts even what they had to offer me. That is my way of moving into any new and strange society, and this way I feel that I have a right to be in my new place. I really believe that. Now that I am in Germany for a short time—away from my present home, and my original home—I still feel at home because I am not away from my big home, the larger community of mankind. So I believe I have a right to be here though I know that legally and politically I haven't got any... But for how long? Because surely this will have to change!

U: I believe you have made a very important point which people in Germany should certainly think about deeply. The stranger, the refugee has a right in the country of asylum because of the human and cultural values he brings with him. Many Europeans now resent the fact that their countries are gradually becoming multicultural. They cannot see that their own society can be enriched by this process.

Ibrahim El Salahi
"THE ARTISTIC PROCESS"

U: There is one more topic I want you to talk about. All this complexity of your expanding identity, how is it reflected in your work? What process is at work when you create a painting? How does the image arrive? What are the stages of development, and how do these different experiences from various cultures and countries merge into one organic whole? You may not, of course, be aware of this at the time, but at a later stage, perhaps...

I: Well, actually I never seem to use an immediate experience. The experience is absorbed, digested and may surface quite unexpectedly. I remember when I first went to England in the 1950s, and I saw the greenness, the intensity of the green and the red roofs of the houses and the pink faces. They all came out much later in my work—these intense and often gloomy colors. For in the Sudan there is such glare that you have to half-close your eyes. Only in certain times of the year can you open your eyes fully. So in the Sudan your impressions are almost half-seen, but I feel them through another eye; I know them by experience of another kind. In England my eyes are fully open; England is a grey world, old houses, dark and sooty. The appearance of things is rather haunting. I took it all in, but never did anything about it in London. It surfaced later on—almost like regurgitating. Some artists will do the superficial thing because they are concerned with scenery or human action, and it becomes a direct thing like, "I see, I draw; I see, I paint; I see, I sculpt, and so on. But there are other people like myself who take it all in, and then let it seep through. I find that when I come to a new place I don't take the ideas in too easily because I have a store within me which is loaded. So whatever I take... it will come later—when I have emptied that store a little bit. Maybe that is why I don't join groups easily. Other artists work in a community; they join the current movement immediately. It makes life easier for them because they want to exhibit, they want to sell, they want to be recognized, and being part of the current trend means that the galleries will accept them, and they can deal more easily with the public. I am not like that. I bring out what I want to bring out—not what the galleries think I ought to bring out.

U: How does the Sudanese element in your experience fuse with the Qatar experience or with the English experience?

I: Well, the Sudanese experience led to the images. As a child I had images of people at dawn. They appeared and I saw them physically. The things I draw are not imagined; they appear in front of my eyes. I draw almost like a medium...

U: But you didn't draw them as a child, or did you?

I: Not as a child, no. I didn't have the tools or the means to do so.

U: Is it that you remember the images, or do you still see them?

I: Sometimes, like a fraction of a second, the horizon opens and I see them. They are watching me, and I watch them. There is something I didn't tell you, but I told Georgina about it. The other day, when you did the final rehearsing for the music of the opening of her exhibition, I came in and I was looking at the appliqué with the two tall black and white figures. When you turned the light off, that thing actually came alive. It is as if something was going to step out of the cloth and move... I quickly moved out of the room. That also reminds me of something that happened many years ago when I was teaching at the Art College in Khartoum. I was working in one of those long studios and I was painting a huge canvas together with my friend, Hussein Sharif. I did most of my work at night, and often I was in the studio up to 3 in the morning. One night I looked at the picture, and one of the figures, a little one in the corner, came alive and was about to step out of the canvas! I thought this was sheer imagination, but I looked at it again, and in fact it was alive! So I turned off the light and went home. Anyway, I work like a medium, so my imagery is not something I would think about. I do not create them, they create themselves... Now, when I came to England I learned two things: I learned about techniques and I learned about people. I was keen to acquire the tools of painting, so I acquired every technique that was available. But I was also anxious to know about people. I wanted to know about European history, the background of the Renaissance, about early Christian painting and the contemporary movement. I wanted to know how people in England think, how they deal with things. I wanted to know about music, about ballet, about opera. When I went to live and work in the Arab world my experience linked again with my early childhood because Arab culture is linked with Arab language, with the Koran and calligraphy. Calligraphy is the most important subject for me because it is an abstracted form with symbols that carry sound and meaning. First, I used to write calligraphy as it is—poetry or words of wisdom. But later on I applied some of the techniques I had learned in Europe. I liked what Picasso had done with cubism—taking the visual form and breaking it into its original components, and then reconstructing it in a new form. I think I did the same thing with calligraphy. At first I wrote gibberish, using the letters without meaning. Then I started to break up the letters. I was interested in the rhythm within the writing. When you write you put down the letters in a line, and then another line. But when you have a closer look and magnify it you find the shape of the letters as well as the shape of the spaces between them, and that gives you another rhythm. Again, I tried to go deeper and break the actual shape of the symbol to its origin, to take it back where it came from. Because these letters can be traced back to animal forms, or water... they are like the hieroglyphs; they are abstractions of so many visual forms. And once I opened this door and went through it, it was like breaking glass! I had to walk carefully because sometimes you can cut yourself. You have to find your way through. I was breaking and breaking and breaking, and figures kept appearing, and the early components of calligraphy began to come to me. Strange enough, they were the same—exactly the same—figures or the same spirits that used to appear to me as a child! They came to me once they were freed of the rigid form of the letter!

U: Most children have powerful visions, but they tend to be frightening nightmares! But yours, I feel, were not like that at all.

I: Mine were quiet. Very peaceful. They'd just stay there, and gaze. Many people told me: "Oh, it can't be true. You are going nuts!" I told them: "Look, I don't force you to believe. I see them."

U: What is so surprising to me about all this is that when you broke up the calligraphy, figures began to appear. I think that must have been the very moment when I first saw your work in Khartoum...

I: ...Yes, indeed, exactly...

U: ...And these images were so strikingly African. You could almost have thought that they had emerged from some ancient culture in the Ivory Coast! There was this extraordinary affinity... maybe there is some deep layer of consciousness that reaches out way beyond its narrow geographical location. After all it was not that you had purposefully gone about to study West African art. There was something welling up inside you.

I: Yes, that is quite true. At first, I was just taken in by them. I couldn't even think about it. Because they wanted to come out and I brought them out, they kept coming and coming. They didn't have color in them; they were always very dark figures. There was no bright light. Always mysterious. Maybe that is why I keep going back to those black and white drawings. Later I thought: "Here I am, thinking of myself as an Arab, but these do look like African masks! How come? I am trying to refine my calligraphy and these kinds of images emerge! Then I got very much interested in the local patterns of the Sudan, I travelled a great deal in the Sudan, and I looked at the patterns in the leatherwork, the woodwork, the wickerwork, the tapestry... I found that there was some distant relationship to Islamic work, but there was another element. The stronger element was different, and when I started to analyze the element and the forms, I realized that they related more to West Africa.

U: What you have described now is that in the creative process there are two quite different—even mutually opposed processes. One is that which is totally uncontrolled by you—an image that just comes. Then there is the other process where you actually go and look at something, where you analyze, break up and reshape. In the one process you just allow yourself to be taken over; in the other one you want to know what's happening. How do these two processes blend with each other? Does the one ever get in the way of the other? Do you find that at times you are becoming too conscious of what you are doing?

I: This can cause a dilemma, this process of weeding and choosing between what flows from within, and that which you have acquired from without. How to weigh the two elements which may be quite contrary to each other, that is the whole nature of the work because ideas are ideas, not art. Art is what you make of the ideas. So this process of making, this factory in which you try to weld this to that, change this, and add that until you feel satisfied that no more readjustment is needed, that is the artistic process. Sometimes it takes a long time. You may even get to a point where you tear up the work because something got drained out of it. On rare occasions it can emerge...complete! Before you know what happened, you're holding the finished work in your hand! But most of the time it's hard labor, and you even begin to think: "If only there was some other job that I could do!" Often you feel caught in the middle— between this forceful element over which you have no control and the conscious process which you try to impose like a discipline. But you have to learn it, slowly, and I would say that the will of God who created you comes in and guides your hand so that you know exactly how to measure right, treat it right, and complete it the way it should be. Many people say to me: "Oh, you are an artist, what a wonderful life!" But I say: "It's hell!" It's hell because it's so difficult to preserve the first vision that you have seen—that first glimpse which often becomes overlaid and confusing and blurred because it keeps growing. Other things also happen to distract your mind. And because that mysterious force only reveals the image to you at a certain moment, the rest is a process of filtering it through all the intellectual processes that go into producing a picture.

U: Could one say that this image that appears—uncontrolled and unsolicited—is really some kind of archaic identity, and that the intellectual process then is to find some common denominator between it and all the other identities that you have acquired through various educational processes?

I: Yes! Let us say that art is the meeting point—just like the child is the product of the fusion of the male sperm and the female ovule. The archaic imagery—hidden, coming through you from the unknown, and allowing you to glimpse it briefly—has to be wedded to the things that you have learned, the things that you see and feel. This wedding is art.

Rowland Abiodun
"YORUBA VALUES"

U: I want to talk to you about your childhood in Owo. About the education you received from your parents, and the type of 'cultural baggage' you have carried through life with you.

R: Well, I don't know. I have never talked to anybody about these. They are very intimate...

U: We need not to be too personal about it. But I think it is important to discuss these things because you are one of the few people I know who have had a very traditional Yoruba upbringing, and yet you have reached the pinnacle of your profession in the Western world without sacrificing your principles. You have gone through the whole complicated process without loss of identity. That is very rare. You have been lucky to grow up the way you did. Compare yourself to somebody who grew up in a working class family in a London suburb, like Georgina. In her home there were no books, no art, and no music. A cultural desert! Millions of people grow up like that in Europe and it takes a superhuman effort to discover the real world, if you come from such a background. And we must recognize the fact that more and more Yoruba grow up just like that today. When Georgina ran a textile workshop at Nike's place a couple of years ago, she took the students to see an Agbegijo dance performance at Erin Osun, and it was the first time that any of them had seen such a performance, even though they live only a couple of miles away from the home town of these dancers and musicians. Now you must ask yourself: "How will these young people cope with Western values, if they have no values of their own to use as a yardstick to evaluate them? Where will they get the sense of security from that enables them to understand a foreign culture?"

Photo courtesy of Rowland Abiodun

When I first came to Yorubaland in 1950 I experienced the reverse situation. There were all kinds of British Colonialists, many of them from culturally very bleak backgrounds. They were bewildered by the indigenous culture, and so they encapsulated themselves in some kind of colonial rituals that helped them to isolate themselves from the new experience.

I first lived in a little wooden bungalow that was a couple of kilometers off the University at Ibadan. The bungalow was located on the farmland of a neighboring village. In the evenings I would stroll through the yam gardens and the palm groves. I soon noticed one isolated house where a public works engineer lived—alone. Every evening I saw him having dinner by himself. He wore evening dress, and the table was elaborately laid with an assortment of cutlery and glasses. The 'steward' who served him wore a white uniform with a red cummerbund. That's what was called 'keeping up British standards' in those days. This type of colonial ritual served to protect people from an experience they did not want to face. The majority of academics in the University of Ibadan participated in it, and accused people like myself—who sat around in Sango shrines or followed the dancing masquerades through the town— of 'going native.'

Discovering the excitement of Yoruba drumming did not make me abandon my interest in classical European music. On the contrary! The more I understood Yoruba music, the more I began to understand my own musical tradition. Those colonialists who had no deep understanding of their own music thought Yoruba drumming was nothing but a lot of noise. The tragedy is that those people educated a whole generation of Africans who thought that rejecting their own culture was an integral part of acquiring Western skills. Abandoning their own cultural base, they had no means of interpreting European culture, and they were left with the grotesque substitute of British colonial rituals. This is how we got the sad phenomenon of what villagers soon labeled *oyinbo dudu*— the Europeanized African, who is often neither European nor African.

R: I think you are perfectly right.

U: So what I want from you is really very simple: What particular Yoruba values you got from your parents have enabled you to cope with Europe in the way you have? In the light of what I said, you will agree this is an important thing to do.

R: Well, let's discuss it, but because it is so intimate, we will have to think about it again before it is published.

33

U: You need not be too personal about it. Tell me what you saw. What you experienced. What are the images of Yoruba culture that remain in your mind?

R: Owo was a town that never had its culture overrun or tampered with—even though it was situated between those two powerful kingdoms of Ife and Benin. When I was growing up the culture was still very powerful and all the traditional festivals were still being observed. We had Igogo festival, Egungun, Ogun, and the Upabi. Upabi was the splitting of the kola nut. It was a harvest festival, a thanksgiving for the new crop. From 1946 on I became aware of what was happening around me. My parents were both Christians and they were very prominent and respected members of the Anglican church. But I had an aunt who practiced the *erindilogun*, the oracle system in which 16 cowry shells are used. Also my paternal grandmother knew a lot about herbs and she helped many women, particularly those of child-bearing age. Also many of my extended family took chieftaincy titles, and I often followed them as they danced around the town in celebration. We lived in a traditional house—a large rectangular building with an open courtyard...

U: With thick mud walls, and courtyards leading into courtyards...

R: Exactly. I was interested in this compound structure. Of course, I wasn't looking at it as architecture then. It was simply home, a place where I felt secure. One other place that attracted me was the Ojomo's palace. Ojomo is the most important chief after the Olowo. His palace was said to be as big as that of the Olowo's—undoubtedly one of the finest palaces in Yoruba land—thick mud walls, polished red mud. The walls, even in our house, were annually painted with a slip of red mud and the floors were painted with cow dung. These houses were cool, and we collected rainwater—like an impluvium. I often ran away from home to go to the Ojomo's palace. I loved to see the sacrifices there, the meetings of the chiefs, the court sessions... In fact they used to tease me at home about it. They'd say: "He'll grow up to take a chieftaincy title in the Ojomo's palace."

U: You have already pinpointed a very important aspect of Yoruba culture: the accessibility of the chiefs. The Ojomo's palace, even the king's palace, would be open to anybody. They were not the exclusive domains of the elite. Yoruba was a very democratic culture. Imagine an English peasant child trying to enter the duke's castle!

R: Exactly! And they always loved me. They enjoyed my interest; my presence. There were always sacrifices. Women were officiating. And then the Ojomo in his regalia! I was overwhelmed. I loved it. The *whiteness!* He came out in these white robes, and the calm and dignity with which he moved!

U: There was a certain stateliness about Yoruba ceremonies. A cool sincerity. But however dignified the king, however holy he was, he always remained accessible. He could never say: "And who are you?! What are you doing here?"

R: Never! If you were a stranger he would have to give you kola nuts. You know, in the Ojomo's palace they had a set of huge drums standing on three legs. In the morning there was drumming, in the evening there was drumming. Everything was enchanting, and there was a special courtyard which I liked to enter, and that was where the Ojomo would talk privately to his chiefs and supporters. I was never barred from it; and when you sat on the Ojomo's right hand, you were overlooking a collection of images: some were *sigidi*, made from clay, some were carved in wood like the Osanmasinmi, and others were bronze heads. Sometimes there was fresh blood from a sacrifice on the altar. To me that man was indestructible! The man who was installed the Ojomo in 1948 had been my headmaster. He had always impressed me at school because he spoke beautiful English. But then, when he became the Ojomo we discovered that his command of our own language was wonderful. Now as the Ojomo, he seldom used the English language. I would always follow him during the Igogo festival. He would come out the day before the Olowo's Igogo. He had to dance from house to house, from street to street through the entire town. I am telling you, he had unbelievable energy. I think he must have been possessed during that period because I don't know how else he could have that level of strength and endurance. He must have had some special medicine. Then at harvest time when the Egungun came out I would follow them around again and again. I would wait at the edge of the sacred grove for them to appear in a blaze of colors. And as I watched them coming out from the darkness of the forest, it was as if *my own life* was being renewed—not just the life of the town.

U: In many Yoruba towns the church actively campaigned against all traditional festivals, and from their pulpit, clergymen would condemn children who had been seen following the ancestral masquerades. Did such a situation exist in Owo?

R: Nooooo! Not at all! Not when I was young. Prominent church members attended these festivals. Nobody had anything against our tradition then. Much later however, maybe in the early seventies, the churches started grumbling. But when I was a child, people thought it was stupid to abandon our traditional obligations. They said: "Christianity does not stipulate that you should abandon your traditional duties." There were several festivals every month—burials and chieftaincy installations. People came out in their regalia dancing and enjoying various types of music. I would follow them around in the street, and I would be among thousands of revelers! When I finally went to Government College Ibadan, I kept revisiting these scenes in my dreams! I sustained myself by visualizing and reliving these festivals in all their details—the movement, the dance and the *colors,* everything! This was really necessary because we learned Latin and French; we learned the History of the British Empire; we learned about America and Australia. I knew the geography of Tasmania! But we learned nothing—nothing at all about our own people! Their very existence was denied. We were even forbidden to speak our language! And anybody who was caught speaking the language would be fined and sometimes those caught three times would be caned and those who were caned for the third time could be suspended or even expelled from the school. There's this interesting incident once when a boy was brought before the housemaster by a prefect. The boy had been caught speaking in the 'vernacular', that is, in Yoruba. The housemaster decided that the boy must be caned. The boy admitted he had been speaking Yoruba but he said he wanted to make a point before being punished. The housemaster agreed to listen. Then the boy said that while it was true that he had spoken Yoruba, he had also heard the prefect laugh in Yoruba. The housemaster said: "How do you laugh in English?" The boy demonstrated a polite chuckle, whereupon the housemaster broke into his own loud, Yoruba laughter. The boy was let off. The only way I could express my own feelings in this environment was through art. I was doing a lot of artistic work then; I won many medals in the Western Region Festival of the Arts. Dr. Olumbe Bassir and his wife, Constance, encouraged me a lot. There was a time when I thought there was no need to study any further, because I was going to become a practicing artist.

U: Let us return to your childhood in Owo. I want to know how children were brought up. How were they treated? In Europe we regulate the lives of children a great deal. They are expected to eat at certain times, they are expected to finish their meal. They must go to bed at a fixed hour. We relegate the responsibility for their education to institutions—even from a very early age because there are usually no aunts or grandmothers around to share the burden. On the other hand Yoruba children move around freely. They wander from compound to compound. They eat when they are hungry, they go to sleep when they are too tired to stay awake, and they participate in all grown-up activities. No child is ever sent out of the room or told "you are too young to understand." At the same time children also participate in the work of adults.

R: Oh, yes. I went to farm only once a week because I was in school the rest of the time. But even when I was quite small I followed my grandfather. You would trek about eight miles carrying something on your head. We would make a few yam heaps, we would also play a little. You would learn how to roast yams and how to hunt little animals. My parents really had less influence on my traditional education than my grandparents.

U: That is very common in Yoruba country. What *was* this influence?

R: I acquired their attitude towards work. I learned the way they thought through the stories they told me. I followed my grandfather when he went hunting. I followed him to meetings. I wouldn't say a word. I sat there, listened and observed how the elders resolved conflicts. I marveled at the language they spoke, the proverbs they used. It was fantastic. And you started learning.

U: Learning without actually being taught. There is something that always amazed me in Yorubaland. Namely, you witness a serious discussion between chiefs in the palace, or you witness a sacred ritual in a shrine; the small children sit there, attentive, watchful, but no child ever disturbs. It is unknown. They don't fidget. How does the culture achieve this? Because children are not repressed; there is no strict 'discipline'. At the same time the children are capable of this seriousness, this calm. You know the poster of an exhibition we had at IWALEWA Haus called "The Face of the Gods." That young girl was no more than seven. She was the daughter of a famous Sango dancer from Ila Orangun. You cannot find a face like that in the whole of Europe. How does the culture produce such a child? In this case, of course, the Orisa has a lot to do with it; but even without that, Yoruba children have a seriousness and a dignity that our children are incapable of. Think by comparison of the German children you met yesterday...

R: Oh yes, they fly off every second.

U: How come European children talk a silly language of their own? Yoruba children do not use diminutives. They speak the same language as adults and they do not whine. How do they do it? Would you have pestered your mother for food? Would you have clung to her wrapper?

R: No, no, no! My mother 'talked' to us with her eyes. And the attentive child would be called omo t'omo'ju—literally, the child who can decode the parents' facial expressions. That is a great compliment. The child who can take his or her clue by just looking at the parents is a well behaved child indeed.

U: Were you ever beaten?

R: No! No! Never! And you know there is one thing called ifarabale—self control; control over your body and mind. When I saw Tunji playing in the Opera House, what came to my mind was "Ah, Tunji ni ifarabale", that is, Tunji displayed complete self-control. This is very important to Yoruba people. So children start at an early age to strive to attain it...

U: Do they learn only by example?

R: I don't really know.

U: Did anybody ever tell you, "Walk like that, carry yourself like this, sit still, concentrate, and so on?"

R: No, I think it has to do with alo (riddles) and storytelling in the evening, because in those days there was no television. When there was moonlight, everybody would gather outside, and all the children would sit there—absolutely quietly. Then one of the older men or women would start with a song and then lead to the real itan, folk tales. In one year I must have listened to at least eight hundred stories. I think that trains you to listen.

U: It trains you to concentrate.

R: It trains your imagination.

U: There is one thing however: the stories are not moral stories. They are not like Grimm's fairy tales, where good always triumphs over evil. *Ijapa* (tortoise), the hero of many Yoruba stories, is greedy, crafty, deceitful, cruel—yet he gets away with it most of the time! So it is not exactly the kind of story that teaches you not to steal or not to lie. After all our sympathies are always with *Ijapa;* we like him for his flamboyance, his imagination and his wonderful sense of survival. In a sense this is remarkable, because the European fairy tale offers a false picture of the world; an escapist world. Yoruba *itan* are much more realistic; they are tragicomedies. The intrigues, the rivalries, the suffering are all there. Maybe they teach us to live with it and to laugh at our weaknesses when we can. After all, we meet these *Ijapa* characters almost every day. The stories merely draw him a bit larger than life... The thing that puzzles me is: how do you grow up in Owo and learn that you don't steal? Because I remember times in Yoruba country when stealing was unheard of. Between 1950 and 1960 I never locked my house in Ibadan or Ilobu or Osogbo. I remember also when I was quite new in the country and I went to give an extramural lecture in Ogbomoso I locked my car automatically, without thinking, when I parked outside the school. Then my class secretary said "You mean that in this Ogbomoso somebody would steal anything from your car?" I felt ashamed and never locked my car again. But then how do you learn such attitudes? Because your parents don't wag their fingers at you all the time, saying: "Don't do this, don't do that."

R: It has to do with a number of concepts. One is *iluti*, the ability to listen, to respond, and to carry out instructions. Another is *omoluwabi,* the child of the source of *Iwa,* character.

U: Chief Delana has defined *omoluwabi* as a person who embodies all the good qualities appreciated by Yoruba people; a man who is good at his profession, whatever it happens to be; a man who shows respect to his elders, who works well with others, whether in a hunting party or a court session; a man who is respected throughout the community; the person of high esteem, 'easily recognized', as the axiom goes, 'by two hundred pairs of eyes'.

R: Good character, *iwa*, is continuously quoted in Ifa as the basis of a successful life, and children hear such verses, not just when they happen to be present at a divination, but also because many of these phrases have entered everyday language.

U: For example, *the man who marries a mannerless woman is a spinster. The man who fathered a mannerless child is a childless man indeed.* But the main question then remains: How does one acquire manners, good character, in Yoruba society? How are manners taught?

R: Through *SUURU*, patience! *Suuru baba iwa*, patience, the father of good character. When you are patient, that means you can listen, you can learn many things, you can absorb many shocks, you can reason, you can respond to any situation. Yoruba people love observing this ability in their young ones; they expect that from everyone. You get rewarded for exhibiting such qualities. You receive praise. Even in the profession of a woodcarver, you cannot be a great artist unless you have *ifarabale*, calmness, self-control, total concentration. You can't be an artist without *ifarabale* and *suuru*.

U: You need the inner peace which I have admired in so many Yoruba elders.

R: Exactly. Without *suuru* you cannot absorb the wisdom your father or grandfather has to impart. Only *suuru* enables you to learn the skills of a great master craftsman. There are different kinds of individual *iwa* and people respect that. But if you want to be respected as a king, as a priest, as a diviner then you have to have *suuru*.

U: *Suuru* is not to be mistaken for passivity.

R: No, no! It is what I would call 'calculated patience!' *It is with calculated patience that one attacks the sand fly perched on one's scrotum!*

U: *Suuru* is a form of pragmatism.

R: That's right. If you take a big stick to kill the sand fly, you end up injuring yourself—and you may even miss the fly. It's not about restraint or self sacrifice...

U: Quite on the contrary. The Yoruba live out everything ... but they know when and how!

R: *Suuru* means that you have the conviction that the world goes on. It takes its course and *your* opportunity will come. Just hold on...

U: Don't hassle.

R: No! Hassling, hustling, being over ambitious, pushy—these are considered to be the worst flaws in a human. An Ifa verse says: *Somebody who carries a basket of eggs on his head has need of composed gait.*

U: And life being what it is, we are all carrying baskets full of eggs, and every time you feel irritated, every time you lose your patience you are breaking some eggs in your life.

R: *It is with care and dignity that the well-raised citizen treads the earth...*

U: One thing I loved most about living in Yoruba country was this. An old man, who may be a priest, comes to visit you. He greets you, " *E ku'le o, Iyawo nko? Omode nko?*" And so on. He sits down. You offer him kola nuts. Maybe a drink. He has not come because he has something to say. He has not come to report some crisis... There is a wonderful Yoruba greeting, "I hope nothing." He hasn't come because he needs money or because he wants to chat. He wants *to be* with you. He sits down quietly. Nothing is said; there is no need for it. No small talk. You may even go on doing what you were doing. He will be there for ten minutes or half an hour. You are not even aware how long it is...

R: Exactly!

U: Finally he says, "*Mo ti rii yin*" (I have seen you), and leaves. Nothing has 'happened', but you feel refreshed, even elated, because you were in his presence. There is a radiation, a strong magnetic field that charges your spirit. And I am sure it is this *suuru,* this inner calm.

41

R: Yes, it is, it is.

U: It's a quality you cannot find in the West.

R: It has been lost. We felt this very much when we first came to America. Even now it feels unnatural—the speed with which people deal with you. "Yes? What do you want?" And they just snap off and move to the next thing. Many people avoid communication altogether. As bad as Nigeria was when we left, people would still just visit as you described. We would have four or five visitors a day, "Ah, it's a long time since I have seen you," and they'd just sit down.

U: Even children can do that!

R: Yes, because they are sent! My grandfather used to send me. Not once or twice a week—I could be sent ten times to greet somebody! So I will go there, to that elder person, and say, "My grandfather has sent me to greet you." He'd say *"Aaah, o se o."* (Thank you.) After about five minutes of silence, he will say, *"Ah, pele o."* (Greetings.) I'd sit there for a long time without saying anything, but now in hindsight, I know that he must have enjoyed the gesture, the attention he was receiving from my grandfather. After a while, I'd get up to leave; I'd prostrate and say goodbye. At home, I'd say to my grandfather: *"Mo ti ki won. Alaafa ni won wa. Won ni ki n kii yin."* (I have delivered your greetings. I inquired after his health. He's well. He sent his greetings and thanks.) My grandfather would say, *"O kare, omo ni o."* (Very well done; you are a wonderful child.) In other words, he was proud of me. The following morning, he might say, "Ah, go and visit the mother near the market place. Tell her that I send greetings. Tell her I hope she's well..." Then I'd go there and say, "My grandfather says I should greet you. He hopes you are well." She'd say, "Thank you. I am well." After some time she will ask, *"Se ko si?"* A way of saying, "Is everyone alright?" Then I'd say, "My grandfather's body is not very well; he has a fever, I think." She'd go into the house and bring some medicine and wrap it. "Give that to him." I would not ask to see what's inside. When my grandfather received the parcel, he'd say, *"Aaaaahhhh, O kare."* (You've done very well.) Then he'd call my grandmother, and say, "Remember that thing we couldn't find a while ago? Here it is!" You see, maybe in the first place, my grandfather wanted to ask for that medicine, but didn't want to be explicit. He didn't send me expressly to collect the medicine, and I didn't really know his intention. But there was a message, a very subtle message, and the subtlety never got in the way of message!

U: At the same time you were receiving a subtle education!

R: I was learning all the time on these errands. On another occasion my grandfather will say again, "You know Lagbaja, Chief Lagbaja? Go and greet him. Tell him I am getting ready for my meeting eight days hence." So I will go there again. I will prostrate. I will sit down. He won't say anything. But, when I am going, I will be given a parcel. Two thighs of the antelope will be wrapped and put in a bag. "The moon has made it difficult to kill anything. All the same, here are two thighs." Then I will take it to my grandfather who will say, "Aaah!" He will call my grandmother and say, "Come. I have something to show you!" And because I carried out all these errands efficiently, my grandfather loved me. He loved me so much that when he was about to die, he asked that all his hunting implements—all of them—be passed on to me.

U: This was the finest education you could ever have. You learned manners. You learned composure. You learned diplomacy. You had to know what to say, you had you sense when the right moment came to leave, you had to be able to convey the spirit of the message, not just the words. You had a great responsibility. A clumsily delivered message could lead to a rift between adults because everything here depended on subtlety and balance.

R: My grandfather told me, "You are a child who has *ifarabale*. The future will bring you blessings." There was another boy, a distant relative. Once in a while, when I was not around, my grandfather would send him on an errand. But grandfather often got annoyed with him. "You send him on an errand, and he doesn't know how to deliver the message." Because, truly, he would rush into the compound, hurriedly deliver his message and he was gone! My grandfather would say, "Did you greet him? How did you greet him?..."

U: So this is how you learn how to become a man, a reliable, secure, well-mannered person.

R: And I enjoyed listening very much. Just sitting there.... When my grand-
      father was very old, he couldn't move much. He just sat in one place for
      hours. He just sat down. He had this long pipe, a long bamboo stick with
      a clay piece at the end. Do you know what discipline it took for me to stay
      by him for about six hours? I would remove the old tobacco when he had
      finished his smoke, then I would get some glowing embers to rekindle the
      pipe. Then I would sit and wait.... I wouldn't be able to doze off.

U: But this is again the magic of just being together, being attuned to the
      world of the other person.

R: And then I learned something else, too. My grandfather was never afraid.
      Sometimes he would be the only one in the entire house, and the doors
      would be open. No thief or anything scared him. And he used to tell me:
      nobody dares! Nobody could come to this house and remove anything
      while he was around. So whenever I was with him and we were the only
      ones in the house, I felt that even though he was frail nobody was a match
      for him. I thought my grandfather was the strongest person in the world;
      he was feared for his supernatural powers. When he was really annoyed,
      he would tap his feet like this and say: "Do you want me to curse you?"
      But he would never curse. He'd add, "If it weren't for your mother, I'd
      curse you...!" Then everybody would be begging. Everybody would pros-
      trate, *"E ma binu baba."* (Don't be angry, father.) This explosion could be
      caused by very little things; like somebody coming in and not greeting,
      "E kaaro" or *"e kuu le o,"* and Baba would feel mortally offended!

U: It may have been a small thing in itself but it upset the tradition, it inter-
      fered with the equilibrium of things and your grandfather was aware of
      the danger to society...

R: It was a manifestation of this strong character, this power. You carry the
      memory of it, the sense of it through your entire life!

U: It is authority emanating from an undisturbed calm, from a perfect
      balance of mind.

R: It is this peace that I got from my grandfather that helped me throughout
      my life, helped me in my work, my research. Most things that I achieved
      in the world happened through the utilization of those values.

U: You were not interested in a rat race.

R: Exactly. In fact I remember my grandfather used to tell me, "The water you are meant to drink will flow in your direction." It teaches you not to join the rat race. When it is your turn you will get it. If you grab it too soon you will lose it. The little phrase, *suuru baba iwa,* explains the very core of the Yoruba attitude to life. It would be totally absurd for a Babalawo to be ambitious or greedy! He simply could not function! His reputation and his effectiveness rest on his modesty, his calm, and his composure. And an Oba, a king, with personal ambitions would be a disaster for his town. Remember the saying, "We made you Oba, and you say you have higher aspirations. Do you plan to become Olodumare, the Almighty?" *Suuru* helps you to appreciate at all times who you are, irrespective of whether you are a cleaner, a night guard, or a town crier. People were proud of whatever they were doing.

U: Muraina Oyelami, musician and artist, told me about a man in Irag-biji whose job it was to get the hay for the king's horse. He was highly respected in the community because he did the job well.

R: Of course! This is something I learned as a small boy. You are respected, not for what you do, but for how well you do it. I learned a lot through proverbs and Ifa verses. And even now, these sayings just come to me when the need arises. The other day I was trying to settle a case between two friends. One had offended the other, but the offender was rather dis-missive, saying that since they had been friends for a long time, the other need not take it seriously. But I told him, "He who shits may forget; the person who cleans it up remembers." You hurt a person, and you say, "Let's forget about the whole thing," but that is often difficult as long as hurt feelings remain...

U: Your traditional Yoruba education has prepared you for almost any human situation. You have learned how to manage a crisis, how to main-tain a calm perspective in a conflict. You can place an individual situation into a wider human context that takes the sting of bitterness out of it. That way you don't have to panic! You know it has happened before, and it has been dealt with, and it can be resolved.

R: One thing I have learned from my grandfather is that there is a reason for everything. You don't trust people who claim to have no motivation. That's what has made me always very uncomfortable with the Western concept of "Art for Art's sake". If you would show my grandfather a canvas which I have painted white on white he would ask me, "Why are you doing it?" And if I told him, "No reason, I just felt like it," he would bluntly say, "You are a liar. There is a reason for it." And he would back it up by saying, "If you see a man running, and you ask why he is running, and the man says, 'I just like to run', don't believe him. He is either being pursued or he is pursuing something."

U: That is a very good example because there is an everyday Yoruba wisdom which applies to the situation in your profession that your grandfather could never have imagined in his life. Your upbringing actually helps you to take a critical look at modem art, and I think that must have helped you to live through a Eurocentric institution like the Art School at Zaria.

R: Exactly. It was this kind of traditional wisdom that made me question everything. I was not prepared to analyze African art by simply dissecting it into shapes and proportions. The study of African art must go beyond that because Africans themselves never thought of it in those terms. It's alright for Western art historians to look at African art like that, but for us, that approach is absolutely empty.

U: It's like grammarians looking at language. They tear it to pieces to discover the rules. But the great writers are not aware of rules. They just write! In my experience, Yoruba people have never really talked about proportions or outward aesthetic qualities of carvings even though the artists clearly worked according to certain criteria. But just as the greatest compliment you can pay a man is to simply say, "*Okunrin ni!* (He is a man)," so priests—when they have installed a new sacred carving in a shrine, and they have performed the ritual for it—will simply say, "*Ere ni*" (It is a sacred image). When you say *ere ni*, it means that you recognize its presence, its force; you acknowledge its *iwa,* its *very* essence.

R: Of course, many things in Yoruba are understood, although they remain unsaid. At a very young age, a child learns to interpret the mother's facial expressions. As a grown-up, one learns to interpret hints—known euphemistically as *abo oro*—truncated phrases, incomplete sentences or words.

Hence the saying, "To an *omoluwabi* (a person of good upbringing and character) we only need to give *abo oro*." *Omoluwabi* can decipher unspoken messages...

U: I think the essential difference between the way Europeans and Yoruba treat their children is that Europeans never give the child any responsibility. They underestimate their children! That is why they seldom listen to their children. They make all the decisions for them, whereas Yoruba children are given the opportunity to determine their own lives. If a child goes to an uncle or aunt and says, "I want to live with you," the elders have no choice! If a child decides he wants to apprentice himself to a wood carver, although he does not even come from a carver's family, the master carver cannot refuse him. When I allowed Tunji to leave school at 15 because he wanted to become a drummer, my European friends thought I was extremely irresponsible. But somehow I felt that he had made a responsible decision, and I had to respect it.

R: The Yoruba would say that it was what his *ori* had chosen.

U: Aha! You see, in Europe they do not respect the *ori* (the very essence of life, head—literally) of a child!

R: In fact they kill it, they wipe it out totally. Then later in life they tell him to start looking for his identity.

U: ...They kill people's identity, and then make a research project out of it! But Yoruba parents are sensitive even to those idiosyncrasies of the child through which the *ori* manifested itself.

R: It starts from birth. When the child is born you take it to the Babalawo. There is a ceremony called *Imori*, during which a diviner foretells a child's future by revealing what his or her *ori* has chosen. The Babalawo may tell you who the child is. He may point out certain food taboos that he should keep. He may tell you that the child has a particularly strong *ori* which you must respect. I don't think that any doctor can do that in the West. And in their education system, they are put through the same mill, the same grinder, and they all come out the same at the end. When I was young, I used to disappear from the house and go to an uncle who was a blacksmith and a carver. He was a carver who specialized in *Ako* (funerary art) figures, and he was said to be the finest *Ako* carver of all times. My father used to say that his *ori* and mine were compatible. Everyone could see that I would rather be drawing than doing school work. Rather than arithmetic, I would be lying under a jacked-up car in a mechanic's workshop. My uncle accepted my artistic inclinations. Everyone knew I was close to Ogun, the god of technology, creativity. So when, at Government College, I decided to become an artist, my father said, "I'm not surprised. Even though we would have liked you to become a doctor or a lawyer, but what your *ori* has chosen, nobody can stop it. Go ahead and do what your *ori* has chosen."

U: The really wonderful thing about the concept of *ori* is that it makes society respect the individual. The individual has a wonderful sanction for doing what he wants to do. After all, he brought this gift, this inclination from heaven, and he must live it out.

R: Even the *Orisa* respects your *ori*. No Orisa can come to your aid without first taking permission from your *ori*.... They have to get clearance from it! So how could the parents try to ignore it? It is foolish and dangerous for somebody to try and ignore somebody else's *ori*. It might even be better to kill the person than to tamper with his *ori!* I think in the wider world, those who have made it are those who have followed their *ori*.

U: Only those can do it whose *ori* is strong.

R: And you have to make sacrifices to allow your *ori* to function. There is a ceremony called *ori wiwe*, the ritual cleansing of *ori*. One's *ori* is bathed with a specially prepared black soap, so that one's destiny can shine. In practical terms it also means you are appealing to the whole world not to interfere with the dictates of your *ori*.

U: I think the sacrifice is also a symbol. After all, if you want to live according to your *ori*, you must also be prepared to sacrifice, that is, give up, other and lesser interests. You must give direction to your life and become single minded—up to a point

R: Of course. That's why I was not at all surprised when I heard about Tunji leaving school, even though other people were asking, "What happened?! What's happened?" I said, "He is doing what he has come into the world to do." It's what we call *akunleyan,* our destiny—that which we chose kneeling down before our creator. *Akunleyan* is that nature with which we were born...

U: Once a person has understood that, he can go through a lot in life without losing direction. And here, I think, we have the answer to my original question: Remembering "what you have received kneeling down" enabled you to travel the long road to Western institutions, without losing your identity. Whether in Government College Ibadan, or Ahmadu Bello University Zaria, or the University in Toronto, you could absorb any foreign ideas, as long as they were compatible with your *ori.*

R: The whole essence in life is just to know who you are, and to fulfill your destiny accordingly. And this is exactly what a traditional Yoruba education helps you to do.

U: I believe that all this throws some light on another important issue. Many observers of Yoruba culture—even a man like Pierre Verger—have said that Yoruba culture is immoral or at least a-moral.

R: Oh no!

U: Well, you can see how it arises. After all there is no "Ten Commandments" in which everything is neatly laid out here. On the contrary moral values are conveyed in a more subtle form. But if you apply the concepts of *ori, iwa,* and *suuru* it becomes clear that a successful life, and therefore a *good* one, is a life in which a person fulfills his destiny by living out his potential to the fullest. An unsuccessful life, and therefore a bad life or a wasted one, is a life in which the person has been diverted from his original path. He has ignored his *ori* and wasted the assets he brought with him from heaven. What I am trying to say is that the person who has acquired the patience and the inner-peace that are derived from a life in accordance with one's *ori* does not need the Ten Commandments because greed, theft and jealousy and all the human failings and offences that arise from them have become irrelevant.

R: That's true. The single minded person simply finds these things meaningless. What a shame it is we have failed to build these ancient values into our modern education system!

Rowland Abiodun
"YORUBA WOMEN"

U: Throughout my life among the Yoruba, I was always impressed by the independence and power of Yoruba women. And yet, there are still many writers, even knowledgeable ones, who see Yoruba society as highly patriarchal, where women are dominated and exploited by men. How does this misconception arise?

R: The fact is that foreign religions have reduced the position of women in Yorubaland in recent years. And Western values and education, Islam, and Christianity have modified Yoruba concepts... They have imposed a new layer of values on Yoruba values.

U: This is true. But even those who experienced Yoruba society three or four decades ago, when Islam and Christianity had not yet undermined Yoruba religion to this extent, were often fooled by the demonstrative show of male dignity in Yoruba society. They see the head of the household, pompously enthroned in his embroidered *agbada* robe, his wives kneeling to greet him in the morning while he casually hands a few shillings to the children to buy schoolbooks. Yet the image is deceptive because it does not reflect the real power or the relationship between the husband and the wives. The women are economically independent; they pursue their own craft or their own trade, they feed themselves and their children. Thus they can be economically independent of their husbands in many respects. They may rise to high positions in the cults of the Orisa they may be leaders in their trade unions, say the cloth sellers union or the yam sellers union, and they can even achieve important chieftaincy titles in the city such as *Iyalode,* the head of women, or *Iyaloja*, head of the markets. In fact they pursue independent personal careers and may carry more respect in the town than their husbands.

R: Another factor may be that men are reluctant to talk about the power of women. They feel a little uneasy about the spiritual power of women.... So researchers who talk only to men do not get a true picture of the situation. How much do we know, for example, about Lobun, the female ruler, in Ondo? She surely was a powerful figure politically, economically and possessed immense spiritual power.

U: Maybe we should talk about this spiritual power....

R: If you look deeper into Yoruba thought, you will find a lot of references to this power. For example, the greeting for every New Year is Odun a yabo, which means, literally, "May the year choose to be, or turn out, female."

U: That is, calm, peaceful ... creative ... harmonious ... and fruitful!

R: Yes! It would be a curse to say, "May the new year turn out to be ako, male!" Nobody wants to hear that. So then, if women are not important, why should we invoke them in this way at the beginning of every important festival or milestone? Simple. We are invoking the powers of 'our mothers' and we do so because we know they wield considerable spiritual power and influence!

U: Immediately it comes to mind that there are so many Orisa who are female, like Osun or Otin, who create order in the society, who bring peace, health, and who are responsible for the perpetuation of the society.

R: In Owo, there is Oronsen, an ancient queen, who married Oba Renrengenjen. She was very beautiful, and she had the power to make the Olowo rich. She was not his first wife. The Olowo had, in fact, married many others before she arrived in Owo. I have the feeling, too, that Oronssen, a truly mysterious woman, had married one or two kings before she married Renrengenjen, whose lot improved considerably as a result of his new marriage. But naturally, the other wives became very jealous and decided to make sure that he would send her away from the palace. They knew her taboos. Okra must not be cut in her presence, and when women carried firewood on their heads from the farm, that load must not be taken down it in her presence. Finally, water must not be spilled in her presence. One day, the co-wives conspired to do all these three things to provoke her. Her reaction was swift. She packed her things and left. When the king discovered that his favorite wife had left, he summoned the chiefs and the hunters, and he asked them to find her. Finally they discovered her in a place called Ugbo Laja, which means literally the Bush of the Head Gear! They called out, "Please stop!" But she refused. They tried to grab her, but she eluded them by sinking into the ground. They pulled, but her head gear was all they were able to snatch. That is why the place was named Ugbo Laja.

Before her disappearance, the Oba had asked Oronsen what Owo must do ensure the continuity of the harmony and security that the town had come to enjoy since her arrival in the town. She let the Oba know that for peace to reign, the town "must celebrate her annually by offering 200 birds, 200 snails, 200 yams, 200 kola nuts and so on...." And it is very interesting. The place where she disappeared is the very place where the Archeologist, Ekpo Eyo, made all those important discoveries of antique terracotta sculptures....

U: So Oronsen is the protectress of Owo, much in the same way in which Osun is the protectress of Osogbo and Otin is the protectress of Okuku.

R: Yes. And every year there is a big festival. We call it Igogo festival. During this festival the men plait their hair like women, and they dress in those big skirts—like crinolines. They put on blouses like women; in fact, they openly acknowledge the power of women! Even the Oba will sit down for hours to have his hair plaited!

U: Thirty five years ago I witnessed an Igogo festival, and I was shocked to see the Oba expose his plaited head! Because for an Oba to show the crown of his head is normally unheard of! It is considered extremely dangerous for anyone to look at his head!

R: Yes, but I think this is an exceptional circumstance. It also shows how much the Oba and the others respect and acknowledge the queen's powers. And for the Igogo festival, lots of potent and protective medicines are applied onto the Oba's head before donning the long white *okin* feather and three red parrot feathers you see in his hair as he dances round the town on the last day of the festival.

U: It seems to me that this is an awesome symbol! For it must signify that the mysterious power of women can *neutralize* the dangerous magic of the Oba's head. I do remember an incident when the Alaafin of Oyo cursed a Lagos lawyer by lifting up his crown and exposing his head to him. The man went mad and died two years later.

R: Yes, at the Igogo festival, women really assert their strength. All the chiefs must plait their hair, too, and they must go and sacrifice at the grove of the Queen. Then the women dance around the town. They plait their hair elaborately, in a very high dome, and they wear literally thousands of red parrot feathers. The feathers of *ayekooto* (parrot) have great magical qualities. This is why one is not allowed to bring them into a blacksmith's forge. It is believed that they can change the chemical composition of the metal! The women dance through the town chanting and accompanying themselves on *agogo*, iron bells. Five or six of them usually go into trance. And I can tell you that this music is so powerful that it will grab you, if you stay near it for long—which, I think, is why one is usually warned not to go near those women. If you stay near them for even 15 minutes, you will feel the music in your intestines and your heartbeat will start responding to it... Some also say that if you stay too near them, you will become impotent! On this day you see thousands of young women dancing through the town, bare breasted. They are dressed only in beads and a red sash around their chest. Even without warning, these women are such a frightening sight that nobody in their right mind would dare touch them. In all, Igogo definitely witnesses the assertion of women's power!

U: You mention the fact that the men plait their hair like women on this day, and they wear skirts. No doubt it's a way of paying homage to women. But, at the same time, it is also part of a much wider phenomenon in Yoruba culture, namely, that though there are male and female roles being played out in society, these roles are frequently blurred or even reversed. I think it has to do with the basic Yoruba concept that nothing is absolute, that all boundaries are flexible, all the truths ambivalent. Sango *is* one of the most male Orisa, extrovert, warlike, boisterous, full of bravado, an Orisa who loves spectacular entries, who revels in dramatic performances; and yet his priests, too, plait their hair like women, they wear skirts and earrings, whereas the priestesses do not kneel before him as women do, but they prostrate like men. In fact, there are towns in Western Yoruba where Sango is worshipped as a woman, where he is the wife of an ancient thunder god called Jakuta.

R: Even the god of the crossroads, Esu, generally considered male, also has female attributes.

U: It lies at the very core of his personality! Esu questions every kind of conventional thinking; he disturbs all complacency in men and constantly forces us to re-think. It is natural that he should also challenge conventional concepts of gender.

R: In English we translate 'Oba' as 'king', but the Yoruba word does not imply gender. It simply means 'ruler', whether male or female. There have been many female Oba in Yoruba history. There have been many female Ooni (Ife kings). The founder and first ruler of Ondo was indeed a female!

R: You know the very ancient crown in Idanre which is said to be the actual crown of Oduduwa? It is more or less a predecessor of the 19th century beaded Yoruba crown with which we are familiar. It has a conical head. But do you know that in Ile-Ife today, the priestess of Owari wears a crown called *ade-afonsokun* that is almost identical to this ancient crown from Idanre? Owari was an early *Owa* (King) of Ife, a powerful, temperamental ruler, who is now worshipped as an Orisa. This suggests to me that if a woman can wear a crown that is identical to the crown of Oduduwa, does it not indicate that women used to wield great political power, and that Oduduwa even could have been a woman? And take a look at Yoruba art. There is a famous bronze pair of figures excavated by Frank Willett at Ile-Ife.

U: You mean the couple with the interlocking legs? The one that was found at Ita Yemoo?

R: Yes, they are regal figures! There is no doubt that the shorter one is a woman. She is wearing a wrapper that covers her breasts. The taller one is a man, but there is no difference in status. They both wear the same type of crown, the same diagonal sash across their shoulders....

U: Almost reminiscent of the Igogo festival in Owo! And the playful inter-locking legs indicate a relaxed, playful relationship....

R: If this was 13th or 14th century, what happened between then and now? I am almost certain that the change in the status of women happened with the coming of the new religions and colonialism.

U: If you go back further—say to the terracotta heads of 11th and 12th century—you find women with the same regal look, the same splendid dignity....

R: Look at their hairstyles. There is a hairstyle called *Owewe*, which means 'finely crafted.' It is very regal, obviously reserved for very powerful people—priestesses, almost goddesses. And it has been preserved right into the 19th/20th centuries. *Owewe* appears on the Epa masks of Alaye.

U: Maybe we should look at Yoruba attitudes preserved in the language itself, in sayings and proverbs and *odu*—Ifa divination verses.

R: Yes, if you look at Yoruba proverbs, you realize that the Yoruba people thought that a man's life did not really start until he was married, and parents would get extremely upset if a man was late in marrying. An Ifa verse says, "Having no wife calls for an urgent and affirmative action. To keep quiet is to invite trouble. What a difference being a married man makes! One without a wife should weep publicly in the market place. To do so is neither an extreme display nor an over-reaction."

U: When I lived in Ede and Ilobu in the fifties, a girl could not be forced to marry a man she did not want.

R: Oh, no!

U: People would put pressure on her, but she could not be forced. More-over, I found that women did not find it hard to leave their husbands. A woman could always run to her father's house, or even to her new husband, and have the case 'settled' later. But it was not as easy the other way round. A husband could not easily send away a wife because usually his mother and other senior female relatives would interfere, and oppose the decision. I don't know what happened in earlier times, but in those days women seemed to have the upper hand. They were often playing with men. I remember one situation in Ilobu, where a young girl was to be married to an important old man. She secretly loved a young school teacher, but she realized that her lover did not have the money to give her an elaborate *Iyawo,* wedding ceremony. So she married the old man, and got herself decked out in expensive clothes, beads, and jewelry; she hired drummers and danced through the town in a triumphant manner. But within a few days, she ran away from her new husband and went to live with her school teacher. This kind of thing was rather the exception, of course, but it does show what a girl could get away with!

R: That reminds me of the story of Osun who descended from heaven with the 16 major/original Orisa. This is a story from *odu* Ifa. After the creation of the land, the 16 major Orisa settled on earth doing their work. All went well, but they paid no respect to Osun. Perhaps because she took up the seemingly unimportant job of plaiting people's hair, she was taken for granted. She was ignored. One day O*sun seegeese*; *olooya iyun,* (Osun the exquisitely beautiful woman; the expert hairdresser with a beaded comb) decided to show them her power. Unbeknown to the sixteen Orisa, Osun had in fact the magic power and ability to make things come to pass. So all of a sudden plants would not yield fruit, diseases could not be cured, men could not produce semen, and the few rain drops that fell from the sky were swallowed by the chickens before they touched the ground. In no time the whole world was turned upside down! Then the sixteen male divinities held a meeting—again without Osun. At the meeting, they decided to go back to the Creator to tell him that things were not going well, that suddenly everything had gone sour.... The Creator asked them why they had come back to him, and they explained. He said to them, "I see there are sixteen of you. Where is the seventeenth? If you do not return and reconcile with the seventeenth person, your problems cannot be solved!" So they returned and tried to woo Osun. They said to her, "Aaah, Osun, you are our mother. You are everything to us. We are sorry we ignored you. We did not mean to do so. We're here to make up for the offense." But Osun was not impressed. "Look I'm not interested in your talk." They started begging her, begging from morning to evening, but she was not impressed. "You think you have power? Go ahead. We'll see how far you get," she scolded. She didn't even ask them what their problem was, but she *knew* because she was the cause of it all. After some time, she felt sorry for them, and she said, "I will consider your request.

I am pregnant. I am expecting a baby. If the baby I am carrying turns out to be a girl, then I will have nothing to do with you anymore. But if it is a boy, he will join you, and work with you to solve your problems." So they began to pray and offer sacrifices that the child should be a boy! She gave birth to a boy whom she called him Osetura. As she promised, Osetura became the answer to the hither-to unsolved problems. He became the bridge between men and women. Now I have done some other work on this, and I am convinced that Osetura is Esu.

U: That makes sense! Esu is the boundary crosser, the natural mediator, the link between men and women. He is the one who carries the sacrifice; he mediates between men and Orisa as well as between the different Orisa!

R: And another thing. In Ifa divination you use sixteen *Ikin,* the palm nuts of Ifa. But there is always a seventeenth, a small conical ivory head called *Olori Ikin,* the chief of the *Ikin.* It is this *Olori Ikin* who always receives the sacrifice for the Babalawo. Now I believe that this *Olori Ikin* is Osun!

U: So that although the men are the diviners of the Ifa oracle, and although they hold the power of the oracle, they can't succeed unless they get the sanction of the female power behind it!

R: You talked earlier about women sacking men, but men finding it hard to sack women. You're right! Evidently, Osun did without the men, but the men could not do without her.

U: I think we should look at sexual relationships in Yoruba society because in Europe people associate polygamy with a seraglio type of male indulgence—a harem filled with ravishing odalisques waiting for their master's pleasure. But the reality was not so at all. A man may have had several wives, but the sexual act was not considered to be an 'independent art form,' as we try to make it now in Europe, or as it was developed, say among the upper casts of classical India. The sexual act served the production of children, and as soon as a woman was pregnant, she could not be touched by the husband until the child was weaned which amounts to three years! So even a man with four wives would live a relatively abstemious life in traditional Yoruba society!

R: And there was virtually no extra-marital sex or adultery in the olden days.

U: I believe there was a very serious reason for this. A Yoruba woman could never hide the identity of the father of her child, because whoever buries the afterbirth of the child becomes the father. No matter who was the biological father of the child, it becomes part of his lineage. So if a woman allows her husband to bury the afterbirth of her lover's child, she is depriving that other family of life. This means that the equilibrium between clans, the harmony of society, is seriously disturbed—a much graver situation than our concept of 'sin' of adultery.

R: The husband was actually a bit left out in the polygamous society. He was rather alone!

U: He was certainly alone, because although the children legally 'belonged' to him, and the woman is said to bear the children 'for him', they were in fact mother oriented, and the father played a lesser role in their lives. Each woman lived in her own room with her children, and the children relied on their mother and on the co-wives for their needs. In the early days of the extra-mural department, we were given a university car and an official driver to take us round the country. And I remember that each one of these drivers would suddenly stop when we were driving through some town and ask to introduce me to his mother. None of them ever took me to see his father. And in a bigger context, when the Olokuku held the annual feast during which his crowns were displayed (for blessing), he must lead a procession in which all eighty crowns are carried by his wives and daughters to the cemetery to pay homage to his mother.

R: Yes, that is right. Women, mothers in particular, are held in awe. A woman is a vehicle for awesome magical power. Even in ordinary children's riddles, *Alo,* the vagina is referred to as "a cup that is turned upside down, but never spills its contents." It's magic, and it's sacred. It's also called "the road that leads to heaven." It is a passage, a sacred passage, through which we came from heaven. So if the powers of this sacred passage are directed against you, your life is in danger. You risk an untimely return to heaven. If a man provokes a woman to such an extreme anger that she suddenly exposes her private part, and utters a curse, the man is bound to be so terrified as to run away.

U: It's similar to the Oba exposing his head. When a woman undresses in the context of a serious argument, it is an explosive situation! A man will

59

most likely not be sexually aroused by suddenly seeing the woman naked. He is more likely to be terrified. The vagina is sacred. It is power concealed. That's why another name for vagina is *Eegun* or *Egungun*, mask or masquerade. It covers a mystery. So being exposed to the vagina is rather like someone trying to lift the mask of an *Egungun* in order to see the person behind the mask. This is an absolute taboo. Now we see why women have lost their status and their power in recent decades: Christianity and Islam have deprived them of their magic. Once a woman loses her Orisa, she loses her power, and she is no longer of weight.

R: Look at another aspect, the woman kneeling down and holding her breasts...

U: As you see on carved Sango dance staffs for example....

R: Many would think it erotic, maybe, but it is not. It is the most sacred position. A woman in a kneeling position, naked, and hold her breasts is the most sacred and powerful thing on earth because in that position she can speak to the Orisa, and her words will come to pass. In other words, these women possess their own power.

U: In that position women pull together the highest powers that no man can withstand or neutralize. It's like an exercise in concentration that allows all her powers to converge.

R: It is a power that is linked with *ikunle abiyamo,* (the woman's kneeling position during childbirth). This position is also linked with the position at which one's destiny is received.

U: So, you could say that in this kneeling position, the woman has the power to confront her *ori,* her destiny. Just as every human being kneels down to receive his destiny before coming to earth, so she now has the power to confront her *ori* again and to change her destiny, or even the destiny of others.

R: In this gesture women can *disarm* the Orisa... That's why women are believed to possess *owo ero,* the hand that sooths and eases hardships, the hand that softens life, the hand that softens the hardest people, the hand that softens Sango, softens Ogun...

U: So the female figure who kneels on the *ose* Sango, proffering her breasts is cooling Sango's temper, softening his power—just like Osun heals a disease with cool water.

R: In Yoruba healing is described in terms of the attributes of water. Water is powerful, yet soft and typically flows gently. There is an association between *ero* (soft) and *ero* (medicine).

U: The water of Osun softens and heals. The brass fan of Osun cools. These are symbols of her power. That is why every shrine in Osogbo has a pot of water from the river Osun. Water from the pot is sprinkled over the *obi* (kola nut) before it is broken and used in divination. The issue that is being confronted through divination is thus calmed in advance; the tension is diffused....

R: *When fire is raging really high, it is with water we quench it;*
When the weather is blazing hot, it is the fan we use to mitigate it.
There is a competition between fire and water.
Fire chases water.
Fire continues to chase water, and refuses to turn back.
A blazing fire!
When fire pursues water, and does not turn back, propitiation is the answer.
Fire cannot maintain its glow beyond the water.
No matter how powerful fire is, once in contact with water it must yield.

U: That is a wonderful image of male and female.

R: You know if somebody is mentally ill, and the Babalawo has tried everything in vain, he will ask, as a last resort, whether the patient's mother is still alive. If the answer is "No," he will say, "This is going to be a most difficult case indeed." But if the answer is "Yes, he still has a mother," he'll say, "There is one last solution." Then he'll prepare a concoction and rub it on the mother's breast, and the patient, no matter how old, will be asked to suckle it. That is the most powerful, most efficacious cure.

U: The healing power of a woman's breast is a very basic concept in Yoruba. Suckling a breast is not simply a matter of being fed. In a society where husbands and wives largely pursue their own separate ways in life, marriage is something akin to loose federation. So it is not surprising that in most women's lives the child has the preference over the husband, and tenderness and even eroticism are directed more towards the child than the man. For the child, too, the mother's breast is a source of reassurance. Children suckle their mother's breast affectionately, long after they have begun to eat solid food. Even when the mother is suckling her new baby, the older child of three or four years, may seek reassurance and peace by briefly sucking the mother's breast. Even grandmothers allow children to suck their breasts, and in certain circumstances, even older women begin to lactate again.

R: That is amazing. Is there a proof?

U: Yes, it was observed by doctors at the University College Hospital in Ibadan in the fifties.

R: Perhaps this orientation towards the mother explains why in every important Yoruba ritual there are some women in the background. Even the Egungun society must, at the beginning of each festival, ask for the blessings of the female—particularly certain old women in the cult—before appearing in public.

U: The guild of masquerade is really all about the placation of women's power.

R: Though charged with political and important judicial functions, the Ogboni society, I believe, also helps to maintain the balance between mother earth, the producer, sustainer of life, and man as the beneficiary of *ile,* the earth.

U: And even in the case of the installation of a king, after the kingmakers have had their say and the Ifa oracle has confirmed the choice, the installation cannot proceed unless the head of the palace women performs the most important installation rites and ceremonies.

R: So we come back to the beginning—the sixteen Orisa descended from heaven to rule the world, but everything went wrong, until they remembered to placate Osun, because she holds the *Ase,* the power of 'yes,' of positive outcome.

U: In the end it is only Ifa that enables men to live with this magic power of women. Ifa teaches everyone to live with patience and coolness; to soften the world and placate the powers of the universe so as to achieve harmony and stability.

Rowland Abiodun

"YORUBA AESTHETICS"

U: This spectacular exhibition of Yoruba Art in the Museum Rietberg here
has sparked off a whole new discussion on Yoruba aesthetics. But so far
the discussion has centered entirely on art, and nothing has been said at
all about the concept of beauty in the everyday life. For example, would
the Yoruba talk of a 'beautiful' flower?

R: I don't think so.

U: Compare that to the cultures in Papua, New Guinea, where people constantly decorate their hair with flowers, where they hang garlands round
their neck, where they use flowers as color! They even plant flowers along
the highway to beautify the road! One the other hand, for the Yoruba,
a plant must either be edible, or have some medicinal use. Otherwise,
they don't care about them. I have not seen Yoruba planting flowers for
decoration. The only tree they might plant in a town is the *peregun,* Dra-
caena Fragans, because it has certain magical qualities, and its presence is
needed in many shrines.

R: That's right.

U: So there is a completely different aesthetic feeling here.

R: Well, aesthetics in everyday life has to start again from *iwa.* The concept
of *iwalewa* goes beyond artistic articles. It goes to the very core of a person's or an article's identity; the *being,* moral fiber, good behavior.

U: Maybe we can apply that to plants. Do you remember that outside the gate to the Osun grove there were three mighty trees? These trees were interlinked in their crowns, and they made a very powerful group. They were very sacred, and you really felt you were in the presence of Orisa. The European visitors invariably said, "What beautiful trees." But Susanne Wenger used to say, "Perhaps we simply call such trees 'beautiful' in our culture because we are incapable of understanding or defining their spiritual being." One night one of those trees suddenly fell to the ground, which to the Osun worshippers was a great disaster. They then commissioned a carving to be placed in the Osun shrine at the king's market as a replacement for the tree. Perhaps the spirit of that tree had to be transferred to that *ere* (the carving).

R: It has to do with the concept of *completeness*. The Yoruba say, "If two people go on a journey, and only one of them returns, the one who returns will feel lonely and ill at ease." It's just like the *Ibeji*, twins. They come into the world as a pair. If one dies, you have to make an image to complete the pair. Otherwise the life of the survivor will be in jeopardy....

U: Because if the completeness is not restored in this world, it will have to be restored in the other world.

R: Exactly! Only completeness can give you assurance. That tree in the Osun grove, once a powerful, has left a gap, a state of suspense by its demise. That power that it once possessed, the spirit that it harbored, where can they go? You have to give them a home. Think of the Ogboni images, too. In the *Edan Ogboni*, there is always a pair, male and female, linked by a chain. The Yoruba have never held the concept that man was created separately from woman.... They are always thought of as having been created together as a pair, a complementary pair.

U: Unlike the Bible, where the woman was merely a divine afterthought, a divine *mistake*, to be precise, because after all, it was woman who destroyed the original divine concept of the world.

R: Whereas in a Yoruba shrine you find mostly a *pair* of images, a man and a woman always go together.

U: Let me ask you about another aspect of beauty, the beauty of women because surely men must see certain aspects of beauty that have nothing to do with character in a woman—aspects that are purely physical, aspects that have to do with forms, and shapes and colors. I know one such criterion of beauty, often represented on carvings, especially on Ife bronzes. They are fine parallel lines round the neck. They are referred to as 'natural necklaces.' Another is a gap in the upper front teeth which is also often represented in wood carvings. Now what other criteria are there?

R: In Ifa divination verses we have a brief comment on this. "Whiteness enhances the beauty of the teeth as rings enhance the beauty of the neck, and as heavy breasts enhance the beauty of a woman."

U: The carvers do indeed represent a woman's breasts as always full and pendulous, like those of a woman who is feeding a baby.

R: Of course. 'Heavy' here means 'heavy with milk'.

U: The beauty lies in the fact that the woman has fulfilled her function as a mother, which is very different from the European concept, where even grandmothers attempt to look like young girls, and where some women feel that feeding a child 'spoils' their breasts. The different concepts of beauty here have to do with different attitudes to age. In Europe, 'youth' is a highly overrated ideal. Not only women, but also men make a great effort to 'stay young.' They actually fight against the natural aging process whereas the Yoruba respect aging and the wisdom that comes with it. They appreciate the calm and equanimity it can bring....

R: Old age is seen as the climax of life, something to be attained, not abhorred or feared! But there is another criterion of beauty which has to do with grace. You know the popular saying: "A person who carries a basket of eggs on his head must walk with measured steps."

U: But actually the implication is that a person should *always* walk as if he was carrying a basket of eggs on his head! He should always walk with grace, with certain poise.... It all amounts to *ifarabale*, calmness of the mind and body, doesn't it?

R: Absolutely! So when you are looking at a woman, you are looking at these qualities.

U: The gait has to portray a kind of calm.

R: Yes, and even when the woman is dancing, her head has to remain very calm. It is sometimes hard to understand how it is possible to control the head when the body moves so energetically!

U: That comes from the ability to maintain calm, coolness of body and soul—*iwa tutu.*

R: Yes, indeed.

U: One thing that is striking about Yoruba carving—something that strikes you if you come to it from another culture—is the profile of the head. The way the head sits on the neck tends to create a line that starts at the back of the head and runs right down to the chin. The head is poised, perfectly balanced on a rather long neck. Often the chin is relatively high—as if the figure were indeed carrying a head load.

R: This is not surprising because as small children we learn to balance things on our heads. The creation of perfect balance is also one of the concerns of the carver.

U: There is another interesting aspect to the Yoruba attitude to female beauty. Whereas in Europe, people have certain preferences of color—say they prefer blondes, in Yoruba, *oriki* (panegyrics), women are usually praised for whatever characteristics are discernible. According to an *oriki* of the Ogoga of Ikere, the Oba is

> ...*the husband of the dark-skinned woman*
> *the husband of the light-skinned woman.*
> *He is the husband of the corpulent woman who sells tobacco in the market.*

In other words, the women are all equally beautiful because they are who they are.

R: You've got it! You have put your finger on the most vital principle of the Yoruba which has to do with conceding to each person his or her own individual character, even if it may not be pleasing to you. We admire Sango, the quick-tempered; we admire Obatala, even though he got drunk and created albinos. We admire Ogun, even if he 'bathes in blood.' We admire Esu, though he can belong to two opposing sides simultaneous and without compunction. So we can admire a woman because she is fat or because she is thin. Thus, Osun is described as a corpulent woman, too large for one person's embrace!

U: There is a hunter's poem in praise of a thin woman:

She falls on a plate; the plate does not break,
She falls on a mortar, and
The mortar splits right down the middle.

It is a joke, of course, but I still feel that it tries to convey the idea that even though the woman is slight of build she is not insubstantial. And here we come to another point where Yoruba ideas on beauty differ very much from those of Europeans. Once a person has reached a certain status in society, he or she is expected to look substantial....

R: You are right! There is an *oriki* in which the Olowo is called 'The father of mountains.' So his size, his bulk, indicates stability.

U: Even the attire of the Olowo..., and the way he is decked out in layers of cloth until he looks like he is wearing a crinoline...

R: Exactly! This reflects the idea of fecundity. The Olowo is also known as 'the prolific banana plant that bears many fruits.'

U: The bigness also means that he is so strong that you cannot shift him.

R: Immovable! He is able to withstand all kinds of crises. It is a metaphor for strength, for endurance; literally, he cannot be pushed around. That is actually what you call *baba*, a stable man, dependable and eternally present...

U: Somebody who has equanimity.

R: A person who has attained the status of *Baba/Aba*—an elder—must not flutter around like a butterfly. At this stage of life one must radiate total dignity. Once you become an elder you acquire a new kind of aesthetic consciousness. It does not matter who or what you had been. As soon as you move into the position of an elder, a chief, a priest, a king, you need this majesty, this composure; you have to radiate the highest level of dignity. The image that is commonly used to describe this phenomenon is that of the elephant, *Ajanaku,* and as the saying goes, "From the condition of the grass on the elephant's path we glimpse the impact of the mighty animal's weight." Or another saying: "When an elephant passes by nobody says 'I sense something fluttering by'."

U: His presence is undeniable. But what it *also* means is that people change their physique as their status changes. This means that beauty is dictated by an attitude of mind. A person looks what he or she *wants* to look like. I can give you another example of it. In 1951 the British Council had arranged a function in honor of their sewing class; and there were all these substantial and dignified Yoruba ladies walking about in rather plain European dresses, which they had sewn themselves. They looked impossible; they just didn't seem to fit into these straight shift-like artificial silk frocks. And I thought then, that Yoruba women should never give up their own traditional clothes, which had been developed for their own type of beauty. But then, only a few years later, you could see young Yoruba air hostesses who looked like PANAM or Lufthansa advertisements. So here again women developed the kind of figure they wanted to have—a case of the mind controlling the body. To give you a much stronger example, many Olorisa certainly begin to look like the image of the Orisa they have in their minds; the image of their own Orisa. A Sango worshipper doesn't look like an Obatala worshipper.

R: No, no!

U: In the fifties, when the Orisa was still very strong, you could identify an Olorisa by simply looking at his face. His physiognomy changed as he got more deeply involved with his Orisa. Even today, a face like that of Sango-dare Gbadegesin Ajala, the batik artist, could not belong to anybody but a Sango priest. So beauty—the specific *type* of beauty a person may have—derives from the inside, hence the axiom *iwalewa*—character is beauty.

R: The character and the beauty, the power and the concentration of a face can only build up over the years. As you know, this cloth you are wearing is almost like *etu*. You know that *etu* is called the fabric of an elder. And they will tell you why. It's because *etu* is not only durable, but it can absorb dirt. So like *etu*, the elder, unlike the youth, is capable of absorbing insults and hardships.

U: As the saying goes:

A young man can own as many embroidered robes
as an elder, but he's unlikely to own as many rags.

R: It's like looking at a masquerader's costume. Never mind the bright beautiful velvet on the top. It's the layers of ancient, faded, and ragged cloth he's wearing underneath that really count.

U: The accumulated power—built over generations!

R: That's right. It's also the history of the mask, the accumulated history. If you carve a new mask today, it cannot have the power of an older one. That power, that spiritual power takes time to build. So we say "The beauty of the *egungun*, the mask, is not in its colorful, dazzling exterior. The real beauty and power reside in its spiritual power." Different masks have different personalities, different characters, and we admire them for what they are. We adore the specific power they represent.

U: If we return briefly to our starting point, the beauty of women, we can say then that a woman is beautiful because she is 'yellow,' another is beautiful because she is 'dark,' one is beautiful because she is 'fat,' another because she is 'slender.'

R: That's right. Only the woman with no character is considered ugly.

U: In fact I remember that some forty years ago when people's lives were still directed by their Orisa, there was hardly a woman who passed our house in Ibokun Road who didn't have a personality, an attraction, some radiation; whereas, if you walk through the streets of Zurich, or, nowadays, Lagos, you may pass a lot of people without being aware of a face. That is

71

because people are harassed; they have neither patience nor *ifarabale*. If they have character, they are hiding it.

R: Only that which has lost its identity can be called ugly.

U: This explains, then, why orisa worship creates beauty—it strengthens the identity! There is an *oriki* (panegyrics) that says, "Sango imparts his beauty to the women with whom he sleeps...." It's a metaphor, I think, for the spiritual power the worshipper, *iyawo*, receives from his or her orisa. In this connection it is interesting, also, that a typical *oriki* of an orisa hardly ever mentions the orisa's physical characteristics. The emphasis is on the spiritual aspects, the power, the personality, of the gods. Very occasionally they talk about things like "dainty feet painted with camwood" or "white cowry shells gleaming on black buttocks". Some *oriki* refer to the eyes, the orisa's sparkling eyes. Osun's eyes "sparkle in the dark like the sun on the Osun River." Obatala's eyes "gleam with laughter." Oduduwa's eyes "shine like 200 stars", and "the light radiating from Ogun's face can cause blindness". Olodumare watches the world with eyes that "sparkle like the sun". Erinle's eyes "sparkle like fire..." Ososi is a "small man with a sparkling spirit and eyes that fill one with fear..." Invariably these attributes all deal with luminosity, with a shining spirit.

R: "Shining" also indicates completeness, *didan*. In Yoruba an article that is completed and ready for use is often described as "shining".

U: Perhaps we could also say "fulfillment", the fulfillment of a personality or the fulfillment of an artistic work. The Yoruba artist aims at a shining surface. He gives the carving such a smooth surface that it reflects the light. Some carvers even nail white metal across the eye of their *ere* to give it that luminous look. But the real completeness of the carving comes with time, ultimately from many generations of worshippers. It is this that generates the patina.

R: That's right. To the Yoruba the work of the carver is only the *first* stage in the completion of a carving. This is a very important stage, but only one stage.

U: There is one other thing that worries me. We all agree that the Yoruba artist follows some very clearly defined aesthetic principles. To what extent he actually verbalizes these principles is really irrelevant. After all, some European artists never talk about their work. Picasso never bothered to analyze his paintings. But the question that arises is this: To what extent do the users of the images understand the aesthetics of the art, and to what extent do they care? Years ago I felt shocked when I saw—in an Osun shrine—a toby jug which some facetious British District Officer "donated" to the priests who in turn placed it in the shrine. Today, and in the light of what you have told me I can understand the priests' attitude more easily. No Osun worshipper could ever imagine another human being to be as cynical as this colonial official. So they must have assumed that the jug represented his orisa, and however weird it must have looked to them, they respected its idiosyncrasy; they conceded its own individual character. But how do priests handle their own carvings? Many of them—during a ritual—are painted with red and white stripes or with dots. They are painted in the way in which initiates were once painted during certain rituals. This does give the images a kind of mystical presence, but the forms the artist created have been obscured. You can no longer see the delicate incisions on the surface because they have been caked up with paint. Lines and dots rudely cut across his shapes and obscure the proportions. During the annual *Ere* festival in Osogbo images from all the shrines are carried in procession through the town and then exhibited in front of the palace for a day. But they are heavily painted, and the general public will never know about the artistic intentions of the wood carver—this being the only opportunity they have to view the images. In the Osun shrine at the King's market of Osogbo the carvings are permanently in this painted state.

R: I have no answer to that. When I talked to Lamidi Fakeye, I asked him to tell me in one sentence what was the greatest thing he ever learned as a carver. After thinking for a long time, he answered, "It is *ifarabale*, calmness, which we go to learn." It is true that the carver takes time to carve certain details. He gives his work a certain surface. And then it is obscured. But there are various categories of carvings. Some are not complete without paint—like *Gelede*, the masks dedicated to the female cult, *Awon Iya*, The Mothers. So for their completeness they need color. This means that the carver's work is only the first stage, though a very important one, towards the achievement of completeness. So the carved image will not be considered complete unless it is painted and then undergoes certain ceremonies. It has to be "empowered," or it will not mean much. There is thus a cumulative process: the carver, the painter, the ritual, and ultimately the user, all contributing to the carving's potency. Later on, the character of a carving may even change over the generations as it is passed from one user to another.

U: But does this not simply mean that in spite of all these Yoruba aesthetic criteria that have been identified in recent years, there is something which is far more important in the eyes of the Yoruba? And does this 'thing' *override* all the aesthetic considerations?

R: That is true. But is this not what we've been talking about—the character of a work, its *iwa*? This quintessence, this *iwa*, has precedence over everything because if a piece of work lacks it then the artist has failed.

U: Alright. Let us put a theoretical case, a highly unlikely one, but worth examining, nevertheless. Suppose a great artist like Olowe of Ise produces a superb *Epa* mask, something that *we* would call a masterpiece; now supposing that during the ritual to empower the carving something goes wrong. Ifa rejects the carving, or the intended owner has suddenly become a Muslim, or whatever, and the ritual does not take place. Then what *is* this incomplete carving? What happens to it? It could only be thrown away because the society has no use for a carving whose value rests *only* on its aesthetic beauty.

R: Yes, it's possible.

U: This reminds me of the famous case of the carver Bamgboye, one of the greatest artists in Ekitiland. He was persuaded by a well meaning British education officer to teach carving in a high school. So he suddenly began to make carvings which he knew in advance would never be empowered by any ritual or put to any religious use. Such carvings were useless, meaningless objects to him, and all one could do with them was sell them to Europeans. And as soon as this situation arose Bamgboye *lost his sense of aesthetics.* His forms became feeble. Some objects were toy-like imitations of his own former works!

R: Well of course, they had no character. They had no *iwa*.

U: We could actually use an example from Yoruba mythology which says although Obatala formed human beings out of clay, Olodumare, the

Almighty, had to breathe life into the forms. So Obatala is the artist; he creates the shapes, but without the ritual action of Olodumare, these beings can never come to life. They remain useless lumps of clay. Therefore, it seems to me, that in all the recent discussion on Yoruba aesthetics, it has been ignored that all aesthetics has a different *place value* in Yoruba society from ours, from the Europeans'. In Europe we tend to place the value of aesthetics so high that we disregard the meaning, content and *iwa* of a work of art completely. And this is what has happened in this particular exhibition here in Zurich: Yoruba values have been turned upside down. The Esu figures, right at the entrance to this exhibition, are an example of this. In a Yoruba shrine these little *Esu* figures hang head down, and they are partly hidden in a cluster of cowry strings. Here in Zurich the figures have been displayed in what is to the organizers consider the "right way" up. We can now admire the skill of the carver, but the *ere* has lost its meaning. The whole idea seems to me that Esu, who constantly upsets the equilibrium, and turns the world upside down, is here again demonstrating his contrariness!

R: That is why I felt it was important that musician Muraina should be here at the exhibition with us because to me these carvings are not complete without *dundun* drums, songs and dance. These authenticate the carvings, and give them sanction. We have to look at them in the right context, that of performance—of ritual performance.

U: You know what Muraina said to us after seeing the exhibition? He said: "If one went through this exhibition lonely—with no other person around, one could be frightened." I said, "What gives you this feeling?" He answered, "It may have to do with the fact that the exhibition is underground, but it is not only that. I almost felt as if the objects themselves ought to be frightened of being there! As you walk down those steps, the first thing you see is *Esu* in a small glass case. It looks captured!"

R: Muraina responded to the isolation of the objects.

U: He responded to what was to him the artificiality of the context. In fact, he said, "It is like some scientist's laboratory—as if the carvings had been taken there for experiments."

R: It is reduced to an academic exercise. The objects have been treated simply like artifacts; a distance has been created between us and the pieces. But then there is always the "usefulness of the useless". It teaches you *one* thing, but then you lose many other things in the process.

U: One could argue of course, that any art work can be evaluated as pure form; that the form as such makes a certain impact on us—whether we understand how it arose or not.

R: Exactly. It has become art history with dates and periods and styles! We are now at a crossroad, at a point where we are stripping Yoruba art of context. We are "leaving it naked" as Georgina says. And that is dangerous! After all *Oro,* a masquerade or spirit does not go out unclothed. *Oro* must never be seen naked. If you ran into *Oro* naked, it spells catastrophe! And this exhibition is not clothed. It is naked, and I think this is why it can frighten. Personally I have to change my way of thinking to be comfortable with it. I have to wear my Western thinking cap.

U: There is now a certain danger, too, that people will use your own work on aesthetics to say, "Well, after all, it was wrong to say that African art has been merely functional. It now has been proved that there have been very clear aesthetic principles which the carver followed." And this justifies an exhibition in which the art work is treated as pure form. It justifies turning Earth the "right" way up. So in some sense they are misinterpreting you.

R: I think you are right, but then you see, things had gone too far in the other direction. Anthropologists and art historians have long been saying that African artists had no conscious idea of aesthetics at all, and that they could not be regarded as individual artists because they were merely *copying* a master. So it has been a very necessary development to point out that African art is not anonymous, and that there are individual masters who can be identified. So this was a necessary development. But I agree; it is equally wrong to isolate the objects from their cultural context because if you do that you mainly serve the interests of the collectors. There are many people who want the objects—but they are not interested in the people.

U: That is very true, and we saw a striking example for that during the last few days. We had Muraina Oyelami here, a great Yoruba musician and artist. Nobody was curious to know how he felt about the exhibition. He was simply ignored.

R: Some visitors used the exhibition like a market place. One of them actually asked me, "This carving here, do you know the owner? I might want to buy it..." Sometimes I feel that we academics become the undertakers of cultures. To some academics these works are mere examples to be used as illustrations in some of their seminars on this or that. But to be fair, we cannot expect others to have a personal stake in the culture—the same way you and I do.

U: If the principle of Yoruba aesthetics is *iwalewa*, as you have explained so convincingly in much of your writing, then we must say that the concept of this exhibition goes right against that principle. And yet I must confess that this "unnatural," and perhaps even uncanny, isolation of the art works does make a powerful impact. It is startling in its own way.

R: Yes, there is something for which we must be grateful. I think even the most skeptical, the most conservative people will be humbled as they go through this exhibition. They cannot help admiring the sheer technical perfection of these antiques, the solidity of concepts, and the consistency of the culture.

U: I think people will ultimately be impressed by the dignity and the integrity of the culture. And maybe, hopefully, the sensitive visitor will become aware of some other force, some other way of life, and the other vision of the world that produced these magnificent works.

Biodun Jeyifo
"DESPERATE OPTIMISM"

U: When we were together at the University of Ife a quarter of a century ago, I think we both took the existence and virility of Yoruba culture for granted. In fact, one could then almost talk of a Yoruba renaissance. Now Yoruba culture is besieged. There are many alarming symptoms that indicate that the culture is in crisis. One such symptom you mentioned the other day—you have met some middle class Yoruba families in Ibadan whose children do not speak Yoruba!

B.J: Let me repeat the story briefly. A former student of mine, now a lawyer in the US, went home on a visit last year. She noticed that her nephews and nieces were unable to converse in Yoruba with their grandmother. And when she asked her sister about this, she was told, "Well, actually they don't speak Yoruba at all, they speak only English." Then she found out that in areas like Bodija, where "upper class" people live, many children don't speak Yoruba, only English, while at the same time their English is not good. What she found most alarming about it was the fact that everyone thought that *she* was the one responding in an abnormal fashion!

U: Surely that is something that in the 70s, when we were at Ife, was unthinkable.

B.J.:   Yes, absolutely unimaginable. And it is a sad reminder of what has been happening since my childhood. The first full-length book I ever read, from cover to cover as we say, was a book in Yoruba titled *Iwe Itan Ibadan* (*The History of Ibadan*) by the late Olubadan Akinyele. The book belonged to a small shelf of titles, all in Yoruba, which constituted

Photo courtesy of Biodun Jeyifo

my mother's small "library." My mother was literate in Yoruba, but not English, which she understood, but absolutely never spoke a word of. I must have been nine or ten then, and my first full-length title in English came about a year or two later. This was a fairly common pattern then in the primary schools of the old Western Region: you were literate first in Yoruba, and then English followed....

U: So what has happened? We are witnessing a neglect of the language, an indifference to it.

B.J.: I think it is serious, but I would qualify that because I don't think you could find that same phenomenon outside the circle of the elite. But it is serious because it is the elite who are responsible for the educational policies and the cultural policies of the society. So, if they don't think it's important, then Yoruba will be neglected more and more in the schools. But I don't think that the language itself is in decline. For instance, the *akewi* (poets) still have a significant following. In fact, during the regime of Babangida, the most significant and potent protest against the dictatorship was articulated by the *akewi*. There was one record album titled *Babangida Must Go* by Olanrewaju Adepoju. It expressed an extraordinarily sharp, eloquent, and witty indictment of that regime and military rule in general, and it was a big hit. Therefore, that kind of vital use of the language continues and has taken on new forms. So, we should not generalize...too much about the decline of Yoruba...

U: I still think it is happening on two levels. There are the elite—or rather those who consider themselves to be the elite—who argue that English is the key to modernization, to class mobility, and to the economy, and so on. But there is another phenomenon, the vulgarization of the language at the other end of the social spectrum by the dropouts, touts and "area boys." Here the language is fast and slurred; the tones have been leveled, the music gone. The language has lost its character.

B.J.: Yes, even the pleasure of conversation has gone out of it.

U: This is a symptom of something deeper. They have lost the patience, *suuru*, which was a virtue of Yoruba life.

B.J.: Yes, but on the other hand, the mass media, like television and radio, have also become a means of maintaining the vitality of the language. There are many programs on television. There is one I know called *Agborandun*, a kind of social conscience program in which people go and publicly lay charges against someone who has defrauded them or given them a raw deal. And the host of the program, a broadcaster who is a gifted user of the language, invokes all the values and virtues of the culture as reflected in the resources of the language, and then asks the accused to show up. And people do show up to defend themselves! Then there is another program called *Eri Okan*, which is a version of American talk shows. The difference is that it tries to interpret contemporary events in terms of the more lasting values of the culture. That also has a very strong following. Then there is a very good radio program on women's issues. All kinds of women participate: market women, professional women, big traders, and so on. And this program is in *deep* Yoruba! So, the vitality of the language is there. Of course, it is threatened in ways that were unimaginable even ten years ago. That threat is real, and it has made its most significant inroad among the elite. But even though I am fully aware of the seriousness of the situation, I remain desperately optimistic.

U: But then even among the elite you have somebody like Akinwumi Isola. I know some people who feel that his translation of Wole Soyinka's *Death and the King's Horseman* even surpasses the original!

B.J.: And there is also a new Yoruba journal titled *Classical Yoruba Studies*. It is already in its sixth issue. And published in Nigeria!

U: So we could really say that the language *is* still very much alive, but that it *is* the educational institutions that have not played their part. But this aspect is very serious because the universities don't function, the schools don't function, and the military displays an openly anti-intellectual attitude. So, what is going to happen is this—you will have a whole generation growing up without a proper education.

B.J.: I feel that one of the responsibilities we now have—and I have found this feeling among other people I have spoken to—is to get a full sense of the dimension of this crisis. I think the dimensions are so staggering that we ought first to get a sense of it. If you take education alone—let me just give a few illustrations of what I see as the scope of this crisis. You know I.K. Dairo, a musician, who died a couple of years ago? He made a hit record album of many tuneful songs in the early 1970s, and the most popular song in that album was one which expressed an open contempt for education. It went something like this: "He says I am uneducated. He says I'm uneducated. What does education amount to now? You have secondary school leavers who are laborers in Ikeja. So what is the worth of being educated?" I remember a time when education was valued both in itself as well as a means of social mobility. When I. K. Dairo made this record, it became a hit because it just gave expression to certain changes in social attitudes toward education. Remember, this was the time right after the Civil War, and many high school dropouts had enlisted in the military and gone to the war? Well, they came back rich, and they built big houses. And let me give you another example. It is now widely known in all the universities in Nigeria that it will have to be a very "courageous" lecturer who will dare to fail a student! There are so many pressures on the lecturer not to fail a student. There is also corruption. Lecturers are bribed to award pass grades to their students. Most of the lecturers are decent, hardworking academics, and grim economic realities have not made them corrupt. But there are a few who have turned to grade-inflation or grade-fixing to supplement their meager income. I went through this, just before I left Ife, when I was acting Head of the Department of English. A father came to the department begging that his daughter should not be failed. I said to him, "Didn't her lecturers tell you that she is a hopeless case?" And he said, "Yes, but you as Head of Department, you can do it for me." Then I said, "You are the father of this girl. You didn't tell your daughter that she was lazy; you didn't ask her why she was so irresponsible in her studies. You didn't do any of these things, and now you've come to beg." Strangely enough, after I said these words to this hapless man, all the tension went out of him, and he said, "Thank you very much. No one has spoken to me in this manner." So the dimensions of the crisis were already quite staggering, even in the early 1970s. The military merely came to worsen the situation—to put the nail in the coffin! For reasons of political expediency, of manipulation, they created more states and each state created its own university. In no time at all, manpower, infrastructure, federal and state budgets were all dispersed. In half a decade the quality of university education was destroyed. This happened in the early 70s to the late 80s when they began to create state universities in Ogun and Ondo states. Everyone knew that this was a joke! And this in Yorubaland, especially in Ekiti where there had been such a high respect for education! Remember how Ekiti people always boasted that education was their only industry? When Ondo State got its University, the science faculty was not as good as the science laboratory in Christ School, Ado-Ekiti. You see, in all these universities once they paid the staff salaries, there was nothing left; no money for equipment or books for the library. Meanwhile people left Ife, left Ibadan, left Lagos to become instant professors in the state universities.

U: And professors left to become Vice Chancellors.

B.J.: So that was the contribution of the military. I blame the military because only they had the coercive institutional power to create more states and more universities that rapidly—and to the detriment of the system of higher education as a whole.

U: Now we are seeing the possibilities of a new political scenario that could at last create a new faith in Nigeria. I found in the past recent years that fewer and fewer people believed in Nigeria as a feasible political unit that could ever do justice to the diverse populations living within its boundaries. But there is still the question: How will Yoruba culture evolve as an identity and growing culture within whatever new political realities emerge? There have been many forces militating against a Yoruba identity that are not even related to the problems caused by the military. For example, there is still a colonial mentality that you find among some prominent Yoruba academics. These academics continue to perpetuate the colonial education system from which we suffered forty years ago. Then there is the very serious situation of the corrupted Oba institution, which is very alarming. How can you reverse the present trend of Oba who are business persons and contractors? It is not necessarily the army that is to blame for this, or even the British. I would actually say that Obafemi Awolowo, Premier of Western Region in 1954-59, himself started this process when he drove the Alaafin, King of Oyo, into exile. In the 1950s I met a generation of Oba like Timi Laoye of Ede, Oba Adenle of Osogbo, the Olokuku of Okuku, and many more. They were Christians, and they understood the changed political situation. They believed in education, but they were also strongly committed to upholding the dignity of their office. They also understood the value and wisdom of ancient Yoruba traditions. They were an impressive group of men, of Kings. They did not use their office to enrich themselves, and they were absolutely accessible to the people. Now, you have a new generation of Oba, many of them political appointments, who have by-passed traditional election procedures in a shameless way. A surprisingly large number of these new Oba have been accountants or big businessmen before acceding to the throne. Some see the office as a means of making money. Various governments keep them in tow by throwing a few contracts their way. You now have an Oba who shamelessly asks:"Where is my envelope?"—a new euphemism for, "Haven't you brought any money to give me?" So how is Yoruba society going to cope with such problems? Should this ancient institution be abolished? Can it be rejuvenated, and in such a way that we can keep politics out of it? Can it still play a vital and positive part in contemporary and future Yoruba society? If not, can it be replaced by something else? And what will that 'something else' be? Who or what will give a sense of direction and cohesion to the Yoruba town? The selection of an Oba used to be a model of democratic practice in Yoruba society. There was no section of the community that did not have a say in it, and it was believed that nobody could be a good Oba unless he had a very broadly based support in the town. Now people more or less buy the office, or they are imposed on the community by government. The other thing that has seriously undermined the identity of Yoruba society is the indiscriminate distribution of honorary chieftaincy titles. A Yoruba title has now become as cheap and meaningless as an O.B.E. (Order of the British Empire). Many politicians and businessmen buy titles from the kings out of vanity. The price a few years ago was a 'V-Boot' Mercedes car. The language problem, as we have seen, is easily solved by comparison! There are Yoruba scholars who have done linguistic rescue work, if you like, and preserved many ancient literatures in written form. Also there are, as you mentioned, writers in the language who are helping to keep it alive, and develop it. But what a new Yoruba leadership will have to do is to assign the language its proper place in the educational system, and time is running out for this! Above all, the Yoruba community will have to be given the freedom within the Nigerian state to pursue its own cultural aims.

B.J.: Well, this is why...we feel that Nigeria should be re-organized into six, or maximum, eight states. We believe that the boundaries can be redrawn, and this can be the basis of a national discussion.

U.: Where would the Yoruba fit into this arrangement of states?

B.J.: Well, at the moment the Yoruba people occupy six states in Nigeria.

U: That is ridiculous.

B.J.: The Yoruba people will constitute one of the six units. But the north-eastern section of Yoruba land will form part of another unit. Kabba, Oka, and Akoko may form part of another administrative unit. We do not want to use the word "state" anymore because of the ideas and sentiments currently associated with it. We also want to avoid "region" so as not to freeze debates and the political horizon around the anxieties and insecurities associated with the former regional configuration. For the moment, we use the neutral term "administrative unit." So, the main Yoruba administrative unit or formation contains the old Oyo State, Egba, Ondo, part of Ekiti, and then once you begin to move towards Owo and Oka-Akoko, that will be part of another unit.

U: Why?

BJ.: Well, it is a matter of administrative convenience. And I think there is also a certain feeling that given a totally different political dispensation, there is no need to contain all speakers of the same language in one unit. The Abacha forces are assuming that we in the external opposition are merely a Yoruba movement. So there is a general sensitivity to that. You may remember Basil Davidson's book, *The Black Man's Burden,* subtitled *Africa and the Curse of the Nation-State.* His thesis is that almost every African country has been incapable of incorporating the most powerful elements of the pre-colonial institutions, whether on the moral level, on the psychological level, or the administrative level. It has been impossible to incorporate the best of the pre-colonial institutions, which worked for hundreds of years! The nation-state has come and superimposed itself, and meanwhile, it has devalued and distorted institutions which were time-tested.

U: Yes, because the politicians went and destroyed these institutions. Nkrumah, leader of the Gold Coast, now Ghana, felt threatened by the Asantehene, King of Asante. Awolowo destroyed the authority of the Alaafin.

B.J.: Yes, and on behalf of the nation-state. You see, Awolowo could not have sent the Alaafin into exile, but for the fact that as the regional premier, he could invoke the authority of a broader power structure, a broader polity than those available to the Alaafin. But the nation-state as we have inherited it from colonialism needn't be anything other than what we make of it. That's why we have to start from scratch because in theory the problem of *obaship* in Yoruba land has been solved. That is, depoliticize it and give it respect and dignity in terms of its ritual functions and cultural role. But because the struggle for ascendancy took place in the nation-state, it became a free-for-all, and some Oba became politicians; they became contractors. Historian Basil Davidson is against the nation-state, and I disagree with him on that point. The implication is that the nation-state, which is a *modern* political creation, hasn't worked in Africa, and therefore maybe it is the *pre-modern* political, social and cultural institutions which should be resuscitated.

U: Well, if that is what Davidson implies, it goes too far. But I think, though, that what he implies is that the African nation-state did not allow for the modernization of those institutions that were capable of being modernized. But we did not test them, so we would not know whether they could, or could not, be modernized. I might also add that if the nation-states had more sensible boundaries, then they would have had a better chance of succeeding. One of the ancient values of Yoruba society, and also of Igbo society, which the nation-state could adopt, is the notion that political power must be strictly separated from wealth. The Yoruba had a saying that an Oba does not build a house! While much wealth circulated through his hands, he was not to accumulate it. He could not pass it on to his children. A parallel statement among the Igbo was, "Anybody can become our king if he wishes, but first he must pay everybody's debts in the community!" So, it ended up meaning that the Igbo tolerated no kings outside the Nri community.

B.J.:   It is an ideal way of social leveling!

U: And even the first set of politicians in Nigeria, they made a lot of money, and most of it surely by devious means, but they also spent a lot of it. I remember situations like this: Say a new secondary school was being opened in a Yoruba town, or some other communal project was to be launched. The opening ceremony was always a fund-raising event, an occasion for citizens to show their commitment. It was also an occasion for ambitious individuals to assert their status. So if the Oba donated, say 100 pounds, the local politician or Member of Parliament would donate 200. That way the money circulated through them. But in a sense, therefore, the politicians saw themselves as super Oba, and by spending lavishly, they tried to usurp the position of the Oba in the local community.

B.J.:   One thing we have left out so far, and which we cannot ignore, is colonialism. And it was not just colonialism, but colonial capitalism.

87

U: Of course that is why colonialism happened: its first concern was always to introduce cash economy.

B.J.: The first period of independence in Africa produced some people who were very clear thinking: leaders like Julius Nyerere, first president of Tanzania, and Samora Machel, president of Mozambique, simplified things, thinking that collectivization and nationalization constituted the automatic solution. Of course, now we know that while they were often far-sighted, they were also rather dogmatic. So if, for the time being, and speaking historically, it's a long way to collectivization, the problem now is a question of whether a rational, human-oriented, and democratic face can be put on post-colonial capitalism in Africa. That is the big question. And because of the collapse of the Eastern bloc, we can start again on a clean slate. We can try *African* solutions, which draw on the lessons learned from the experiences of other nations and peoples in the modem world. What we have now in Nigeria is peripheral capitalism, capitalism without its traditional efficiency. Even banks in Nigeria do not operate in terms of strict capitalist rationality. For example, you go to a bank simply to deposit your own money, to save it; you are not there to borrow money. Yet they make you wait for hours! The banks operate on capitalization of loot from the state, and therefore work with the logic, the mentality of the state, dispensing largesse and patronage.

U: They may even ask for a bribe before you can withdraw your own money.

B.J.: Yes! And you may even have to beg to be given the privilege to bribe!

U: But this is an attitude that started from the very beginning of independent. For example, a simple thing like taking a passport was not considered a citizen's right, but a favor granted by some petty clerk. It is worse now and will be very difficult to wipe out.

B.J.: I don't think so. Everywhere in Africa, people are beginning to recognize that there must be a distinction made between the state and civil society. One of the lessons we have to learn now is that the sphere of the state has to be substantially circumscribed. I mean, beyond minimal regulations, who are *you,* as a state functionary or official, to order people around, and to make life a hell for people? So, we need a new definition of the social contract, where people voluntarily decide to come together and there is only a minimum of regulation and legal-judicial constraints. Leave the rest to the people to work out their lives. Then people will respect their Oba again. They will no longer have to prostitute themselves because they know that they are accountable—not to the state, but to the community. So I think we have to focus on the notion that the state has to have very limited powers, and leave the people to their own institutions, which they can build, which they can revitalize. Whether they are Igbo, Yoruba, Edo or whatever—you leave them their own autonomy.

U: There is so much competence at that level! How are huge cities like Lagos and Ibadan fed? The market mummies have worked out a smooth and efficient system for that, which no government in Nigeria can ever match.

B.J.: And if somebody wants to be an Olorisa or Christian or Muslim, let him or her be. And all these vital elements that you see in Yoruba culture— with the *akewi* (poets), the *Alarinjo* masqueraders and the travelling theatre—they will then have room to flower. Let me come back again to the *akewi* I mentioned earlier, Olanrewaju Adepoju. When he first released that big hit *Babangida Must Go!*, the government was looking for him all over Ibadan for two weeks. But then, when the record became such a big hit, they did not dare to touch him. This same poet had somewhat prostituted himself in the past, singing praise songs to loud mouthed, unpopular politicians. Now he had caught the mood of the people and was expressing their deepest feelings, and that made him extremely popular, So think under these new conditions, an Oba who proves himself useless will not have that state to run to in order to prop him up. He will be responsible for the community, and he will be accountable to it. He will also no longer have policemen (*akoda*) who will ring themselves around the palace like an army of occupation, chasing the people. We experienced all these in the past, as you know.

U: Actually one reason why independence went wrong is that this kind of thinking did not take place at the time. What was going on in the minds of the politicians was more like this. There were these British colonial masters who were getting all these plum jobs and perks; now we are occupying the same positions that they used to occupy, so it is right that we should also get all the perks! So there was no willingness to change anything; it was all merely a change in the color of faces: black faces have replaced white ones. It all validated George Orwell's famous insight: "You become what you fight." So the new politicians and civil servants just moved into what used to be the European reservation. They moved into the old European Club and started their own elitist and exclusive society. And whereas the colonial government was corrupt, they became more corrupt.

B.J.: You know, Tony Enahoro (an anti-colonial activist) put the matter very simply recently. He said, "The problem with independence and the post-colonial government is that in pre-colonial times, you could not steal the people's property and remain there; now in the modem nation-state, the property of the state is loot, booty for everybody. You can take your own, come back to the village, and everyone knows you are a thief, but they see you as a hero."

U: The state is anonymous.

B.J.: Yes, the state is distant. How are we going to remove that distance between the state and the community? So, we must set the limits of the state: the state can only go this far and no more. Maybe provide registration of certain things, provide regulations of certain activities in certain areas, so that anybody in the service of the state who oversteps these boundaries will be clearly known as an offender and be removed. In the same way in which—in pre-colonial society—you were held responsible for a function within the community, and once you overstepped those bounds, people knew how to deal with the situation. Just remember how an Oba who had overstepped his bounds was presented with an ultimatum....

U: He had to commit suicide. But one thing which has made the situation rather difficult is that the state has simply become too big. Even though the Yoruba city-state would have up to 70,000 inhabitants in the middle of the 19th century, it was still manageable as far as democratic processes went. But Nigeria today is no longer of manageable size. The checks and balances don't work. It is impossible for people to know what is going on in these mammoth bureaucracies. Then, there is the involvement of foreign corruption, which is even more difficult to control for the exploited citizens. In a way, I am beginning to feel that independence was given tongue-in-cheek. The colonial government had already groomed a certain class that would play into its hands after independence. It had created, through its educational system, a privileged class of conspicuous consumers, who were alienated from the people, and who would betray their own people in order to uphold, and even augment, their special status. So the type of education provided at the University of Ibadan before independence was not just from incompetence, it was deliberately designed to be so. Then there was that additional pressure that any politician who attempted to go his own way, Like Nyerere, would immediately be ostracized, or even demonized, like Castro.

B.J.: Well, what you have just said relates to Africa's place in the modem world at different stages. Roughly speaking, we can say that we are now in the stage of "globalization." I have an attitude about globalization that fills me with deep pessimism, and I see it in the following manner. Suppose you live in a small community in which you have a very powerful neighbor while you are a poor man. If there is no way in which the vast disparity between you and your powerful neighbor can be rectified, you are permanently at the mercy, or contempt, of your powerful neighbor. This is how I see Africa with regard to globalization. We all live on the same shrinking planet, but Africa is totally marginalized. You are living down the street from your rich and powerful neighbor who has everything. Your children will go begging there. It would be a reversal of everything we know about human nature for that excessively rich and powerful neighbor not to dominate you, not to condescend to you. And that is my greatest worry. As the planet gets increasingly smaller and more interconnected on every level, that arrogant and rich neighbor is bound to become more oppressive.

U: It reminds me of an image used by a Canadian at a conference many years ago. He said that being a Canadian is like sleeping with a friendly elephant. However well meaning the elephant is towards you, he may turn in his sleep at any time and squash you. Well, in this case Canada is not even friendly at all. In fact, Canada, like the rest of the West, uses his tools—the IMF and the World Bank—to keep you permanently poor and dependent. I think that when the opportunity arises, and the Nigerian exiles will be returning, at least many of them will...

B.J.: No, I don't think they will!

U: Really?

B.J.: I don't think so because middle class professionals are the most oppor-tunistic in a globalized economy. They go where the highest salaries are. The more patriotic of them send money back home and are thus putting something back into the home economy and society. But the overwhelming majority will not go back. Some may go back to build a house in their village or state capital, but they will not go back in large numbers to rebuild the Nigerian university system. I think the universities will have to be rebuilt afresh by those who have stayed at home during the bleak period, plus a few who will go back from their voluntary expatriation.

U: That's depressing.

B.J.: It is, but let me tell you the standard joke here. When a Nigerian academic arrives in this country, the USA, and is asked how much leave he was given from his home university, the prompt answer is always, "One year." Then after a brief pause comes: "In the first instance!" In other words, the intention is not to go back.

U: So what will be their contribution to Nigeria?

B.J.: Almost nothing.

U: Okay, let us assume now that the time comes when you will be ready to return home. And you will find some like-minded people who will want to tackle the task of rebuilding the universities. What would your priorities be, and what do you think a Nigerian university should be and do?

B.J.: One precondition is that people get a sense of the scope and scale of the problem. If they don't understand that, people will take half-measures.

U: And also the *nature* of the problem. Because for a long time people have not understood the nature of the problem, they have merely put their efforts into producing more of the same.

B.J.: Also, what they see is only a part of the problem. They see the problem of gross under-funding and think once that is solved, everything will be okay. During the last ten years, the level of funding has increased, maybe by 20 to 25 percent. But the number of universities has doubled! So, one very concrete problem is that once salaries are paid, there's nothing left. So people see underfunding as *the* problem.

U: But the primary problem is that people have not thought about what kind of a person they want to produce in the university. How will he become a responsible citizen rather than a mere academic technician?

B.J.:   The first thing that needs to be done is to reduce the number of universities drastically, and also to re-deploy some of the staff because all that the universities now amount to, in terms of the basic function, is reproduction of mediocrity.... Once we have solved this initial problem, we then have to debate how to relate the universities to economic production, to the training of relevant manpower skills, the development of perspectives, which will generate fresh initiatives. What we have at the moment is just mere *certification* in place of real, substantive education. Frankly speaking, I cannot see the kind of cultural and social revolution that will drastically change the contents and objectives of universities on the horizon of the present expectations. At this point in time, it may be that we can see what needs to be done on the basis of experiments in selected parts of the whole system, rather than a complete overhaul—which is what is really required. For example, if we have six universities producing engineers, we should be able to find out which of them produces the more competent, more employable, and more all round engineers relevant to the needs of a developing society. At the moment, we just look at certificates, and we do not distinguish between the products of the different universities. Where else in the world do you have a situation, where there are no criteria to distinguish the difference in standards and viability between, say the University of Ibadan and Ago-Iwoye? Another issue which has been raised, but only superficially, is the question of private universities. I think it will just be a moneymaking caricature. They will put a few symbolic and highly visible figures there, and collect absurd fees, and the wealthiest will send their children there. Therefore, it will become an apparatus for producing glorified mediocrity.

U: So let me ask you: Which of these issues would you consider a priority, if and when this period of reconstruction starts?·

B.J.: Good question. But let me first ask you, as an older and much more experienced man, because the crisis of Yoruba culture, the crisis of the Nigerian state, and of the whole continent raises fundamental questions for me: What is it to be human? What is the future of the human race? What is the nature of community? We now understand that we live on a planet whose resources are not unlimited. We have to use them wisely. But within these finite resources there is the infinity of human imagination and human creativity. The problem I find in all this, both in relation to Africa and the rest of the world, is that we seem to have raised a younger generation that is no longer in touch with the beneficial, altruistic traditions of creativity and inventiveness. So how can we nurture the hope that no matter how terrible the decay and deterioration in the quality of education, in the quality of life, the human spirit is so outstanding in its capacity to rejuvenate itself, that even if the present degradation goes on for another decade, we will always be able to pick up and start all over again? Each time I go home, I witness a further degeneration and impoverishment. When Georgina asked me the other day, "What do people eat?" I had to say, "I don't know." This is because most people live below subsistence level. Among those who still have jobs, some are not paid wages and salaries for months. And of course, within the national pool of employable labor, and in the formal sectors of the economy, far many more are *not* in employment than those who are... And this is the basic picture throughout Africa. So my question to you really is this: In the face of this massive deterioration in the quality of life for so many millions, in the face of the suffering of the majority of the population, in what way can art and language and culture still feed and uphold the human spirit?

U: The deterioration in the quality of life is a universal problem. The difference between the industrial, affluent societies and the third world is that the former suffocate in superfluous wealth and in a useless accumulation of materials and disposable goods, while the later live below subsistence level. But the wealth of Western societies, their scientific achievements, their computerized living, cannot give them a sense of belonging, cannot give them a cultural identity, and cannot fill their lives with any real meaning. "Culture" in the West has been replaced by the entertainment industry. The result is that young people are disoriented; they opt out of society and seek comfort in drugs or even drift into crime. So the brutalization of Yoruba society is part of a global phenomenon. The reason why it strikes us as so much more tragic in Yoruba society is that within my own personal experience, I still lived in a Yoruba society that functioned with many of its values intact.... Cultural manifestations were common property, and poetry was not confined to big festivals. *Oriki* are an extension of greetings. You don't just recite Ogun's *oriki* when you bring him sacrifice; you recite a few phrases while you pass his sacred *peregun* tree. Hearing your own *oriki* recited strengthens your personality, reassures you in your sense of identity, places you firmly within your lineage, and establishes your place in society.

B.J.:   But part of the problem is that language and culture are usable as means of socialization precisely through their being "packaged" in certain *forms* or *modes*. Values do not exist in a void; they exist in the forms and modes of expression, which ensure their transmission. And then some ideas, which came from the West, came in specific forms, in cultural packages which collided with Yoruba forms and ideas. And of course, a lot of these came by way of colonial conquest, by the use of arms....

U: And also by trade.

B.J.:   Yes, but we live in a universe where languages collide and cultures clash and victory does not always go to the wisest. And the ideas that are most valuable for the human race do not necessarily survive in this conflict. So, all the values and ideals of Yoruba culture that you so eloquently enumerated need new forms and modes for their transmission and perpetuation. Television, radio, computers—these are forms and media for packaging ideas. I mentioned earlier this television program called *Agborandun,* in which people go and make allegations and lay charges and ask defendants to show up. This is one instance where television reaffirms the moral responsibility of every individual to "show up." You cannot hide, because if you have lost your name, you have lost everything.

U: But that is very traditional Yoruba wisdom. So it does show very clearly that a culture that has retained its vitality *can* use these new media for its own purposes. Remember, all the new cultural forms that we have both witnessed in our own time. Look at the Yoruba Travelling Theatre. Starting from rather naive dramatizations of Bible stories mounted by the *Aladura* churches, it developed into the sophisticated analyses of contemporary society and human character in the plays of E. K. Ogunmola and into the grandeur of Duro Ladipo's historical plays. Now, remember, we were talking about the tragic and self-destructive mistrust between Yoruba and Igbo. Duro Ladipo in his play *Moremi* reinterpreted an historical or mythological event and applied it to a topical political crisis. He brought Igbo dancers into his play, and the conflict between the two cultures was resolved in a ceremony of reconciliation that echoed the historical reconciliation between the Yoruba and the original inhabitants of the land. Again, look at the development of musical styles of *juju* and *fuji* (Afropop). Look at Yoruba-Brazilian architecture of the 1920s to the 1940s. Look at the Osogbo art movement. All these represent ways in which Yoruba culture has extended in different directions without losing its character. Take the case of the plays of Wole Soyinka. He is surely one of the most international characters I know, and yet, could anyone but a Yoruba have written *Death and the King's Horseman?* It is true that he wrote it in English, but he could never have created this type of English poetry if he hadn't known Yoruba.

B.J.: I am in agreement with you. But you see, what worries me is that right now, after this TV program *Agborandun*, there will be obituaries and announcements of social functions, and you will have people trumpeting how much they have donated. This shows that the culture contains antithetical ideas seeking transmission in these new forms and media....

U.: But then you are saying it depends on the Yoruba people themselves; it depends on what they want to make of television. Just as it is up to you what you want your universities to be. Of course, in most parts of the world television is used to advertise Western products and to brainwash people into becoming consumers. In Nigeria, TV has also been used to advertise the various military governments. One thing is careless planning. Western Nigerian TV, which started in 1956, was boldly advertised as "First in Africa." It was to be the Action Group's showpiece. But what happened is exactly what would happen later with the universities. They had money to put up buildings, buy some equipment, and pay staff. But there was no money to produce eight hours of television programs a day. So they had to buy old soap operas from America that had been shown all over the world already and therefore didn't cost much. But what that did was to promote middle class American values in Nigeria. The Action Group politicians didn't see that. I argued with them saying, if you can only afford to produce one hour TV locally, just broadcast one hour until you can raise the money to broadcast two hours. But of course they wouldn't see that. They only thought having TV was a sign of being progressive, more "progressive" than the other regions in the country. But these are avoidable mistakes!

B.J.: But that is the thing; are they really so avoidable?

U.: Totally. If you have analyzed the problem, and if you have the determination not to succumb to cheap Western values. It's not an intellectual problem, it's a political one.

B.J.: You are proceeding from the standpoint of the most positive values in society, while the medium is dialectically open to all the negative values as well.

U: But you are underestimating the intelligence of the average Yoruba man and woman. Remember that it is not the viewers who determine what goes on TV; it is not even the producers, but it is the government that decides what people should see. Remember the rediffusion boxes? A particularly destructive medium, because you pay a monthly rate regardless of how many hours you listen to it. So at first, everybody kept it permanently on, and it blared out its programs from 6 a.m. to 11 p.m. But because people wanted to sleep, they mounted the boxes on their verandas and then closed the shutters at night. I remember it very well, because in those days we could not start rehearsals in the Duro Ladipo theatre until after 11 p.m. But when Akintola, Premier of Western Nigeria, began to use the rediffusion boxes for his political propaganda, people returned their boxes by the thousands. The whole medium died! And again, the *Daily Mirror* in London owned the *Daily Times* in Lagos. But then it was a much more serious newspaper than the parent newspaper, because the Nigerian public was not interested in petty gossip and sex-and-crime stories; they wanted to know what went on in Nigeria. The *Daily Mirror* then pursued a painstaking policy of trying to corrupt the Nigeria public's taste, and to a point it succeeded. But the Nigerian press then bounced back, and we then had *The Guardian* and all kinds of weeklies, which were very courageous and full of integrity. We have seen Nigerian journalists going to jail and at least one murdered. So these young, mostly untrained journalists have shown us how a medium can be used.

B.J.: But let me be very blunt about this. And it is almost un-Yoruba to approach you in this manner because you are now an elder. I think you do not leave enough room for what I call the radical nature of evil.

U.: That may be true. But what is the answer to that except to fight it step by step? And I think you can, and you must, fight it in your own sphere of influence. Now if you go back to Western Nigerian television, there was a lot wrong with it, but within that institution, a single person like Segun Olusola, Africa's first television producer, made a lot of difference. For a long time, he produced a short play by Duro Ladipo every month, sometimes every week! That kept the company alive during the most difficult years. So, every person can make a big difference if he uses his imagination and inventiveness and energy where he stands.

B.J.: That's why I started by saying that I believe that no matter how great the destruction, no matter how many evil forces militate against you, human creativity will pick itself up, dust itself off, and start again. But having started from that, I still think we have to leave room also for the existence of evil—without feeling defeated. But we must leave room for it because it is so *powerful*. And you know that Yoruba metaphysical traditions leave room for this problem of evil, for instance in the saying that "evil and good walk side by side." This idea is given perhaps its most powerful exploration in Soyinka's *Madmen and Specialists*. Without being paralyzed by it, I have come to believe more and more in the last few years that you have to deal with the radical nature of evil.

U: You cannot change an institution single-handed. I could not change the University of Ibadan in the 1950s and 60s. I could not persuade them to teach African literature; but I could teach it outside the university, and I could start *Black Orpheus,* and I also helped found the Mbari Clubs. So, you can often sidestep these powerful conservative institutions, and in the end, these little steps build up to something. It is true that now we do not have the cultural dynamism that made life so exciting in the 1960s.... A future government of Nigeria will have to find a way of curbing the exploitative capitalism that dominates the country at the moment. It would have to create a fairer distribution of the nation's abundant wealth. In some areas, it may even have to introduce drastic land reform. It will have to learn to live more simply and avoid enslaving the country by taking more and more loans.

B.J.: I am still worried about the power of evil, even at the existential level. It takes ten times, fifty times, longer to create a pot than to destroy it.

U: That may be so, but remember that Germany recovered from Hitler and World War II. And let us not forget one thing. In spite of all the corruption in Nigeria, the exploitation and crookedness in high places, there is another level of society in which people still trust each other and rely on each other. I know a wealthy Yoruba trader who may return from overseas with thirty, or even forty thousand dollars in cash. She goes straight to a Hausa moneychanger in Lagos and deposits the whole sum with him. Any time she needs some Naira she sends a boy or girl down to him to ask for it. Nothing is written down. There are no receipts and no accounts. Everything is recorded in both their heads, and she has never been cheated.

B.J.: I can corroborate that story. I once gave Femi Osofisan an envelope that contained $400 to take back to Nigeria and give to a friend who lives in a village near Ife. For several months I did not hear from this friend, so when Femi returned to the US, I asked what happened to the envelope I gave him. He explained that he did not meet my friend when he called at his home in the village, so he gave the envelope to an old woman who said she was a neighbor and would deliver it. "How could you do that?" I said. "I haven't heard from my friend!" Osofisan replied that the woman looked honest, and this upset me. But now, just a few days ago, I heard from my friend that he had received the money. The woman had handed it to him—and that in a situation of dire poverty. So I'm going to write Osofisan and tell him. "Our faith should not be destroyed!"

U: I think this is a good note on which to conclude our conversation. And I would like to thank you for remaining "desperately optimistic" in these hard times.

Chinua Achebe

"THE WORLD IS A DANCING MASQUERADE"

U: There is a well-known Igbo proverb, which says, "The world is a dancing masquerade. If you want to understand it, you can't remain standing in one place." This proverb seems to be a central image of the Igbo world. Can you elaborate on its meaning in traditional society, and also tell me to what extent it is still relevant to Igbo today?

C: Yes, you are absolutely right in thinking it's a very important statement. First of all, the masquerades. The masquerade is, perhaps, the most typical of all the Igbo arts, because it contains so many things. It is theatre; it is dance, music, architecture—anything at all. The masquerade is motion; all kinds of motion—athletic motion, graceful motion. Then there is the religious aspect. The masquerade is a representative of the ancestors—of eternity. It comes to visit the living, thus establishing a link between the past and the present. History is one continuous flow. Now, the spectators in the arena, they cannot stand rooted somewhere or take a seat.... They must get up and follow the masquerade around, if they want to see it in all its magnificence and from all angles. So that's the literal meaning. But now the symbolic meaning, and why it is a proverb—not just a statement. The proverb is applicable to other things. You use it when you are telling people not to get so deeply rooted in one thing that they don't see the possibility of change. The world is in a continuous state of flux, and we, as inhabitants of the world, must learn to adapt, to change, and to move. So the whole concept of mobility in Igbo culture is enshrined in that proverb. Even old customs—customs that are wonderful—may at times no longer be useful. We must be ready at any moment to try

Photo by Don Hamerman, courtesy of The Publications Office, Bard College

something new. That is basic to Igbo culture, the idea of change—you know, that "no condition is permanent"...

U: Yes, a favorite statement of the Onitsha pamphleteers....

C: It is a modern statement of the same idea. In Igbo culture, nobody is allowed to inherit the titles of his father....

U: Everybody starts from the beginning; everybody has to achieve.

C: All that is contained in this statement. Society judges you by your own work, not by your ancestors. So you see, it gets very...sort of succinct. It sums up everything about the Igbo people—the fact that they are restless, the fact that they believe in change, that they believe in "improvement" whether as individuals or as groups.

U: So you get this competitive spirit amongst Igbo communities: Which village can first build a secondary school? Who can first install electricity or a water supply? Igbo communities have never waited for government grants!

C: Now the problem of course is how do you accept change without losing your identity? Remember, everything has its deficit side...

U: It's a very pragmatic culture; it's open to everything. It's rather ironical, because it's the exact opposite of the European cliché image of stagnant, primitive cultures...

C: Yes, the idea that we have sort of been trapped in savagery; the image that the "sweep of civilization" is going on somewhere else, and we have been totally unaware and untouched by it. That's absolute nonsense. It's a very pragmatic culture, even individualistic! We think that individualism is something we learned from the Americans. That's not true! Igbo individualism goes so deep, you see, it's not even "We are all equal in the sight of God." *Every single person, man or woman, is a unique creation.* We are not just created by the same God, but each person has his own *chi*, a personal god. We are made by our *chi*, so not two people are the same, not even blood brothers! This is individualism taken to its utmost!

U: It seems to me that one particular strength of Igbo culture is that they don't accept any truth as absolute. I cannot see a fundamentalist movement or fascism taking root easily amongst Igbo.

C: No, the Igbo do not believe in anything absolute. They believe that "Nothing stands by itself"; that "Wherever one thing stands, some other thing will stand next to it." It's again the idea that you don't stand in one place; that we don't hold to one belief. Igbo people don't say, "This is it. This is the answer"; rather they say, "There must be something else."

U: They believe in the possibility of simultaneous truths.

C: Yes, so again it is *movement*... in the metaphysical sense! We are not fixed in a particular idea of truth.

U: You can grasp an aspect of truth, but not *the* truth.

C: Yes, I am sure that "I am the way, the truth, and the life" must have struck the first Igbo people as a heresy.

U: Certainly they would have thought it represented a simplistic view of life.

C: Yes, and I am convinced that the only reason the Igbo went under was the fire power of the British army who came with the missionaries.

U: Even then... I can't see that even today, Christianity has succeeded to kill Igbo individualism or Igbo pragmatism...

C: No, no! It's not possible. People have been living in a particular frame of mind, and it is not possible that someone would come and uproot it all in a year or even in a generation. The basic individualism still exists.

U: Certainly the competitiveness is as alive as ever today!

C: Yes, yes, but what one regrets, I think, is that in the past it was kept within the bounds of a certain spirituality. There was a kind of composure....

U: A certain dignity....

C: Yes, you can lose that and become rather frenetic in your pursuit of the new things ....

U: Of course, in traditional society there was a limit to the amount of wealth a man could acquire, because there was a limit to his physical capacity to work. How many yams can even the strongest man grow?

C: Yes, we have lost the relationship between wealth and work. Nowadays you can become rich without work, simply by manipulation....

U: Traditional wealth did not involve selfishness, because there was the corrective mechanism. People didn't mind anybody becoming rich, but if he then wanted to have political power as well, the community made him shed all his wealth first. If you wanted to become influential in the society, you couldn't remain rich at the same time.

C: Yes, that's very true. And after all you "took" the title. It was not the community saying, "You're a great man, we make you a lord." You, yourself, decided that you had acquired enough property, and you now wanted to become one of the titled men in the clan. And they would say, "Yes, but there is a fee!" So you bring out all the wealth you have acquired and you throw it back into the community through feasting and through fees you pay to the older members of the association and so on. At the end of the period of celebration, you are really a poor man again. But you've got your title, and you wear your anklet, or your red cap, or whatever! But you are no longer rich, and you cannot be a threat to the community.... And another interesting point: Even within the narrow scope given you in taking titles, every title had its taboo! This in itself was an imposition of a spiritual nature on your activities.

U: And severe.... As the titles got higher, so did the restrictions. They became more severe....

C: Yes, the things you could not do! Like, you could not sleep outside your compound. Your movement was limited. And so people would then limit their ambition. They would say, "Why should I impose more restrictions upon myself? It's too much trouble. I shall limit myself to my present title; I won't go any further."

U: So the acquisition of power was not only made incompatible possession of wealth, it also imposed its own automatic discipline...

C: Yes, the highest title was, of course, that of the king!

U: *Eze!*

C: Yes, Eze. But to become their king, you had to pay the debts owed by everybody in the community! They said, "If you want to become king over us, then we will tell you what we owe.... Then, when you have paid all our debts, you can become king!"

U: It is an amazing concept. A man who wants to hold supreme power is being prepared to shoulder that much responsibility, and to endure such severe discipline that in the end people feel, "It is not worth it!" This control mechanism was so effective, that in the end most Igbo communities managed happily enough without a king, because no one wanted the job. So the result is a democratic government! Europe could learn a lot from that. Another thing I find remarkable about this is the extent to which the Igbo man or woman is left to decide his or her own fate. There is a great concept of individual freedom here! It reminds me of another Igbo proverb which is quoted by Victor Uchendu, a historian, in his monograph on the Igbo: "The world is a market place, and it is open to bargain." In other words, under whatever circumstances we are born, we have the right to manipulate our lives...our fate! How different from the kind of attitude you find in lower middle class England, where mothers tell their daughters, "Don't think you can better yourself!"

C: Is that so? You are not supposed to aim?

U: You are not supposed to aim high because you find yourself embedded in a rigid class structure which you have been taught not to question. It's an attitude that would be unthinkable amongst Igbo.

C: Yes, that's right. The idea of bargain is very intrinsic; it goes beyond the everyday reality we see around us. It reaches back into the very beginning, into the cosmology of Igbo land. There is a bargain...

U: A bargain with your creator...

C: Yes. With our *chi;* with your creator...

U: It is similar to the Yoruba idea of "choosing your *ori*." There is the concept of a garden in heaven, in which the "good" heads and the "bad" heads are kept, and before a man enters the world, he is led into this garden..., and he has to choose his *ori*, fate. And again you may remember Gabriel Okara's story of *Woyengi*, the woman who had chosen her fate before birth, and then went back to the creator to try and change it. So there seem to be related ideas in many West African cultures—and yet there are significant differences, too. Now how exactly is the myth of heavenly bargaining related among Igbo?

C: Your *chi* is the representative of the almighty, and it is your *chi* who is assigned to be your companion through life. And this relationship starts at the very beginning, the moment you choose your career—because life is viewed as a career with the possibility of....

U: Promotion!

C: Change, yes. So you decide this is the kind of person you want to be in life! Then on your way into the world, there are distractions—there are temptresses who try to shake your resolution! You could fall there already, but again you could resist. Your *chi* will be keeping close to you, but not so close as to deprive you of your own free will.

U: But you can get support from your *chi*!

C: Yes you can! And now, when you come into the world, and you discover that you have a different ambition from....

U: What you have planned....

C: Planned, yes, in fact what you had sworn to! Then it's not easy ... but here again this is where the Igbo pragmatism comes in: strong as that pact is, it's not absolute.

U: It's negotiable!

C: It's negotiable, but very difficult. That's why we say, "If a man says 'yes' very strongly, his *chi* will also say 'yes'!"

U: You have to be pretty single minded to bargain successfully with fate! And this single mindedness is another strong Igbo characteristic. When they say "yes" very strongly, they are prepared to go with their head through the wall! At a certain point, when a strong decision has been taken, you are supposed to carry that through to the end; there is no turning back again. I have read in a book about the slave trade that three hundred Igbo slaves, chained together, decided not to accept this humiliation, and they jumped overboard together and drowned. Now this kind of determination, this ability to draw consequences to the bitter end, seems to me a very pronounced characteristic of this culture!

C: Yes, it is! But you are not supposed to invoke it every day! It is only permissible when there is no way out, when, as another proverb says, "The back is broken and hung over the fire!"

U: When you have exhausted all your options!

C: Yes! And that's when you can have the incident of "The Igbo Landing." That's still the name of the place in South Carolina: "Igbo Landing".

U: That's why people did not want to buy Igbo slaves; they fetched a low price because they were reputed to commit suicide.

C: Yes, particularly the titled men with the *ichi* marks. They would not, they could not possibly, be slaves. That's why there is this ultimate—this suicidal element....

U: At a certain point, the Igbo reached that stage during the Biafran war— or so it seemed to me.

C: Yes they did, they did. It's interesting that you could raise this, because the story of the Igbo slaves who walked into the sea was told at a meeting which I addressed in the South in the United States, during the war. I was travelling there, trying to explain what was going on, and at the end of my lectures this old man, this old black man got up and told the story of the Igbo Landing. It was a very strange feeling! Nobody knew what to say after that! He didn't say, "Your people have done that before," or anything like that. He just told the story and sat down! So there have been such moments in Igbo history. Fortunately, Igbo culture makes sure that it does not encourage people to adopt that attitude too often.

U: Then how do they stop people from adopting this single minded last stand?

C: By creating alternative views that almost contradict it. For instance the proverb which says, "It is good to be brave and courageous, but we stand in the compound of a coward and point to where a strong man used to live." You see? He is no longer there. He has been destroyed by his strength and courage... So it is saying be strong, be powerful, be prosperous. But it is also saying it carries a penalty.

U: But then people also know, that there are moments in life, that there are situations when they must be willing to pay the penalty. There are some cultures which have a clearly marked bottom line where people exercise a lot of tolerance, but then there comes a situation where you have to kill. Certain cultures in New Guinea are like that.

C: It's what the Igbo call *abomination*. Everything else can be sorted out peacefully by some sort of arrangement; but when an abomination is committed, the community cannot tolerate it. Murder is an abomination, and a man will have to pay for it with his life! Only if it can be proved that he did it by accident, then he will be sent into exile for seven years!

U: That is a harsh punishment because where does a man go? What role can he play elsewhere?

C: It's the harshest kind of punishment because your life is supposed to be lived within your community. There is a Bantu statement: "A person is a person, because of other persons." That also applies to the Igbo concept of a community. If a man had no community, he would be an animal! It's society that makes you human...

U: It's only in relationship to other people that you could be right or wrong, good or bad.

C: Nobody says that a lion is wicked, because it does not apply. The Igbo actually believe that it was agriculture (and the communal effort in

109

making it succeed) that humanized us. There is a story that human beings used to wander around in the bush like animals. And one day *Chukwu*, the supreme God, gave yam to the king of the wanderers and to the king of animals, and told them to plant it. They tried, but they did not succeed. Then the wanderers went back to Chukwu and said, "We cannot do it. The soil is too soft, too watery...." Then Chukwu said, "Go and bring the blacksmiths from Awka, and let them blow the soil dry with their bellows." They did, and the soil became drier. Then they grew yams and all sorts of other crops. So this is how civilization began, according to this tale. Once people settled down and began to plant, they then had to make tools for use in agriculture, and this is how the arts and crafts are developed...

U: Now this is interesting because it defines art as a communal activity or as an activity that serves a very practical purpose in the community. But there is another characteristic of Igbo art that has always fascinated me: The Igbo artist often likes to work *against* his material. Compare, for example an Igbo Mbari house with an Olokun shrine from the Benin area. They are both similar in that they consist of assemblages of mud figures, often life size; the one being dedicated to the earth goddess Ala, the other to the god of the sea, Olokun. Now the Olokun mud figures, or Yoruba mud sculptures representing Esu-Elegbara, are all carved out of a lump; the shapes are rounded, heavy, with the arms usually close to the body, and the shapes undulating which is what comes naturally out of the process of molding clay. But in an Mbari House you will find the earth goddess enthroned, with her arms outstretched wide, holding a sword in the right hand, or a leopard pouncing from a height and supported tenuously on its small paws. Here the artist is defying the limitation of the material; he is exposing it to a stress it cannot stand. But he does not care if the figure collapses after a few days, because he feels that "it is then simply time to make a new one." Or again, if you see a Yoruba carving of a horseman, it's carved out of one upright trunk, and the horse is reduced in size and shortened, so that it can fit into the shape of the trunk. But I have seen an Igbo shrine where a horseman was carved out of two pieces of wood. The horseman was carved separately and placed at an angle onto the horse, and one arm was carved out of the third piece of wood, thus allowing the artist to create a series of intersecting lines, and thus exploiting all possibilities of creating tension.

C: Oh, I see. Yes, yes....

U: Or if you look at Igbo face painting, if you look at the cover of my book on mud sculpture, there is an image of *Ala* from an Mbari House and the *Uli* design on the face cuts right across the eye. The painting is used to destroy the anatomy! Compare that to the Yoruba tribal marks. They will always underline the anatomy. They follow the bone structure of the face. But the *Uli* artist imposes his own vision onto the natural shape of the body, so that you forget certain aspects....

C: Of the body itself! Yes, yes that's very interesting.

U: It's highly sophisticated, and I think there is also an enjoyment of the tension.

C: It's a dare! Well, I think you put it very well. It's also obviously part of what you might call the ambitiousness of the Igbo people—to go beyond what is given....

U: An element of provocation!

C: Provocation, yes; that's really what art is to them ultimately. You are given something—the human form—but you want to go beyond.... I would describe it as "giving yourself another handle on reality." The more you go beyond what is given, the more tension you create, and thus the more vitality is introduced into what you create! It's not composure that the Igbo artist is seeking. His art is full of vitality and motion.

U: Yes, I think you are very right when you said earlier that the masquerade is the most typical, the most central art form of the Igbo. Even today when much of the religious significance has gone out of the Igbo masquerades, even now! What energy, what constant surprises, when the masquerade stands still, and then it suddenly seems struck by some lightening energy, and it bursts forth.... This explosive movement is quite mind blowing. And the colors! The violent juxtaposition of reds and yellows and oranges! Again it's this enjoyment of a clash, of tension!

C: It's like Igbo women dancing. There is this undulating, flowing motion of the choreographed group, which is satisfying to the eye.... But then there are these individual outbursts, where a single woman comes out and dances against the beat in a truly *antagonistic movement*! It requires courage to do that! And again, it's an attempt to go beyond....

U: To challenge the given order. But to go back to those colors, two generations ago those colors could not have been available to the Igbo artist; yet they seized on this new opportunity and used it to express something that had always been inherent their culture.

C: Well, this kind of creativity comes straight from the source. It's like those Igbo who were asked by some of us in the university to paint a shrine at Nri, with *Uli* paintings. Now the art of *Uli* painting had practically died out in that village, and none of them had ever done it before; only one old woman had some vague memories of being involved in a painting when she was a young girl. And yet they were able to create the *Uli* forms again! Perhaps that call gave us some courage, because it seems to show that our culture is not all that fragile after all!

U: Of course, we are actually witnessing a kind of regenerative process of the culture now. There is a process of rethinking—a new consciousness. I am thinking of artists like Uche Okeke and Obiora Udechukwu. They have been objecting to certain aspects of colonial art teaching, certain methods of imposing another way of seeing onto the culture. And they have gone and looked at *Uli* design, and the traditional wall paintings of Igbo women. And they are trying to find a new starting point from there. Some people have compared this quite wrongly, I think, to the Negritude movement, but I don't see it like that. There is, of course, theoretically the danger of such a process turning into mere rhetoric, and I think that with some of the lesser Nsukka artists, this has become a mere stance—a pose, rather than a genuine development. But with the major artist like Obiora it's not like that at all. Now, you have been quite close to the artistic movement. How do you see it?

C: Well, it's difficult to put into words, but it's *not* like going back to something "primitive." We must explain the need for this movement from our recent history. The change in our society has not been a gradual development; it's been rather brutal—like a violent incision, a breach of continuity. Through colonialism your initiative is taken from you; you are thrown out of your history and into somebody else's history.

U: All the decisions were suddenly made by other people.

C: Yes, and it was a very traumatic experience, and we are only just beginning to wake up from it. So this artistic movement is part of the process of saying, "Let's discover who we are...."

U: Of making a connection with your history...

C: So that you can then decide which way to go. You see? We cannot *preempt and say*, "This is the way to go...." But we have to establish a kind of awareness of who you are—after this period of total dehumanization.
    We have to find the measure of things again, find out just who we are. That does not solve all our problems—or even most of them. But it's a beginning. It's a point from which you can find a direction. And it's not a personal decision, it's a whole generation involved in it. To put it in literary terms, when I travelled to Kenya last December, my publisher invited me there, and I must have seen every school child in Kenya! They came out in hundreds and thousands in every centre. There are about twelve schools in every district, and they all came together in one place with all their teachers, and it was like they were saying, "We found ourselves in literature." I had the biggest book signing in my life. So something has happened to us through this literature, no matter how imperfect it may be, and these school children found themselves at the centre of a story! So they can go and develop it later whichever way they want. We have to reestablish again that we own this, this territory. After that artists can go on, and go their various ways....

U: You know that I started some modest courses in African literature in the early fifties in the Extra-Mural-Department of the University of Ibadan—before your books were published. And some Nigerians would come to me and say, "You are trying to put the clock back." They did not want to know about Tutuola or Fagunwa let alone about *Oriki* (panegyrics) or hunter songs or Igbo ballads. And I tried to explain to them, "I am not trying to tell you to ignore what has happened or undo what has been done because that is not possible. But I want you to *evaluate* what happened. I don't want you to accept the interpretation of your colonial masters who are telling you that what has happened is simply a change from bad to good, from darkness to light." But some of them are already reacting the way they had been taught to react...

C: Yes, of course, it's brainwashing of a very serious nature.

U: So what the young Nsukka artists are doing, what the young writers are doing, is opening everything up again. Everything is open to question again; nothing is taken for granted any more. You are open to different kinds of change, and that is the basic Igbo attitude again. What happened in colonial times is that you were deprived of choices. This is why your novels have been so very important. They made people aware; they helped people to re-examine the colonial process. They realized that the tragedy was not so much that they lost this or that art form or this or that custom, but they'd lost their ability to make decisions. But while the intellectuals begin to resume some kind of initiative, politicians all over the Third World still have decisions made for them by bodies like the IMF.

C: Well, you know, in March, I was to a meeting of the Organization of Economic Cooperation which is really a meeting of rich nations—Europeans, Americans, Canadians, Australians—all the people who are doing well in the world. They were celebrating their twenty-fifth anniversary in Paris. And for some reason I was the only one among them who was not an economist or a banker. They were reading their papers, and they were talking about the "structural adjustment programs" which they impose on the Third World. They say to us, "You are not managing your affairs well; you are in debt. So if you need more loans, this is what you will do: You have to remove subsidies on agriculture and this and that. And if you obey our rules, more loans will come your way." So they tell us, "There are a few things that you will have to adjust; it may impose some hardship on you, but we know it's going to work." Then the Chairman of the Central Bank in Kenya said, "A country like Zambia has been practicing this for ten years, but they are no better off after off this." But they said to him, "No, you have to give us a little more time... This thing has to work in the end!"

      Then I got really angry and said, "I am beginning to understand why I am here. I have been wondering what a fiction writer is doing among world bankers and economists. But now I realize that what you are doing here is *fiction!* You talk about 'structural adjustment', as if Africa was some kind of laboratory! Some intellectual abstraction. You prepare your medicine, you mix this into that; if it doesn't work, you try, out another concoction. But Africa is people, you know? In the last two years, we have seen the minimum wage in Nigeria fall from the equivalent of fifteen pounds a month to five pounds a month! That's not an abstraction: Somebody is earning that money, and he has wife and children, you see?" And it was amazing because the person who had been speaking was shocked! As if he had realized for the first time that Africa was not just a conglomeration of different formulas... I said to them, "You are punishing these countries because they are in debt, but America is the biggest debtor of all; and nobody is asking America to adopt politics that would bankrupt their citizens. But Africa, the Third World, they are places where you can try out things. Africans are not really people.... They are expendable!" And that's the mentality that created our problems. Whether in literature or economy, people think we are expendable: "We can go there and straighten them out. Give them the gospel, give them this and that." Then they go and forget us and carry on with their lives.... In the meantime, our own lives have been messed up.

U: The situation is much more serious than in colonial times, because the bankers exercise much more power than the colonial district officers.

C: The power is greater ... without the responsibility! They don't have to explain to anybody why there is a coup in the Sudan, but they control the Sudan nonetheless.

U: A colonial officer could get killed. Think of the governor of the Gold Coast who was captured by the Ashanti. At least they had to stick their neck out....

C: And explain themselves in the House of Commons! But today they are totally faceless! Our first generation of nationalists had a go at it, but they did not make a good job of it, and now we have to persuade ourselves that we can actually run nations. There are people now in Africa who doubt that we could ever do it; after all they say, they were there in the first place because we were savages. But the assessment is not quite fair, because if our leaders failed, they were not the leaders we have chosen; it was the leadership *they* installed.

U: It was certainly the leadership they had educated in their own image. And certainly, they did not question the political or social or economic processes they found themselves involved in. I remember that I had a lot of arguments with my friend, S.O. Awokoya, a science teacher, who became the first Minister of Education in Awolowo's Government in the

Western Region of Nigeria. He was a very nice person and very intelligent, and I did admire this extraordinary drive he had. But he had this theory: Yoruba society was becoming a kind of class society because the few who had been to school despised the majority of the farmers who had not been to school. The answer to that problem, he said, was to send *everybody* to school, so that school would cease to confer any artificial distinction on anybody. And with enormous energy and efficiency, he organized "universal, free education" in the whole of western Nigeria within two years! An extraordinary feat! But I said to him, "Is it not far more important to think about the content of education than the quantity of it? Instead of saying, "Within two years I want every child to go to school", is it not far more important to ask, "What kind of citizens do we want to produce in our schools?" Or "what values do we want to impart to the school children?"' For if school children go to school, and end up despising their grandparents, does it not indicate that something is wrong with the content of education? And by multiplying schools without correcting the content of education, are we not multiplying the problems? Schools and universities can become places in which irrelevant knowledge is passed from generation to generation.

C: Yes, that's the mistake of the first years after independence—not realizing where our priorities lie. The idea of "school" not being just "school"; rather "what kind of school?" We cannot afford to make these mistakes again. The most important thing for us to aim at is the mind. We have to say to our children, "Look, we had this kind of society in the past. Late as it is, we must find out what we can..." There are still little corners of knowledge where the values exist, where the poetry exists! It is the question of content, again. There are young people nowadays, who are trying to invent a new Igbo language, which they call "Central Igbo". They are not familiar with the work of great Igbo poets, but they start to invent! They invent a word for university which literally means "knows everything!" This shows how tired the minds are, how unhealthy. And this is what we are trying to battle!

   There are certain university professors who are setting up the society for the study of Igbo culture, but they don't know anything about it, and they don't care. Their only interest is to get together and set the exams for the West African School Certificate; mark the exams, write their books, and make money on them. But they are not struggling for the survival of those elements of our culture, on which we can build! For example, they don't even know about the great poets in Anambra State, and how relevant and topical their work is today! There is one story—just an excerpt of a long epic.... It is an epic story about how the heroes got together to discuss a threat, a threat that was coming from the sky....where a certain ruler, a tyrant, had established himself. He had built steps up to the sky, and from there he was sending down decrees. One day he dropped down a piece of paper to the community telling them that they must not eat for the next twenty-eight days! There would have to be complete abstinence from food and drink! Why? He was holding a feast up here, and while he's feasting, nobody on earth must eat.

U: Almost like the IMF!

C: Exactly! And the people obeyed, you know; they felt helpless! And he said, "If I see even one person drink even water, or chew a chewing stick, I will destroy the entire community!" So the people started crying. Those who could read started to cry, and those who could not read took it to the ones who had learned to read, and when they read it to them, they all started crying! And they started their month of starvation, and the children began to die. The heroes came together from different parts of the land and said, "What are we going to do about this? We must go and find out what's going on up there!" Then, first of all, they started quarrelling over who should lead them—the usual sort of thing. And the boisterous ones became the leaders, but the real hero was the one in the back, with his flute in his hands. But after weeks of arguing and moving about, but getting nowhere, they began to say, "Well, we better go home. We better give the whole thing up!" So they turned around, and they met the man at the back who asked, "Why?" And they said, "We don't see any point in this. We are going home!" So they all went back—including the spirits that had come from the spirit world to help them. But the real hero continued the journey. And the amazing thing is, when he arrived in heaven, the tyrant was not really all that strong! You would have expected a cataclysmic kind of struggle, but there was none at all! The fellow was actually a coward!

U: So it was a bluff! And the real heroes of the Igbo society are the artists and the writers who have been telling everybody that colonialism was just one big bluff!

C: Yes, and if we win the battle for the minds, the first thing which will go
     is that rigidity of mind that has come to us with the so-called "higher
     religions", this fanaticism that can make a man go to war over a matter
     of belief!

U: Then you might recreate the spirit of the culture, not by going back to
     some antiquated custom, but by making people realize again that the
     world is a market place—open to bargain!

C: Yes, and by rediscovering the meaning of the old saying, "The World is a
     Dancing Masquerade!"

Wole Soyinka
"YORUBA RELIGION"

U: I wanted to talk to you about Yoruba religion because you seem to be the only writer who has seriously tried to come to terms with it. Even many of the Yoruba scholars, who do research into language, literature, history and religion of the Yoruba, shy away from the subject—as if they were embarrassed by it...

Now in your own case, given the type of upbringing you had, I have asked myself how you became interested in Yoruba religion. There is an image in *Ake: The Years of Childhood* that has made a very strong impression on me. You were living in the Christian school compound that was surrounded by a high wall, and when the Egungun masqueraders were passing by outside, you had to ask somebody to lift you onto the ladder so that you could watch the procession going on outside. Your upbringing was designed to shield you from the realities of Yoruba life, and later on your education in the Grammar school, the University in England—they all were designed to take you further away from the core of your culture. How then did you find your way back into it? How did you manage to break the wall that had been built around you?

W: Curiosity mostly, and the annual visits to Isara, a very different situation from Abeokuta! There is no question at all that there was something, an immediacy that was more attractive, more intriguing about something from which you were obviously being shielded. If you hear all the time, "Oh, you mustn't play with those kids because their father is an Egungun man," you become curious, and then you discover that there is nothing really "evil" about it..., that it is not the way they preach about it. Even my great great uncle, the Reverend J.J. Ransome Kuti, whom I never met, composed a song whose refrain was, "Dead men can't talk...." One was

Photo by Remi Omodele

surrounded by such refutations of that other world, of that other part of one's heritage, so of course you asked questions about it. Yes, and even if I realized quite early on, that there was a man in that Egungun mask, that did not mean that a great act of evil was being committed any more than saying that Father Christmas was evil. I had this rather comparative sense, and I wrote in *Ake* that I used to look at the images on the stained glass windows of the church: Henry Townsend, the Rev. Hinderer, and then the image that was supposed to be St. Peter. In my very imaginative mind, it didn't seem to me that they were very different from the Egungun.

So one was surrounded by all these different images which easily flowed into one another, I was never frightened of the Egungun. I was fascinated by them. Of course, I talked to some of my colleagues, like Osiki, who donned the masquerade himself — from time to time. The *Igbale*, the masqueraders' grove, was nothing sinister to me; it signified to me a mystery, a place of transformation. You went into *Igbale* to put on your masquerade. Then when the Egungun came out, it seemed that all they did was bless the community and beg a little bit for alms here and there. Occasionally there were disciplinary outings. They terrorized everybody, and we ran away from them, but then, some distance away, you stopped and rested.... Maybe my dramatic bent saw this right from the beginning as part of the drama of life. I never went through a phase when I believed that traditional religion or ceremonies were evil. I believed that there were witches, but I was convinced that there were good apparitions. And, of course, I found the songs and the drumming very exciting.

U: You never really took to Christianity at any stage....

W: Never really—not even as a child. I remember distinctly my first essay prize at secondary school—that was in my first year. My essay was entitled, "Ideals of an Atheist." Yes, I went through all these phases. I just felt I couldn't believe in the Christian god, and for me that meant I was an atheist.

U: How old were you then?

W: I was eleven! But I also enjoyed being in the choir. I was a chorister. I went regularly to rehearsals. I enjoyed the festive occasion, the harvest festival, etc. Then we processed through the congregation, rather than sneaking in through the side entrances. At Christmas and New Year, I enjoyed putting on the robes of a chorister. On the way to church I went to see my friend Edun, who lived in Ibarapa. And my Sunday was made even more interesting when we met the Egungun masquerades on the way—which was quite often.

U: Do you remember we went to a conference in Venice? It must have been in 1960 or 1961....

W: Oooooh, yes....

U: There was a writer from Northern Nigeria.... I think it was Ibrahim Tahir. And he made a statement, the gist of which was that Nigeria was, or was about to become, an Islamic country....

W: I have actually forgotten that, but it wouldn't surprise me.

U: I am not quite certain what his real argument was or how it was phrased. But I do remember your rather fierce reply. Your point was that both Christianity and Islam were conservative forces that actually retarded Nigeria's ability to cope with the modern world, whereas traditional religions—Yoruba religion at least—was something much more open, and much capable of adaptation...

W: Yes, and for that very reason liberating! I am glad you brought up the issue of Islam, because that was also contributory to my entire attitude to imposed foreign religions. You know all this nonsense of religious intolerance which is eating into the country now—it didn't exist in my youth! During *Ileya*, Id el Fitir, we celebrated with our Muslim friends. They would send us meat from their ram; the Oba would go to the mosque, even if he was a Christian, and vice versa. During Christmas and Easter, our Muslim friends would come to the house. There was always equality between the religions—acceptance. And that in turn made it impossible for me to see one as superior to the other. And of course, the more I learned about Yoruba religion, the more I realized that that was just another interpretation of the world, another encapsulation of man's conceiving of himself and his position in the universe; and that all these religions are just metaphors for the strategy of man coping with the vast unknown. I became more and more intrigued, and it is not surprising that, when I went to study in England, I nearly took "Comparative Religion" as one of my subjects. But then I decided that I would enjoy it more, if I just read into it and visited all sorts of places.... I remember going to this small Buddhist meeting. I visited the so-called fundamentalist religions, the spiritualist churches.... I went to one or two séances. I have always been interested in the spirituality of the human individual. So when people like Tahir—and there have been many of them—have made that kind of statement, I have always risen to counter it very fiercely. Traditional religion is not only accommodating, it is liberating, and this seems logical, because whenever a new phenomenon impinge on the consciousness of the Yoruba—whether a historical event, a technological or scientific encounter—they do not bring down the barriers or close the doors. They say, "Let us look at this phenomenon and see what we have that corresponds to it in our own tradition which is a kind of analogue to this experience." And sure enough, they go to Ifa, and they examine the corpus of proverbs and sayings, and they look even into their, let's say, agricultural practices, or the observation of their calendar. Somewhere within that religion, they will find some kind of approximate interpretation of that event. They do not consider it a hostile experience. That's why the corpus of Ifa is constantly reinforced and augmented, even from the history of other religions with whom Ifa comes into contact. You have Ifa verses which deal with Islam; you have Ifa verses which deal with Christianity. Yoruba religion attunes itself and accommodates the unknown very readily, unlike Islam or Christianity. In Islam, whatever is not found in the Koran does not exist. The last prophet was Mohammed. Anybody who comes after this is a fake. And Christianity! The Roman Catholics—until today they do not cope with the experience and the reality of abortion! They just shut the wall firmly against it. They fail to address the real problems of it; they refuse to adjust any of their tenets.

U: The Yoruba people have always been willing to look at another mythology and equivalents in their own tradition. For example, when I first met Aderemi, the late Ooni of Ife—that was at Easter 1951, he told me about the different shrines in his town, and he said, "You know, in Yoruba religion we know the story of Mary and Jesus," and he told me the myth of Moremi who sacrificed her only son in order to save her town. And he said, "Really, Moremi is Mary." I was impressed, because he could see that there was some basic metaphor that remained valid across a variety of cultures. He knew that the basic truth is the same—only the trappings are different.... The Yoruba had no hostility to the piety of other people.

U: Yoruba religion, within itself, is based on this very tolerance. In each town you have a variety of cults, all coexisting peacefully. There may be Sango, Ogun, Obatala, Osun, and many more....

W: Even in the same compound!

U: Even within the same small family—because you were not supposed to marry into the same Orisa! But there is never any rivalry between different cult groups; they all know they are interdependent. Because they are like specialists, everybody understands specific aspects of the supernatural world. Nobody can know everything. The Egungun know how to deal with the dead; the Ogun worshippers know how to handle the forces that are symbolized by iron. But for the Ogun worshippers to function, it is also necessary that Sango worshippers, and Obatala worshippers, and all the other Olorisa to perform their part. Only the concentrated effort of all of them will bring peace and harmony to the town. So naturally, when the Christians first appeared, the Olorisa could hardly suspect...

W: How hostile the new religion would be.

U: I think that tolerance is one of the big qualities of Yoruba culture. Even the treatment of the handicapped or mentally disturbed people all shows how much more tolerant Yoruba culture was than Western cultures which absolutely block your entry into new progressive fronts. Yoruba religion just doesn't do that! It is interesting that when the Yoruba refer to a religious sect as *Igbagbo*, belief, they are referring to "Christianity" because it is nonsensical to say "I believe in Sango" or "I believe in Ogun." The Yoruba are too secure in their traditional worldview to engage in this sort of affirmation. I think I once mentioned to you that remarkable reply of an old Olorisa when his grandchild said, "The teacher said your Obatala doesn't exist." He simply answered, "Only that for which we have no name does not exist." He could not be shaken.

W: That is a brilliant way of putting it. You have been to Brazil and Cuba. In that part of the world you find Europeans, not just Mulattoes, but people of pure European descent, who accept the humanism of this religion and who recognize it as their own way of truth. And they cannot conceive of any other way of looking at the world. This is a proven ability of this religion, and it is well documented.

U: A few days before I came to Nigeria, I received a letter from a Portuguese student at the University of Munich. She came across a small community of Olorisa in Lisbon, and again she found this a more realistic and intense way of looking at the world.

W: I know a number of people like that. On the other hand, what you said earlier on about Yoruba scholars and their reluctance to come to terms with Yoruba religion ... It is a very curious phenomenon....

U: So you agree with my estimation?

W: Oh yes, I agree with it absolutely. And the worst part of it is that those fellows who speak about "false consciousness"—and I don't just mean the dying breed of Marxists—are all totally preconditioned. Even when they are trying to be objective about African religion in general, or about their own traditional belief system, they are totally incapable of relating to it. They say, "This is a contemporary world. What use is our traditional religion today?" And I feel tempted to say to them, "What use is a system of beliefs like Islam and Christianity in the contemporary world?" Obviously they cannot see that they have totally failed to make that leap, to take Yoruba religion on the same level as any system of belief in the world; they cannot see that they are committing a serious scholarship lapse or that they are totally brainwashed by what I call "elaborate structures of superstition"—Islam and Christianity particularly. They have accepted these as absolute facts of life which cannot be questioned. They lack the comparative sense of being able to see Yoruba religion as just another system—whether you want to call it superstition, belief, world view, cosmogony or whatever. You have to do it on the same level with any other system. Once you do that many questions which are being asked with regard to African religion become totally redundant. Sadly when our scholars come up against their own religion their faculty of comparison completely disappears.

U: There is a whole body of prejudices which have their roots in the ignorant or malicious misinterpretations by the missionaries. These misinterpretations still persist in the minds of many Africans. A typical one in Yorubaland is the accusation that the Egungun try to "deceive" women and children by pretending that they are spirits. But, of course, every child knows that there is a man behind the mask...

W: Absolutely! I did.

U: Everybody knows that the mask is carried by a dancer who is specially trained for that task, but at the height of the dance, he becomes the ancestor. That is a totally different matter. Can't people see that during the Egungun festival, these "wicked" men—who allegedly try to intimidate women—are in fact blessing women and children?

W: And again, if you take the communion—a thing that happens every Sunday and sometimes twice a week—in which the officiating priest actually gives you a wafer and says, "This is the flesh of Christ," and then gives you a drop of wine and says, "This is the blood of Christ...." And you believe it!

U: Another defamation of Yoruba religion is the notion that it is a form of exploitation of the people. But surely it is much less so than Christianity! Take a *babalawo*, an Ifa priest, for instance. When you consult a *babalawo*, you put down three pence, a token fee! There is no money involved in divination. Have you ever seen a rich *babalawo*?

W: Laughs

U: A traditional *babalawo* was a poor man. He was not even interested in being rich. In fact the whole society did not even know wealth in our modern sense. What kind of possessions could you own that others didn't have? Another *agbada* robe? Everybody had enough yams to eat. Everybody lived in a spacious compound that would accommodate him, his wives and children. Everybody had enough clothes to wear... Everybody had access to land. What else could you want? There was nothing to buy. The grand old Olorisa priests I knew in the fifties—the Ajagemo of Ede, the Akodu of Ilobu—they were poor people, in spite of their influence. There was no such thing as a fat priest. Whereas now, some of these new churches really do exploit their congregation. Only a week ago one of these self-styled "prophets" went to see a friend of mine, and told her: "I had a vision. The child you are carrying will be born dead and you too, will die in childbirth. The only way you can survive is to fast for three days without water and to give money to the church!" Now here is not only exploitation but also blackmail!

W: It is happening all the time. All the time! This whole spate of prophesy-
     ing, this competitive mortification of people is nothing but an attempt
     to bring powerful and wealthy people under the control of the priest.
     Even ordinary individuals are not exempted. They have succeeded in
     some cases. Oh yes. They rush to them and say, "You must do this and
     that." And sometimes when people take no notice of them their relatives
     will! There was a relation of mine who got so frightened—when one of
     these prophets predicted a likely death for me—that he ran to him, and
     asked him what to do. And I said to him, "I will curse you if you go again
     to that church. I will follow you there and break up that ceremony." So
     they do succeed on so many levels, and it has become competitive...

U: Now let us talk about the way in which some of these traditional Yoruba
     concepts have been used in your plays. If I am not mistaken, it was in *A Dance
     of the Forest* that you first used some kind of Yoruba symbolism in a play.

W: Yes, of course. By that time I had written the draft for *The Lion and the
     Jewel*, but that was a very different thing. It was on a different level...

U: The striking thing about *A Dance of the Forest* is the character of Ogun.
     This image of Ogun has accompanied you through your later writing,
     but it has been said that the Ogun of your play is a rather personal,
     "unorthodox" Orisa; that you have, in fact, created a new kind of Ogun.

W: Hmmm. That is true.

U: But of course, even in purely traditional Yoruba terms, that is quite a legiti-
     mate thing to do. Ogun has never been a rigidly defined being. The Orisa
     can only live through people—by "mounting somebody's head". You could
     even say that when the Orisa fails to manifest himself in this way through
     his priests and worshippers he ceases to exist. If the priest who personifies
     Ogun is an unusually powerful Olorisa he can modify the image of Ogun.
     So in Yoruba tradition, Ogun consists of a variety of interrelated personali-
     ties. Any traditional priest would accord you the right to live Ogun your
     own way. In fact they would think it the normal thing to do. You recreate
     Ogun, or perhaps one could say you are sensitive to other aspects of his
     being. After all Ogun is a very complex being....

W: Yes, indeed.

U: It is again the typical Yoruba openness and tolerance that we are talking about. It applies not only to the relationship between the different Orisa cults; it also applies to the variants of interpretations within one and the same cult group.

W: And in the Diaspora, of course— the same thing. The concept of Orisala or Osun are very different in Brazil or Cuba, and in turn the manifestations of the Orisa over there have affected the interpretations of some of the scholars, and they in turn have transmitted some of these ideas to our most traditional priests. So that when you speak to a babalawo, you may notice a new perception, a slightly altered perception.

U: Actually Pierre Verger (ethnographer, photographer and *Babalawo)* was instrumental in establishing contacts between Brazilian Olorisa and their families in Dahomey and Nigeria. Messages were sent back and forth which were ultimately followed by exchange visits. Today, there is quite a bit of movement between the two countries. Look at Sangodare, for example, the young Sango priest who grew up in Susanne Wenger's house. He was invited to Brazil four times by different groups of Olorisa.

W: Take Esu for instance. The stature of Esu has grown considerably, so that the original myths of Esu that I knew as a child have grown even more colorful. I believe Esu became so strong in Brazil because he had to defend himself against this very facile Christian interpretation...

U: The "devil"...

W: That's right, and again Wande Abimbola admitted once that these new aspects of Esu are now found here in Nigeria as well...

U: And of course it shows that the whole thing is alive. But you know what Melville Herskovitz thought about Verger's travels between Brazil and Nigeria? "Terrible man," he said to me, "he is destroying laboratory conditions."

W: Oh perfect! That's perfect. That's beautiful! It really sums up the whole lame battle scholarship faced with a living phenomenon.

U: Now the Ogun you created in *A Dance of the Forest* stresses particularly the creative aspect. He is not merely the warrior, but also the creator.

W: This was for me very obvious, because the instrument of sculpture belongs to Ogun. Many sculptors are his followers, and so is the blacksmith, again a very creative person, not just an artisan. And then of course there is the *Ijala*—he is therefore, by implication, the father of poetry. All this made me delve more into the complexity of Ogun, and given my own creative bent, I explored that a lot more. And given my own acknowledged combative strain, I found a fine partner in Ogun. It was a kind of liberation for me—having grown up in a narrow form of Christianity.

U: Which is very simplistic...

W: Very simplistic. Everything has to be black or white. You are either a good child or a bad child. When I grew up, and was given a little bit to self-analysis and introspection, I wondered why I should be inclined towards the creative—I really feel alive when I am creating—while at the same time I would readily drop my pen or typewriter without hesitation and pick up whatever combative instrument necessary.... Yoruba religion made me see that there was no contradiction. It was the most normal thing in the world to have within the same person these two or more aspects.

U: Each Orisa contains and bridges contradictions, and human beings are the same. To pretend otherwise is hypocrisy. People don't realize how unrealistic Christianity is. Yoruba religion portrays the world as it is and makes you live with it the way it is. It teaches you how to turn a dangerous situation, how to diffuse tension, how to turn a negative situation into something positive even. But in *A Dance of the Forest* you created another character called Esuoro. I find it hard to relate this figure to any Yoruba tradition. I am tempted to say you simply invented him.

W: Oh, that was purely dramatic. That is something I have not taken beyond the pages of the book. It's purely dramatic. I created him in the same way—I suppose—in which Puck was created by Shakespeare, taking parts from various mythological beings. As you know, Oro is one of the most intangible beings.... So I fleshed him out, somehow.

U: By far the most important statement you have made about Yoruba culture is your play *Death and the King's Horseman*. I don't know whether you remember this, but it was Pierre Verger who found out about this famous incident in Oyo. He was even able to verify it by writing to the District Officer who was then living in Canada

W   I do remember that you gave me a kind of summary of the story....

U: I thought that the material was crying out for a play. But for several years, you didn't do anything with it.

W: Well, I wasn't ready for it.

U: I then gave the material to Duro Ladipo who produced *Oba Waja* in 1964. Then, maybe a decade later you wrote *Death and the King's Horseman*. What was it then that prompted you to go back to this material finally? What new insight had occurred? What new preoccupation with Yoruba religion, maybe?

W: That's a question that's always very difficult to answer because it has to do with the entire active creative process—gestation, something that takes place on different levels of consciousness or subconsciousness. But don't forget, I wrote this play in Cambridge when I was there for a year as a fellow in Churchill College.

And it could have been the resentment of the presumption! Because you know in a Cambridge College named after a personality like Churchill, you have encapsulated the entire history of the arrogance of your colonizers—the supercilious attitude towards other cultures, the narrowness, the mind closure. It could be all of that. It was not a year which I enjoyed particularly. There were a few stimulating intellectual contacts, which made it worthwhile, but I think there was the basic underlying question, "What the hell am I doing here? What the hell are we doing here?" I felt like a representative; a captured, creative individual having to deal with another culture on its own terms, in its own locale. And passing the bust of Churchill on the top of the stairs almost every day—with all that Churchill meant! The big colonial man himself! It could have been all of this that brought back the memory of this tragic representation of the way their culture would always impinge on ours. The artist is in many ways similar. Each time he discovers a proto world in gestation, it's almost like discovering another world in the galaxy. The artist's view of reality creates an entirely new world. Into that world he leads a raid. He rifles its resources and returns to normal existence. The tragic dimension of that is one of disintegration of the self in a world which is being reborn always, and from which the artist can only recover his being by an exercise of sheer will power. He disintegrates in the passage into that world. He loses himself, and only the power of the will can bring him back. And when he returns from that experience, he is imbued with new wisdoms, new perspectives, and a new way of looking at phenomena. I was using Ogun very much as an analogue. What happens when one steps out into the unknown? There is a myth about all the gods setting out, wanting to explore and rediscover the world of mortals. But then the primordial forest had grown so thick that no one could penetrate it. Then Ogun forged the metallic tool and cut a way through the jungle. But the material for that implement was extracted from the primordial barrier. This I took as a kind of model of the artist's role, the artist as a visionary explorer, a creature dissatisfied with the immediate reality, so he has to cut through the obscuring growth, to enter a totally new terrain of being—a new terrain of sensing, a new terrain of relationships. And Ogun represented that kind of artist to me.

U: I can find parallels to Yoruba concepts here on several levels. The artist as the "creature of dissatisfaction with the immediate reality" is really very reminiscent of the Orisa, who starts life as a human being—a king or a warrior—but because of his dissatisfaction with the immediate reality "leads a raid into that other world," losing himself on the way. Sango hanging himself at Koso, Ogun descending into the ground at Ire, Otin turning into a river at Ota Ayegbaju—all these are examples of the creative human being breaking through the limitations of ordinary human existence. Of course, the Orisa does not return. He undergoes a metamorphosis and becomes a divine being. But he is there to remind us of the existence of that other world, to remind us that we can dare to penetrate, however briefly, that other sphere of existence. Similarly the Olorisa going into trance crosses the border, "rifles the resources" of the divine world, and returns with a new understanding. His personality undergoes significant changes through such repeated experiences. The maturity of the old Orisa priests, their wisdom, tolerance and insight into the human mind are the result of these raids into the divine sphere.

Am I right in thinking that this is something very similar—almost identical to the experience you have described in the *Fourth Stage*?

W: Yes, definitely!

U: I think you can describe the act of the priest who goes into trance also as a creative act because he has to personify the Orisa, recreate him through his performance, through song and dance. So in that sense there may be some real hope left. For a while we must helplessly watch the culture crumble in front of our eyes, there are still some individuals, like yourself, left who can capture something of the spirit of this culture through the very individual process you have described and who can keep the Orisa alive in some new form of existence.

W: There is a lot of hope left. I'll give you an example. When I gave a lecture in Ibadan recently titled *The Credo of Being and Nothingness*, when I explained certain aspects of Yoruba beliefs, the role of the Orisa, the reaction—the forcefulness of response which I could see on the faces of the young people—was really very encouraging. It was more than just an expression of their misgivings towards the way in which they were brought up; more than just a feeling of deprivation. These young people are really looking for new directions in their lives. I believe there is real hope.

Wole Soyinka

ON *DEATH AND THE KING'S HORSEMAN*

Introduction

Wole Soyinka's play, *Death and the King's Horseman*, is based on an historical incident that took place in the Yoruba city of Oyo in 1946. According to an ancient custom, the Elesin Oba, the commander of the King's cavalry, was to follow the deceased Alaafin (king) into the other world, so that Elesin Oba could lead the Alaafin across the final threshold into the world of the ancestors.

As soon as an Elesin Oba has this important title conferred upon him, he commissions weavers, tailors, and embroiderers to make the splendid gown in which he is going to die when the appointed time comes. Throughout his lifetime he enjoys great power and privileges. When the day comes on which he has to follow his master, he dresses in the gown of death, dances through the town with drummers and praise singers, and is given the highest honors by the entire population. As the sun begins to set, he returns home, sits down amongst his relatives and friends, looks into the sinking sun, leans back, and dies—by an act of will. His death is the climax and fulfillment of his entire life.

When the ritual was to be celebrated in 1946, the British District Officer went out and arrested the Elesin Oba and threw him into jail because, according to British law, attempted suicide is a criminal offence. The Elesin Oba's son, who was at that time a trader in the Gold Coast (now Ghana) rushed home in order to bury his father. On seeing his father alive, the son was so horrified by this abomination that he committed suicide on the spot. The Elesin Oba, in desperation over his failure to accomplish his sacred task, also committed suicide. But it was too late to accomplish his ritual mission.

These are the historical events as they were originally researched and related by Pierre Verger in the early sixties. The conversation between Wole Soyinka and Ulli Beier touches on some of the cultural, religious and ethical issues raised in the play.

U: In your introduction to *Death and King's Horseman*, you issue some very fierce warnings to would-be producers. You tell them in no uncertain terms that you do not wish the District Officer to become the key figure by making him "the victim of a cruel dilemma." Above all you object to that facile cliché of the "conflict of cultures." As for the role of the District Officer, it seems to me that Pilkington is too banal a character to be even capable of becoming the victim of a cruel dilemma. He is far too convinced that he is right. The other point you raise is more complex because on the surface, at least, there is a conflict of cultures here. Do you see this play as an internal conflict of Yoruba culture that is merely sparked off by an external event?

W: First of all, there is a background to this particular note. It was written after an extraordinary blurb on my novel, *A Season of Anomy*. I did not think that it would be possible for any human intellect to read *A Season of Anomy* and say this novel was about the conflict of the old and the new African culture. As you know we have been through this a lot. Many poets in a certain period have indulged in that shallow cliché. They could not see any other issue at all and some of it was really awful literature.

U: Dennis Osadebey: "My simple fathers in childlike faith believed all things" and so on...

W: Mabel Imoukhuede!

U: But she basically only wrote one poem in that mood.

W: But the others carried on for so long. We have been discussing that phenomenon and its short-lived influence a lot. We thought we had dealt with it. Then years later this novel (*A Season of Anomy*) was published in America, and I could not believe what was written so authoritatively and implanted on my book. Not just a review, which I could ignore. But my book was actually made to carry the burden of this reductionist summation. So that's why the introduction to *Death and the King's Horseman* was so strong. I wanted to caution everybody! But having said that and explained the source of it, I also consider it true, and it has historical justification. For example, one of the major wars of the 19th century was triggered by a very similar event. In this case, it was the Aremo, the eldest son of the Alaafin, who refused to commit suicide, and he was even supported in this by his father whom he was to succeed to the throne.

U: Yes, it was Alaafin Atiba, who in 1858 abolished the age-old custom that the Aremo, his eldest son, had to die with him. For many centuries, the Aremo was considered as the King's co-regent, but he had to pay for this sharing of power and privilege by dying with the king, just as the Elesin Oba died. Atiba loved his eldest son because he had been a very loyal son who had shared many dangers with him, even before he, Atiba, became king. So he got the support of the powerful war chiefs of Ibadan to help him change the custom.

W: But Kurunmi, the ruler of Ijaye, declared this to be an abomination! He never accepted this change, and when Atiba died, and Adelu was actually installed, Kurunmi went to war over it. But what is significant about this is the fact that this king, Atiba, was not a Christian. There is no record of European or missionary influence on his decision. In other words, this was a revolt against certain acceptances within the traditional set up. So if you want to look for the root of certain tragic experiences in Yoruba history, you don't have to go outside. The story of the Elesin Oba, which you told me years ago, takes on a global dimension, and this enables me to interrogate the morality and the history of those who point the finger at the Yoruba as being barbaric and having primitive customs. It gives me that combative dimension to examine the whole meaning of existence and how different people interpret it. It enables me to look at the conflict of honor and obligation. You are quite right in saying that at the beginning I do make the District Officer (DO) rather a cardboard figure, but, towards the end, I do hope that I succeeded in giving him some moment of dignity. He is now confronted by a situation, which he has never in his life anticipated, and he responds to it with a little more sensibility. I even make him best the Elesin Oba in an argument. I did so by making the DO utilize a proverb of the Elesin's own people to silence him!

U: "The elder grimly approaches heaven, and you ask him to bear your greetings yonder. But do you really think he makes the journey willingly?" But you are very right in saying that a culture constantly transforms itself, and a situation arises when an age-old custom becomes difficult to carry out and eventually becomes unacceptable. Remember that in the mid-fifties, the Ogun worshippers in Osogbo found it hard to carry out the sacrifice of a dog, and they employed somebody from outside the cult to do it for a fee. Another, rather more severe example is the conflict between politicians and traditional rulers in the mid-fifties. A century earlier Kurunmi of Ijaye, as we know, was unable to dislodge Oba Adelu, and the people of Oyo accepted the new ruling that the Aremo should not die. They insisted, however, that in future the Aremo should be sent into exile after his father's death and that he should be disqualified from succeeding his father. Now you remember that in the 1950's the Action Group government ordered an enquiry into the affairs of the Alaafin of Oyo. The British commissioner could not find much evidence of the alleged corruption and exonerated the Alaafin. But the politicians did not accept the verdict, and eventually they sent the King into exile in Ilesa. Then they went ahead and brought the Aremo back from exile to be installed as the next Alaafin. In other words, they installed the one person who was not supposed to become king! I sometimes wonder whether this was done from ignorance of the customs, or whether it was a deliberate calculated attempt to destroy the institution of kingship.

W: I think this was a deeply calculated move to break a certain mould, a certain tradition, through an act that amounted to an "abomination" in the eyes of many. They were a very anti-feudalist party. They operated not merely through such negative, aggressive means, but operated also by catapulting some powerful monarchies, like the Ooni of Ife, into the political arena where they now came under control and became themselves enticed and absorbed in the new dispensation. The politicians were very wily; they knew what they were doing. And even from the very beginning—before they officially embraced socialism—they were at heart pretty republican.

U: Now the play has several controversial issues, and one of them is found right in the first scene. I am referring to the demand of the Elesin Oba to have a new bride before following the Alaafin into the other world. I don't know whether this goes back to the tradition, or whether it is merely a dramatic device that you invented. One thing I know is that the Elesin Oba enjoyed certain privileges during his lifetime, and one of them was that he could claim any woman—just like the Oba himself.

W: Oh yes, the traditional *gbesele*, (I place my foot on her), a privilege that applied not only to the reigning monarch, but also to the Aremo and the Elesin Oba. The head of the king's cavalry could go to the market at any time, and demand any goods or any woman. And you would be surprised how many Oba who are still trying it today. I know one instance in recent years—I am talking about five years ago. This Oba went to Ibadan to visit his daughter, a student at the University of Ibadan. The daughter introduced one of her friends, a girl who was already married, to her father. The Oba later sent two of his chiefs with staffs of authority to her, summoning her to his palace, and telling her in plain terms that he had decided to marry her. When she explained to him that she was already married, he said, "Oh that's alright. I'll send for your husband and let him know my decision." The girl refused, but he harassed her so much that in the end she had to send a delegation of elders to the Oba asking him to desist.

U: Yes, but surely whatever the traditional privilege of the Elesin, there is a clear indication in the play that at that moment this was not appropriate— because at that moment his thoughts should have been somewhere else.

W: Oh, of course!

U: His indulgence, in fact, weakened his resolve.

W: He himself actually admits that at a later point.

U: He blames his new wife for the "mystery of the sapping of his will."

W: But my position on this is somewhat dual. First, there is a kind of image in my mind. There are the *Abami Omo*, the supra normal children who from childhood on are considered *agba*—old and unusually mature. They therefore enjoy unusual privileges. They can sit down with adults, and participate in their conversation. Tunji Oyelana has such a child. She utters the most unbelievably perceptive statements about things. There are children like that and of course, Yoruba society has a place for them. Naturally I have always wondered about such children. And in a drama like this, when human weakness comes into conflict with a sense of duty and one's perception of being virtually one step away from the land of the ancestors, there is a hovering sense of symmetry.

U: Between the child that has just come from the other world and the old man who is about to go there?

W: Yes. All this is just part of the metaphysical aesthetics operating in my mind. I try to use this ambivalently also as an expression of the man's weakness. In other words, how do I make it happen? Of course, I could have just made the woman donate the daughter to the Elesin, and not make him feel guilty about snatching her from someone else, but then I would lose the element of humanity in the man. He becomes self indulgent—with the connivance of the entire city, he tries to prolong his sensuality which is his definition of his being at that moment. I put myself in the man's position—not just as a human being, but also as a product of that particular environment, both the physical environment and the spiritual one. And at the back of my mind there is the constant awareness of this *Abami Omo*—the extraordinary child. At that moment I could not resist the proposition that the loss of this person from the community would be compensated for by the planting of a seed; not just in the sense that one man dies and a child is born, but in the sense that this child will also be something special, something extraordinary. A suggestion...

U: ...that the child would become an *Abami Omo*.... Of course, the Elesin Oba himself is a very unusual person.

W: And he believes also that he is creating something very unusual.

U: The child could even be the same person reborn. After all, the Elesin says to the Iyaloja, "Let my going be like the death of the plantain," meaning that he will renew his existence constantly like the plantain does.

W: It could be the same, but in any case it would be a very unusual person. So, yes, there is this man's weakness, and he indulges himself, but at the same time, when Iyaloja says, "What I hear is no longer the voice of the living...."

U: She has to honor that.

W: This is something different. This is not just a self-indulgent old man. He has prepared himself for this in the proper way, and he is ready to do it. I wanted to leave it as ambiguous as possible—all the various suggestions.

U: The point is that Yoruba culture can perform such a feat and produce the kind of mind that is capable of....

W: ...sustaining it; a mind that totally believes in it, finds it viable, and is able even to hold it up against another culture. In fact one thing that convinces me of the validity of such a world view is the fact that it can stand up to the alien, with all his arrogance, his claim of superiority which is not based on any evidence anyway. In some sense the District Officer and his interference reinforce the values of that society. These values have been true for centuries. There are converts, no doubt. But on the whole..., look at Yoruba society today—even in Lagos—that society still holds on to certain elements of tradition.

U: Let us return to the District Officer. It is true that towards the end you make him more sensitive, more responsive. But he never grasps the simple fact that the value of life is not its length. To him the prolongation of life is what life is all about. Even a meaningless life must be prolonged at all costs. It has not occurred to him that life has a natural span in which it must fulfill itself.

W: Yes, but the problem is that in Europe, the dissidents from this point of view, the so-called euthanasia volunteers—they are also problematic, like that doctor in the United States who virtually sets up suicide gadgets to enable people to kill themselves. I followed that very carefully. There are doctors who are being faced with the evidence of the uselessness of existence at a certain point, whether it is age, or terminal disease, or coma, I respect their point of view very much. But unfortunately they cannot conceive of how to integrate their philosophy into society. The result is this American doctor who hawks around his suicide machine. That in itself is for me part of the decadence of society. If you read his pronouncements, he's a man on an ego trip, a man on a power trip! He's a man who enjoys wielding power over life and death. He's invented his little machine, he's appearing before the cameras, and he says, "Take me to court!" He does not know that this requires a communal answer; that it requires a communal mental reformation. This seems to confirm the belief in Yoruba society—that life has an end if there is no more purpose left in it.

U: And again, death is painful when the person is too young to have fulfilled his purpose. Death can be joyful if the person has fulfilled his life. And who can have a more complete life than the Elesin Oba whose death is not an accident but the climax of his life? I cannot imagine such a total fulfillment in any other society.

W: Right. I cannot think of any...

U: And then there is this other misunderstanding that is embedded in the European position. There is the notion that the Elesin Oba is enslaved to some bloodthirsty potentate who forces him to commit suicide. But on the other hand, the District Officer with his superior morality, arrests the Elesin because he is committing a crime—not against himself—but against the Queen of England!

W: That is correct. The Elesin is depriving the Queen of one of her subjects!

U: How absurd can you get! Is it not a worse enslavement if the Queen can say, "You can't kill yourself because your life belongs to me"?

W: That's why I make Sergeant Amusa—who is the comic figure in this play—insist that it is a crime: "You are committing death, it's against the law!" But whose law?

U: But that was the position. You actually got jailed in Britain for attempting suicide.

W: Yes, until recently. It was not treated as a form of disturbance or illness. Nobody was looking for the cause; it was simply treated as a crime. The first time I read about it was when I was a student in England. Somebody tried to commit suicide and was jailed. It blew my mind! Now, in Nigeria there was a similar case. The judge was obliged to sentence him to three months, but if you read the judgment you could see that there was a very different attitude. No moral indignation. The judge was trying to help. He told the man, "Life is not as bad as all that. You have a family, and you have friends. Try and make a new start. Maybe, he said, "These three months will be a time of reflection for you." It was a humane attitude.

U: Europeans have another difficulty with this play. They cannot believe that the Elesin actually dies by an act of will. They are convinced that he must take poison. I have no difficulty with this at all. Having lived in Nigeria for so long, I know that people are trained to develop certain faculties of the mind which our society has always suppressed.

W: I have experienced many similar incidents with persons quite close to me. I know that wives decide to die after their husbands and mothers after their children. There was a time when my sister was very ill, and it looked as if she might never recover. She had been operated on, and for days she was suspended between life and death. My mother used to sit by her bedside, watching her. And when I visited my sister in hospital, I could tell that the woman had made up her mind: If my sister was not going to survive that illness, she would go before long. She would certainly not remain alive to see one of her children dying. I could tell. It was very obvious. The way she sat there, sighing from time to time; the way she looked at me when I came in.... She seemed to be saying, "Fate has played a dirty trick on me." Not long after my sister had recovered, my mother and her circle of friends held a feast. My late friend Femi Johnson was there and he observed the things between the two of us. She had cooked a special vegetable, *efo sokoyokoto*. She was serving around this vegetable—like a communion! When she came to me I refused to take any of it. And she said, "Alright. That's your business." She was implying, "I know you know why I am doing this; if you don't want any of it that is your business." I just turned away. I knew that woman had made up her mind, and I wasn't going to partake of her ritual!

Not long after that, I was travelling to Ghana. I was teaching in Ife at the time. It was an early flight, and I was standing in a queue a long time before the counter opened. When I approached the counter, I suddenly picked up my bag and said, "I am not travelling." I told the driver, "We are returning to Ife." I went home, and sat there for a long time. I wasn't sure why. I hadn't spelled it out, but I just knew I wasn't going to travel. I sent the driver to pick up my mail, and shortly after that Yemi Ogunbiyi came to the house. He started talking to me in a consoling voice, and I said to him, "What are you talking about?" Then he said, "Oh I thought you had heard!" That was the moment I knew that my mother had died!

But that is not the end of the story. I had spent the previous night in Ibadan with the Aboyades. So when Yemi spoke to them, Aboyade said, "Don't talk nonsense. He left before 6 o'clock this morning." But she insisted, "No, he hasn't travelled." So you see it is not uncommon for Yoruba people to decide on the time of their death. Sometimes they call their family together, they distribute their property among them, and then they go! Or they do it more secretively, like my mother.

U: It reminds me of another recent incident. You know that Asiru Olatunde, the Osogbo artist who died recently? He had been ill for some time, and his daughter, Sinawu, got very worried. Every weekend she came up from Lagos to visit him. One day he said to her, "You don't have to come here every week to check up whether I am still alive. I am going to die next Saturday at five o'clock." And he went exactly at that hour.

W: Yes, yes. I know very precise announcements like that.

U: Then there are the very old Olorisa, priests and priestesses, who have acquired tremendous spiritual power during their lives. They are so old that their body has nearly wasted away, but their mind is very active and very strong, and they rule the household with great power—lying on their mat. When they decide it is time to go, they send their eldest son to the farm or the bush and say: "Dig under such and such a tree. And when you find this medicine that I have buried there, destroy it." The moment the medicine is destroyed the old priest releases his hold on life.

W: There are these various moments for cutting through the thread of life. In *Death and the King's Horseman* it is the dance of death, through which the transition is accomplished. But it is not only old people who can accomplish this. There are even children...

U: *Abiku*! A child who is born to die; a spirit child who is born to a human mother, but has to return to its companions in the spirit world at an early age...

W: Yes, the *abiku* not only threaten to die, they sometimes announce the precise time of their death. They warn and suddenly go. But the *abami* do it more gently. They may say to their mother: "I hope you won't mind. I hope you won't worry too much, but I will be going at such and such a time..."

U: Of course, the real tragedy in this play is not death, but the man's failure to accomplish death. Elesin Oba has to face the horrendous fact that he could not accomplish it, and that in the history of the Yoruba he was the first person to fail. The sense of continuity is very strong in the culture and even in less potent situations—say, during an annual sacrifice for Ogun—the people pray: "We have met here today and we have done so again as our forefathers before us. We pray that we shall meet again next year to perform this sacrifice." So for somebody to suddenly realize that he...

W: ...It is the end of his life.

U: More than that even. It is the end of the community itself, up to a point. I have witnessed situations not dissimilar to this. Many of the feats Olorisa accomplish during ritual performance can only be achieved if the entire community is concentrating on this one action. And if that kind of communal concentration is not there anymore, then the individual performer cannot carry it any more. I am thinking of the Baba Elegun Sango, for example, during the annual Sango festival. I have recently seen a Sango ceremony in Ilobu. Ten years ago these festivals in Ilobu were mind blowing events. But now nothing happened. The small crowd that had gathered was part curious, part hostile. They did not participate in the event. The handful of priests could no longer evoke the power of the god. Sango did not manifest himself. The ceremony was a sham. I remember even in the fifties, when such feasts were still very powerful, how disturbing the presence of a single alien person was. I never took Europeans or upper class Nigerians into such ceremonies. But when one of them found his way there by chance, I felt extremely disturbed by the alien presence. How much more disturbing must they have been to the person who had to carry the burden of the performance.

W: Yes, I made this point in one of my essays in *Myth, Literature & the African World*. What I tried to do is to define the thin line between the possessed actor and the possessed representative of a god. That very grey area when the ritual role that has already been predetermined is carried out almost with the precision of a rehearsed piece, but indicating that the possibility only exists, when the potency of the crowd, that is. the communicant chorus has reached a certain height, a certain level, a certain pitch. Then it becomes the reinforcement of the individual. They transmit their own communicant force onto the head of that individual, and at that moment—there is no question at all that—the individual becomes the voice of the entire people. It's like the transfer of all the individual tendencies to the protagonist who then moves into the arena of the gods. But for him to attain that level when he becomes the embodiment of the deity, where he crosses the threshold into the world of the deity, it requires the complete and total potency of that communicant crowd. That is for me the real meaning of the chorus in ritual Yoruba Theater. It's not just people repeating refrains and sympathizing and empathizing with the individual going through his travails. No, the chorus is in fact the force which enables an actor to become the embodiment of the role.

U: The proximity between religious ritual and some kinds of theatrical performance that you are talking about, became very evident in the late Duro Ladipo. Over the years his performances of *Oba Koso* became more and more like ritual and he became more and more a personification of Sango.

W: That's right. And Duro, having separated the audience from the stage, compensated for it by the charge which, through rehearsal, had given his actors who were equally possessed. They were oblivious of the audience. Something was taking place on that stage which could use the audience, but which did not depend upon it. It was Duro himself, his wife Abiodun, Tijani Mayakiri and Ademola Onibonokuta who between them carried this charge. I believe you were not around when Duro died, but did you hear what happened?

U: Yes, thunder!

W: Unseasonable and of unprecedented dimension. It was incredible. Such incidents really make you wonder...

U: But let me come back to the Elesin Oba. Was he being carried by his chorus? Or was the crowd wavering?

W: Oh no! The support was there. It had not reached its climax before the intrusion came. But there is no doubt that left alone he would have accomplished his task. He was ready; he was prepared. And again, he could have made it in spite of this intrusion if, however, his weakness had not been present.

U: The terrible thing is that once such an ancient ritual cycle is broken it can never be revived again. This is really frightening. Because for centuries a powerful ritual has been carried out that binds the community together, and that strengthens its ties with the ancestors. Then something interferes which in itself is rather trivial, and the person causing it is himself rather banal; and yet this trivial incidence has this enormous negative power.

W: Yes, it is often the trivial incident that has the most profound and far-reaching consequences! And that's why for me the play is not just a thing in itself; it's a parable, a parable for many things that have happened to Yoruba society; a parable of history.

U: There is a photograph in Ajisafe's *History of Abeokuta*. It shows the Alake Gbadebo with Governor MacGregor. The Alake is a giant of a man, not only physically, but spiritually; a really powerful man. And next to him is the British Governor, pale, spindly, in a kilt, looking a trifle silly, perhaps. And yet this man, through his negative thinking, can destroy the whole powerful and meaningful world that his opponent stands for!

W: Of course we must never forget that the colonialists were able to utilize the dissidents who had their own motivations, their own ambitions. You don't just do it frontally with guns. You can rely on the meanest, the weakest individual to exploit the situation. But basically every society carries within it the possibility of change—positive or negative. And that's why every society must constantly reexamine itself, its values, its customs, and its procedures so as to reduce as much as possible these drastic changes, these insertions of alien solutions to their problems.

U: West African societies were in a relatively strong position to handle such processes because of their very size, their highly organized political structures and their flexibility. In the tiny communities of Papua New Guinea these confrontations were much more dramatic. A typical case is the village of Hopaiku in the Papuan Gulf. In 1930 the missionaries had made very little impact. There were only about 30 converts in a population of several hundreds. But one night, the Christians went and burnt down the sacred Eravo, the ceremonial house in which all powerful objects were kept. One of the women began to talk incomprehensibly and incessantly, claiming that her head "is growing big, and has separated from [her] body…" Her husband got alarmed and took her home immediately, but in the car she spoke more incomprehensibly…

W: Speaking in tongues!

U: Yes, and she continued for three days and three nights until the priest, who must have imposed this state on her, released her.

W: It is very taboo to use your spiritual powers in this way, but the priest, whoever he was, acted under extreme provocation.

U: One final thing. This European notion of "suicide" is very far removed from the ritual that takes place in *Death and the King's Horseman*. If you look at the mythology about the Orisa you find that there is always some form of so-called "suicide" involved. Sango actually hangs himself. Otin, deified as a river goddess, throws herself on the ground and becomes a river. Oluorogbo ascends to heaven on a chain, and Ogun descends into the bowels of the earth. In each case there is a metamorphosis from one form of existence to another. It always arises from a sense of tragedy, from a feeling that without this transition you cannot become what you are meant to become.

W: You have come to the end of your mission in this particular existence. How you come about that knowledge varies. But as you pointed out, it is unusually in the tragic mode. And it is true that tragedy in Yoruba mythology and culture is not perceived as the termination of existence. Yoruba tragedy exists in a world that believes very much in the interflux and almost equal partnership or collaboration between the living and the world of the ancestors. It believes that one world cannot exist without the other. If you have a world which accepts this totally the word "suicide" is meaningless. The tragic experience then leads to a new sense of awareness. That is why the Egungun come out in our midst as a reminder of the world of our ancestors. People realize that there is a man underneath the mask, but it is a symbolic representation. It may require less energy, a lesser act of the will than, say, the priest who becomes the embodiment of Sango. But at the same time, you know, after going through the ritual in the sacred grove, some Egungun have to be restrained when they come out in the mask. So it's a whole world of perception. Suicide in European terms is a negative act. It's of no interest except for the individual concerned, and it's terminal. What we are talking about in *Death and the King's Horseman* is an experience of an entirely different kind: a widening of the horizon, and a progression from one sphere of existence to another.

Wole Soyinka

"THE CRISIS OF YORUBA CULTURE"

U: There was a short time in Nigerian history—between Independence and the first military coup—in which we lived through a period of great optimism. Financially the people of Nigeria were relatively well off, and they assumed that with independence things were going to improve steadily. In the West people believed in the benefits of universal free primary education. They were proud of being the "First in Africa" to have set up a television station. The University of Ibadan was functioning and had a good reputation. Night life was boisterous; people could afford to go out, drink beer and listen to really good bands. Even in Osogbo, which then had 120,000 inhabitants, one could hear three or four bands at weekends. The Yoruba Travelling Theatre was booming. A decade after independence, Biodun Jeyifo counted about a hundred Yoruba theatre companies—all managing to survive somehow off their performances. People actually preferred the theatre to the movies. But then those were the days of Ogunde, Ogunmola, Duro Ladipo and the Orisun players. Where in the world could you find a comparable constellation?

W: There was ferment!

U: There was no official planning; little government interference. It was a natural growth. If you now think back to this period, how do you view it with hindsight? Why does it appear to us now as a "golden age" rather than a mere beginning?

W: My immediate reaction is: if only we knew what we had then! And how fragile it could become! Not that it was fragile, but how fragile it could become under the buffeting of the rapidly changing political and economic situation. We took our values for granted then. Let's talk about, well, let me not call it "family values" because in America that has become almost a dirty word. Let's just say: "family sense". So first of all, at the core of Yoruba society there was this family sense. It was something that extended beyond the borders of Nigeria. Remember when I was travelling around in a land rover, doing research into West African theatre—Togo, Ghana, the Ivory Coast? It never failed to strike me, this sense of Yoruba existence and solidarity; of self cognition.

U: So you found it even in Abidjan? In Treicheville?

W: It was incredible. Yes, even in Treicheville people would ask about their cousins at home, as if they just lived a mile or two away. There was this kind of I hate to call it Pan Yoruba feeling because then you think immediately of an artificial creation. It was the recognition of something that had obviously existed for hundreds and hundreds of years and which had survived the imposition of colonial boundaries. So that took a buffeting, first of all, as the sense of the independent nation grew more and more rigid. Ghana, for instance, began to take the lead in a particular direction, becoming ideologically hermetic. We use ideology here in a loose sense, but Ghana identified itself out of the West African community.

U: Starting with the breakup of West African Airways...

W: The Bank of West Africa...

U: The West African Cocoa Marketing Board. All these institutions became national.

W: So I think that within Nigeria the Yoruba sense of belonging became stronger—first of all. At the time the Yoruba within Nigeria, including even immediate neighbors in Dahomey, had a sense of themselves as a distinct entity. This attitude was shared also by most other communities in Nigeria. In Lagos the Igbo community met weekly, had their cultural societies who contributed money towards the higher education of some of their children, and supported all kinds of community projects. They organized the Atilogu dancers and they rehearsed strictly; the same thing with the Agbor dancers and the Itsekiri dancers. In the South at least, there was hardly any community that did not identify itself through such cultural groups. This was carried, of course, into politics. The Action Group was based undoubtedly on the Egbe Omo Oduduwa, and it was founded as the political wing of that cultural organization in order to rival the NCNC which was based on the Igbo State Union. You know very well how all these different groups had a competition of self-cognizing, shall we say "nation states", within Nigeria. That rivalry was very palpable, no question at all. You could touch it, you could feel it.

U: And if you think of some of the politicians, like Akintola, his use of the Yoruba language...

W: Oh yes, even the worst of Akintola's enemies had to admit that this was an exemplar of Yoruba linguistic acrobatics! And the fight between him and Awolowo, at the beginning, was like a fight within the family.

U: People took pride in their language then. And another thing was that the Oba...

W: Ooooooooh yes!

U: They were still proper Oba. Some were Christians and some were Muslims, but they took their office extremely seriously. If you think of someone like Timi Laoye of Ede, Oba Adenle the Ataoja of Osogbo, they were wise men, tolerant and true peace makers. And Moses Oyinlola, the Olokuku of Okuku, I have not seen a man anywhere in the world of whom one could have said so convincingly "every inch a king". And the Ooni of Ife then, a man of the world, a diplomat, a politician and a businessman—but a man of great stature and dignity.

W: Yes. The Oba were not beggars and they were not cultural relics. They were authentic spiritual leaders. The occasional fight for succession was conducted very tersely, in a very tough manner; occasionally also using some people's political clout. But there was no betrayal to external sources of the institution of kingship. There was no cheapening of it. On the other hand the Ooni of Ife today is an embarrassment.

U: I don't know whether you have come across this French picture book on African kings. It shows royal figures from Ghana or the Cameroons, even those extravagant figures from the Nigerian Delta who sport European top hats. But they carry it off with panache! The only exception in this book is the Ooni of Ife. He had himself photographed, slouching on a sofa, like an Odalisque.

W: I may never have told you this, but during the coronation of the Ooni I saved that institution from a serious embarrassment. Elufowoju, who was the photographer of the African Studies Institute at Ife, took the official photographs for the occasion. One day, when I was sitting in my office, a bunch of postcards arrived. Elufowoju had sent them, in case I wanted to send them to some of my friends. I looked at this picture and nearly fainted with embarrassment. You have to see it! It was a composite photograph. There was the crown, which was photographed separately and the Ooni was looking at it with his mouth wide open... I said to Elufowoju: What is this? Is there a war going on between you and the Ooni?" He said, "No, I took several pictures and the Ooni himself selected this one." He added that the Ooni had ordered a vast quantity of them and that he had already sent out some of them. So I sent my staff out, you know, the acting company, especially those who were from Ife; I sent them round the town to all the shops to collect whatever they could find of these pictures. And I asked Elufowojo to let me have all those he had left in his office. And I said: "I will pay for all the other work. But this one, forget you ever did it! Just bring me the negative." Then I went to the Ooni and said: "By the way, I have seized all those postcards." He said: "Ah didn't you like it? I thought it was rather good." I told him: "If I wanted to construct an image of *omo oju o r'ola ri,* someone who has no dignity, that's exactly what I would do." And I added, "This photo does not represent you."

U: Think of his predecessor. When you entered his palace you knew you were in the presence of an Ooni. He had a position even beyond the confines of his sacred office. He knew how to combine his traditional duties of an Ooni with those of a minister of state. Yet he was totally accessible. He would receive you at any time. He knew that an Oba must be available for his people and for strangers, unlike the present Ooni. I once accompanied the Timi of Ede, his close friend and a business associate. But even he was kept waiting endlessly!

W: And another thing. Let's spend a little more time on the Ooni because he is the symbol of everything that happened to the Yoruba people during the last two or three decades. Remember, some years ago, during the regime of Buhari, the Ooni of Ife and the Emir of Kano, Bayero, went to Jerusalem together. That was before we established formal relationships with Israel. They were received very well there, by the government and by the Prime Minister himself. Of course, when they came back, Buhari was furious! Never mind that some months later they started negotiations with Israel. But at the time they had to make a gesture and so they restricted the movements of the Emir and the Ooni. The governors were ordered to issue restriction orders: They had to remain confined to their towns for six months. I know that Buhari visited the Emir of Kano. I don't know what he said but I am quite sure that he apologized and explained that for political reasons this had to be done. And the Governor of Oyo also visited the Ooni and explained that it was an unpleasant duty he had to perform, but that as a Yoruba son he had to pay due respect to the Ooni. In any case the restriction was administered very leniently. The Governor knew very well that the Ooni went to parties in Lagos, but he never said anything.

But the moment the six months' restriction was lifted, the Ooni gathered his chiefs and went to Oyo to thank the Governor. It was a day of shame for the entire Yoruba nation. OK, you have to accept the fact that they are powerful enough to force the restriction on you. You bear that humiliation. You don't say a word. You just sit there. A true Oba would even have refused to travel immediately after the lifting of the ban. He would have considered it cheap to jump into a car at once. But the Ooni went to this Governor and said: "I have come to thank you for lifting the restriction. It has been a good lesson and I have brought my chiefs along, because I want them to see that they are subject to discipline also. So when I tell them that they must have discipline, they will know what I mean." It was shameful! Photographs, the lot... And this Governor, who at the time wasn't even a Yoruba, repeating those cliché phrases: we want our Oba to be respected and so on and so on. I went to the Ooni yet again and said: "Did you really have to do that? What was the point? What did you think you would gain?" And he said: "But you heard what I said. It was for my chiefs. I wanted them to understand..." And he went on and on and on. But of course it was a lie. All he wanted to do is look for some contracts... The man who is occupying the most important throne in Yorubaland is unfortunately also the man who has presided over the demise of Yoruba self-worth. He has been parading himself all over the world, even campaigning for Sanni Abacha. He goes to America and says: "Look, I am the leader of the Yoruba people and I tell you that this is our position: we are in full support of the head of state."

U: He seems to be the symbol of the Yoruba malaise. Other Oba also give way to these immense political pressures. And many attach even more importance to their business deals than to their royal functions. But all the other Oba now have retained some dignity, even when they are forced to compromise.

W: He is the *Saka jojo* of Yoruba Oba. You may not know that expression. When I was a child silent films were introduced—Charlie Chaplin, Buster Keaton and many other comedians. We were inspired by those films to produce our own shadow plays. We made cut out figures from card board and moved them in front of a lantern. So if I call him *Saka jojo* I mean a cardboard piece of humanity clowning, making movements across the wall. There is something else I want to say about this Yoruba crisis, namely, the figure of Awolowo—his activity, his position in those years. It is true that some people declared he was nothing but a tribalist who cared for nobody but the Yoruba. But even some Igbo compared him favorably to Zik. The parameter is Awolowo's pride of race which was something Zik never had. Zik was a compromiser. In fact he compared himself once to a beautiful bride who was being courted by all those political parties. Can you imagine Awolowo sitting on the fence like that? It was something even the Sardauna of Sokoto once acknowledged. He said that he would never forgive Awolowo for making it necessary for him to get up from his exalted throne and campaign like a commoner during the first post independence election in Nigeria. You see, Awolowo had made inroads into the North by allying himself to NEPU while Azikiwe had a kind of pact with the Sardauna that they would not campaign in each other's region.

U: But let us go back to the 1960s now and talk about the events of which you said before: "I wish we knew then what we had!" It was a period of intense theatre activity and one of the big events of the period was a kind of festival you staged in Ibadan in which you brought Ogunmola, Ogunde, Duro Ladipo and the Orisun players all together into one big event. What was the motivation behind this theatre summit?

W: The idea was very simple. You remember I had been travelling all over West Africa and had seen the various travelling theatres—like the "Trios" in Ghana—and I was impressed by the movements across the borders of many of these companies. I would arrive in Abidjan and find Ogunde performing. I would arrive in Ghana and meet a group from Abidjan. So I had the idea of organizing a big festival of all these various groups, but of course, that was far too ambitious, and it was not easy to arrange either because they were travelling theatres in the real sense of the term. I thought of this as a pilot festival which would allow people to enjoy the richness and the variety of travelling theatre in the Western Region because Western region was easily the richest region in that kind of activity.

U: How would you assess these three companies? How would you describe each company's specific contribution?

W: Duro Ladipo was obviously the tragic genius. His plays were densely poetic. He really explored the origins of his people.

U: Before Duro the popular Yoruba theatre always treated *babalawo* or Orisa priests as comical figures or even as despicable ones. In Ogunde's plays it was always the school teacher type who was flaunted as the progressive hero. Duro was the first to restore the balance. He gave Yoruba culture back its dignity.

W: He made his audience understand the role of an Orisa priest in the community. Ogunmola was of course the great comedian. I don't think that he ever denigrated traditional aspects of Yoruba culture...

U: No, he just left it out.

W: For Duro, on the other hand, every single aspect of Yoruba life formed part of the—I won't say jigsaw—but the composition of Yoruba society. And the thing about Duro was that he didn't just play the role. He was inducted into the rite of Sango. So when he entered the stage he was virtually in a state of possession.

U: And he had this enormous presence.

W: Yes, and is it not interesting. Duro died in Ibadan in March—during the dry season. And in Ibadan—only in that town—there was the most unbelievable thunderstorm the very night he died. And everybody remarked that "Sango has passed." It was remarkable. The storm discharged itself that night and there was no more. It was really interesting...

U: I remember one night we met in Lagos, and I took you to see a performance of *Love of Money*. It was a very long time ago because it was the first time you actually saw Ogunmola perform. And I remember how excited you were, particularly by the scene with the wedding preparations. Ogunmola created the impression of a bustling household of fifty or a hundred people, all milling around, doing different jobs, carrying things here and there, and getting into one another's way. Yet all he had at his disposal to achieve that effect was an empty stage; no backdrop, no props and just two actors—himself and his wife—to suggest a crowd!

W: Yes, that is what attracted me to his theatre—the real innovation and the economy with which the effects were produced. And that is what I wanted my own actors to absorb—the seamlessness of it; that the theatre is a seamless continuum, and that when it comes to innovative devices there isn't really such a thing as Yoruba theatre or European theatre. And, of course, we were also aiming at this economy of expression and at creating a travelling theatre. So it was a tremendous experience. I remember that organizing this little festival took so much of my energy, and there was so much tension too, that I under-rehearsed my own team. We performed both *Brother Jero* and *The Lion and the Jewel*. *Brother Jero* was okay, but I realized on the night of *The Lion and the Jewel* that it was horribly under-rehearsed. Nevertheless, it was certainly one of the great theatrical heights of that period.

U: What do you think about Ogunde's contribution to the theatre scene? Of course he was the initiator of the whole movement!

W: Well, one thing about Ogunde is that his plays deepened towards the end. He became more and more aware of the possibilities of the Yoruba tradition. I never found that he succeeded in integrating his theatre. In other words, he took elements of the traditional theatre and planted them in his normal dialogue theatre. As you know, he began with a kind of Vaudeville tradition, and only later began to bring in *egungun* and various aspects of Orisa tradition. At this point he delved deeper into the liturgy and dramatic incantations...

U: His weakness, as far as I am concerned, was that he was not really an actor.

W: No, never! It was always Hubert Ogunde's personality on stage—no matter what he was doing. Whether it was a role from history, from mythology, whether he was a politician or a victim of British colonial rule—it was always Hubert Ogunde. He had the least expressive face of all of them. He had a handsome face and a handsome figure...

U: There was a bit of vanity about it too...

W: Absolutely! The cock of the roost and his entire harem around him on stage! Yet he gave an entirely new dimension to the theatre scene in Nigeria.

U: When did you actually found the Orisun players?

W: OK. The first thing I did was *A Dance of the Forest*. First of all I wanted to set a standard, a high standard of professionalism from the word 'go' so that the young actors I would later train would understand from the very beginning the high standard that we wanted to take on tour. So in spite of these immense logistical problems of dealing with a cast that was partly living in Lagos and partly in Ibadan, and all of whom had senior positions as teachers, public servants, broadcasters or oil company executives, we staged this play with senior people like Yemi Lijadu, Olga Adeniyi-Jones, Patrick Ozieh, Segun Olusola, Ralph Opara, and Francesca Pereira. I had to take advantage of Nigeria's Independence celebrations to get letters which released them for rehearsals. It was sheer opportunism, but it was a chance once in a lifetime. So I said, "Let's take advantage of this now and do something big with a high level of profes-sionality and then start training a new generation." The young actors, Femi Euba and Sola Rhodes, were already inside as understudies. Jimmy Solanke and Tunji Oyelana came a little later. And I told Yemi Lijadu and the rest: "We want to bring up this new generation and you will be the *Babaasale* and the *Iyaasale*—the fathers and mothers behind the scene. It's amazing how they actually understood and played that role. And then later, when I came to extract Orisun Theatre from the parent body, the 1960 Masks, they were the ones who handled publicity, sold tickets, while Orisun actors devoted themselves purely to their artistic responsibilities. And again, they were able to work in tandem with the 1960 Masks. As the 1960 Masks staged a play like *Dear Parent and Ogre* by Sarif Easmon, the Orisun Players went on to do political sketches...

U: *Before the Black Out!*

W: By this time Akintola had gone wild. I actually had to train my actors in self-defense on stage because Akintola and Fani-Kayode frequently sent thugs to break up our performances. They also sent the Attorney General to our performance to see whether they could bring a charge against us...

U: For sedition?

W: Oh yes, sedition was very popular then. Remember Sam Aluko had been charged. But when they had their caucus meeting, they decided they didn't have a strong case in court. So they chose to deploy thugs to break up our performances. That's why I called my boys together, and trained them in self-defense.

U: Orisun was much more than a theatre company.

W: Oh, absolutely. It was a family—apart from the politics.

U: It was also a total way of life...

W: Completely. Those boys, Jimmy Solanke, Tunji Oyelana, Yomi Obileye, Yewande Akinbo... It was a commune. Whatever we had, we shared. You remember we took over that house in Agodi, the one you engineered as "Headquarters for Black Orpheus". They lived there—the ones who had no homes. And they cooked there. And whatever food I could get I brought into the house. There was no replication of that period! And the real tragedy is, you know, there is no possible replication! What is left is the reality of something valuable, which still exists in the careers of Tunji Oyelana, Yewande...and any time I have a production, anywhere I can, I call them; I rely on them. They form the core of the new company, and they immediately help to form a community. In fact, I recently had an Orisun production in London.

U: You can actually say that of all the companies who were active in the sixties. They had a total commitment to this new way of life. If you think of Duro's company, many of the members came from routine jobs—as shop assistants, petrol station attendants, pools manager—where they had earned more than they did in the theatre. They didn't really have any career opportunities in the theatre either, as far as they could see, but they saw a new meaning to their lives when they joined the company. And that became more important to them than money.

W: Tunji Oyelana had been the private secretary to an Oba, but he just turned his back on that kind of life. Orisun became a microcosm of Yoruba life, of extended family Yoruba principles. And of course, it wasn't just Yoruba people in my kind of company.

U: No. It was a remarkable time from that point of view. As you pointed out before, artists from Yoruba, Igbo, Efik all put a lot of effort into maintaining and projecting a separate cultural identity within the larger nation state. But there was also a genuine faith in Nigeria at that time, and many organizations cut right across these groupings. After all, we also had Mbari!

W: Thank you. Mbari cut across the languages and also across the different arts. In Mbari we had the painters, the poets, the musicians and the actors. And once people came into that kind of community, they simply absorbed the principles. And as I said earlier, none of us at that time knew what a great thing we had; nor could we imagine what a terrible level of national disintegration we could reach.

U: For a while, I think, Mbari was a worthwhile institution.

W: Oh yes, it was terrific!

U: Of course, we did use outside funds, but it was not really very much.

W: Mbari was a shoe string operation—considering the achievements. And comparing it to art institutions in Europe and America—I know what kind of budgets they consume.

U: You know when the idea of Mbari first occurred in my mind? I had sent the script of "A Dance of the Forest" to the Nigeria Council, suggesting it as the official play for the independence celebrations. The secretary returned it to me with the commentary: "We can't make heads or tails of this." Then I thought, "If this is the official Nigerian body making decisions on cultural matters, then we must create an independent organization in which a few like-minded young artists can have the freedom to pursue their own aims."

W: Well, the timing was perfect. If you remember, I was looking for premises to start an arts club and you arrived from Paris. You had made contact with a foundation and you said: "Look, give me a proposal quickly. Can you and Chris Okigbo and J.P. Clark get together? So things just came together at a propitious moment. But there is something else I want to mention that was very important at the time: The Cooperatives in the Western region. I have never before, or since, seen an organ that operated at regional level—and we are talking of a region with a population of at least 20 million—and still succeeded in keeping its roots firmly in the community. Remember the Coop in Ibadan? That was the most prominent, but there were branches everywhere. The farmers and the craftsmen brought their goods, and the Coop paid them generous prices. The leather workers, the carvers, but mostly it was food, and I am not talking of cocoa now. That was a thing of its own. I'm talking of the petty producers who brought their food stuff to the Coop and were paid immediately. And they could actually see what was needed, what was moving. I cannot remember any complaint about it. There was never any scandal about the running of it. And it integrated the peasantry, the smallest tier of productivity in the entire Western region, with the highest level of distribution in the state. These cooperatives were the symbols of the cohesion of society because when you have productivity organized on that level, and in such a way as not to alienate the people, that is a real testimony to the family feeling within the community. And when that goes, something really serious has happened to the community itself. Under Akintola the Cooperatives began to decline because the government began to dip its hand into the purse. The farmers weren't paid any more, and they stopped bringing their goods. One after the other the Coop shops disappeared until in the end even the one at the centre of Ibadan also closed. First the goods became fewer, less varied, and finally it was turned into just another shop. It was like a symbol of the disintegration of our society.

U: And this happened at a time when the region was pretty well off. There was no financial crisis. In fact even junior clerks, primary school teachers and farmers were living comfortably. So it was really a willful destruction. But let us return to Mbari for a moment. Two of the absolute highlights for me were the first performances of your *Brother Jero* and J. P. Clark's *Song of a Goat*. *Brother Jero* with Yemi Lijadu as Jeroboam and Ralph Opara as Chume. That was a performance bristling with energy and wit and irony. One of the greatest theatre performances I can remember anywhere. J.P.'s *Song of a Goat* was something else again. It was no longer a performance; it became a ritual and a distinctly uncanny experience. Francesca Pereira went into something like a trance.

W: Oh yes. That was an incredible experience. I think we were all a little bit possessed that night. Certainly Segun Olusola was sufficiently terrified during the crucial moment of the ritual...

U: When you actually sacrificed a goat on stage...

W: You remember that Segun Olusola played the part of Tonye, the young man who cuckolded his senior brother. There was a scene where he was to escape through the window—the library window which adjoined the stage. I played Zifa, the senior brother. When I was charging him, instead of just escaping through the window, he began to barricade himself in by piling chairs and tables against the window. When I tried to get in but couldn't, I got wild, and smashed the window down. At the other end of the library there was a door, that narrow door that led onto the street. And as I climbed through the window I saw Segun standing there with his hand on the door and the next thing, he was running up the hill towards that church, you know, St. Emanuel's Church. I saw his fat, waddling bottom disappear over the horizon, and at that moment I came to myself. Later I asked Segun: "What happened?" And he said: "I took one look at your eyes and I decided I wasn't staying around that night! That was no play acting."

U: Well, it started off as play alright, but it was the spilling of the goat's blood that 'got into Francesca's head.

W: Yes, she was the first to get wild and that affected everybody else.

U: I believe that this kind of thing could only have happened at Mbari. On a proper stage the artificiality of the situation, the presence of technicians and stage hands would have kept everything within prescribed limits. To me it was the informality of Mbari that was its great asset, and it made such extraordinary experiences possible. I guess after the civil war it was not possible to resurrect this anymore.

W: There was an irony about the loyalty during the war. Somebody like Dapo Adelugba, who became a senior director of the Orisun players, arranged with television to have a weekly play to keep the company alive. First of all it's impossible. You can't have enough material for a half hour play every week. And what kind of rehearsal time do you get...? So the standard really went down. And when I came out of prison I took one look at it and I was appalled. I immediately terminated the whole thing. Better to have no theatre than to have a theatre at that level. The ensemble playing had disintegrated, and even the core members had lost their standard. Wale Ogunyemi turned out plays at an appalling rate!

U: The civil war destroyed a lot of things. The artists and writers of Mbari dispersed in different directions, had different loyalties, and found themselves suddenly on opposing sides. It was not so easy to restore the same kind of trust after the war. But Mbari itself had begun to disintegrate before the civil war. Personally I lost interest in it when they decided not to renew the lease of the original premises, but to move to the Central Hotel. I thought it was too big, too ugly, and it had the wrong atmosphere. I conceded the point that one could build a proper stage and that Demas Nwoko could make good use of such a stage. But it was expensive. It took up virtually the clubs entire grant, and with it one also bought a lot of useless space. All those hotel rooms...! Besides it was a nouveau-riche concrete monster. I couldn't see how the atmosphere of Mbari could be recreated. So even though Chris Okigbo tried to offer me the chairmanship of the new club at least for the first year, I decided to leave and concentrate more on Osogbo.

W: It had become a committee thing then. You could never recreate that atmosphere: the combination of that old Lebanese man and his own enclave there and then being situated in the middle of the market. It was right in the heart of throbbing Yoruba life. They didn't see what they were losing. The size was totally irrelevant. The very makeshift quality of the original Mbari was a challenge. And it didn't alienate anybody. Moving into the Central alienated a lot of people.

U: "Threshold fear. In the old Mbari everybody could feel at home. There was no class or clique that dominated the place.

W: You had students; you had the Peace Corps. You had crooks, you had con men, and you had pickpockets. I described a scene in Ibadan when a whole lot of con men cheated women who had come to do their shopping in Ibadan. They came from Ondo or Ekiti or even further afield. The crooks came with lucky dips. You were supposed to bring one Naira and pick up your luck in a box. Of course it wasn't the dip itself that was the business. It was very good psychology. They would watch those women who had come from the interior, having collected money from their fellow traders, to do their Christmas or Ramadan shopping. They would watch and assess which of them had money. Suddenly they would cause a commotion, and her purse would be snatched. It was through our own self-policing that we were finally able to invite the police to come and arrest them. They were heavy thugs, and difficult to tackle on one's own. And of course they had friends in the police also. But eventually we were able to break up that ring, and one of their leaders became a very good friend of mine!

U: I gather it was the Orisun boys who broke up the ring. They were a wonderful link between Mbari and the wider public, It was they, also, I feel, who spread the popularity of the Mbari shirt. In the fifties Adire was worn exclusively by women. And even when we started wearing it as shirts, it did not catch the imagination of a wider public. It was only when the staff of Mbari, like Ademola, the Alake's grandson, started wearing them, and above all, when the Orisun players also began to wear Adire shirts did we see people hawking the shirts on the street. Young boys with long poles with twenty, thirty shirts of different sizes hanging from them...

W: A whole culture developed. You could go to East Africa or South Africa at the time and see the Mbari shirt. You remember Herb Shaw? The American who taught drama in East Africa? I think it was in Makerere. He was the one who spread the Mbari shirt in East Africa.

U: Now we have said that the civil war destroyed many things, and caused some irreparable damage to the different cultures. But in some sense the country emerged from it intact. In fact there was a kind of high spirit. Think of the University of Ife under the leadership of Dr. Oluwasanmi. It was highly motivated.

W: There was some optimism because there was the feeling of "Oh *even* a civil war, yes, we can overcome."

U: A sense of indestructibility... It was exhilarating to visit the University of Nsukka after the war. It was a tremendously inspiring place when the students first went there, cleaned the place up and more or less twisted the government's arm to reopen the university.

W: A determination to rebuild.

U: Remember the Ant Hill, the Uli Art Movements. The place was bursting with creativity.

W: It was still the Mbari spirit that carried on. They had been involved in it, were therefore able to set up their own centers. All that was encouraging, but the economic productivity had gone to pots. War had become a business. You remember the famous cheroots, the cigars that used to be manufactured behind Bamgbose Street in Lagos? We used to go there and purchase them for about 10 shillings a hundred. I went there when I came out of detention and a found the shop closed down. Why? The woman had become a trader supplying materials—insert, food, clothing, blankets—to the army during the war. Before the war there had been this little industry. She personally supervised it and she did very well on it. But the war was much more profitable than that. And she didn't just go there, make big money while still running the little cheroot factory on the side. No. She stopped it completely. She had become an army contractor. And that was true of many small scale industries. When the war was over they never went back to it. They simply continued to chase contracts. Their whole life was entirely commercialized. They took up more and more contracts with the corresponding bribery. The famous 10 percent became institutionalized.

U: It became a hell of a lot more than 10%.

W: Thank you. It went to 15, 20, and 25 percent. And they became agents rather than producers. And to make things worse, if the economy had remained at that level, some of them might have returned to their former trade. But then the oil money came. That finished off the entire productive responsibility. Remember the Ikorodu ceramic factory? Never mind what you thought of the quality of design at the time. But things were being produced there that were put to immediate use in the country, and that cut out some of the imports. But all that just disappeared. Let's not talk about Abuja. The war industry, followed by oil, totally distorted our lives.

U: It also meant that the states just relied on their share of federal oil money which was enough to keep them going. They allowed their small industries and even their agriculture to go to ruin. In the late seventies Nigeria even began to import palm oil. The West was particularly affected. Land became an object of speculation. Whole villages lost their land, selling under pressure or seduced by their own greed. In the Osogbo area you can't see a yam field anymore. The yam people eat comes from the Midwest or from the North. With this new commercialism other things started to happen. Money began to play an ever increasing part in the installation of Oba with the result that most Oba in turn have to become businessmen. One of their lucrative businesses nowadays is to sell chieftaincy titles...

W: To all and sundry!

U: The popular currency for a chieftaincy title is a V-Boot3. Another alarming symptom of the disintegration of Yoruba society is the language itself. If you listen to a Lagos area boy or a taxi driver, the language has become hard. The rhythm has gone, the tone levels have been flattened, the text interspersed with English words, and uttered at tremendous speed.

W: Even the language of music doesn't sound like it anymore. The lyrics have gone. It is linked thoroughly to commercialism. A new phase of praise singing has developed. This is different from the spontaneous praise singing we used to know in the night clubs of the sixties, the one which was bestowed on you the moment you appeared on stage or entered the bar. The singer did not really expect any reward; it was part and parcel of the performance. Maybe you put a few token coins on his forehead or you bought a couple of drinks for the band. But now what it means is that the singer takes the same *agbada* (robe) of praise singing he has just bestowed on you, and puts it on the next person. No inventiveness; he simply uses the same sequence of praises for each individual.

U: This has been triggered off by this obnoxious "spraying."

W: Thank you. I was coming to that.

U: Lavishing money over the performer has nothing to do with the quality of the performance or with the personality of the singer. It is a form of self-display of the nouveau-riche: "I can spray more than you!"

W: Why should the singer waste his creative energy when all his fan wanted to hear was his name interpolated into the same formulistic singing?

U: I remember how well-informed the old *Juju* bands were about the fans' lives. Black Morocco would refer to recent events in your life. He certainly knew your *oriki*. He even knew who your recent girlfriend was.

W: That's right and his praises would be specific to her: the texture, the complexion, her specific variety of beauty as opposed to that of the last girl. But now it is standard. They will sing about anybody you bring—as long as she is a sprayer. She can be as thin as a rake, but if the praise they used last had to do with a real market mammy type, they would just repeat the same phrases without shame or sense of impropriety. And the girl would be basking in it because all that matters is that her name is mentioned. And from there music moved into the sanctimonious. It's almost as if to compensate for this worship of money and of status. It is very difficult to analyze the relationship or what stimulated what, but I have observed that the music now also indulges in fulsome prayers, the standard invocations to hope and good luck. These have now become the centerpiece of the new social music repeated *ad nauseam* and inflated in its worth. In other words you can have that thin phrase repeated with the most unctuous kind of voice. A new religiosity whose literacy is of the lowest has been born through new social music. This music in fact has no imagination whatsoever. So you can have the whole thing going on for 15 minutes or in fact longer, but consisting of nothing but: "May I not encounter evil in my life." And that will be repeated throughout in a more and more unctuous manner. No more imagination, no more creativity. And then a combination of that with all the new technical effects! Compare that with the beautiful music of Tunde Nightingale, Black Morocco, and Orlando Owo with his beautiful husky voice. Compare the original *Juju* music with the social music of today, and you can see the collapse of the group personality, the total social decay.

U: One problem is that the public no longer demands the imagination and creativity we used to know. Another reality is the political hopelessness and frustration. People have lost their faith and their sense of belonging. So they just play along with whatever corrupt government is in power, and try to get out of it what they can for themselves. They become Muslims or build other pragmatic relationships necessary for securing contracts in Abuja.

W: Yes that's another phenomenon. Changing your name so you can be associated with the feudal power...

U: That amounts to a deliberate negation of your own identity. The question is, with political power permanently concentrated in the North and with the money monopolies centered more and more in the North, what chances has Yoruba culture got to survive? And more seriously, how much do Yoruba care about their culture and their identity nowadays?

W: Now here we come to the positive side, or the negative one. I don't know what to say because it depends upon whether you look at it as a Nigerian nationalist or a Yoruba nationalist. The reverse process has begun. There is now a feeling of self-disgust by the younger generation of the Yoruba, and in that I include the forty, forty-five years olds who looked at the entire phenomenon and said: "Wait a minute. We are Yoruba people. That bastardization of our existence—the lowering of the quality of life from our original existence, the humiliation of our people by those traitors who go begging cap in hand and betraying the political cause for their own profit—we will not stand for it any longer." There is a swell of reaction. It is exemplified in the most frightening way; in the kind of experience we encounter today when we try to mobilize political opposition to the dictatorship. Our people, particularly the youth mentioned above, say clearly to us: "Listen, we are ready for struggle, but we are not willing to struggle for a Nigerian nation. There is only one nation we are willing to recognize and that is the Oduduwa nation." In the States alone there are at least four Yoruba movements that I know: Egbe Omo Oduduwa, Yoruba Progressive Union, Oduduwa Nation... One of them was so blatantly Yoruba that I had to say to them: "Listen, at this stage, at least, this is a national struggle. If you want to become affiliated to NALICON ("National Liberation Council") you have to change your name." I cannot accept a sectional-based organization. You know what they did? They went and had a meeting and they came back and said to me: "OK. We've changed our name. We are now 'Action Group for Democracy."

U: Very clever.

W: Look, I roared with laughter. I thought it was one up on me. I had no choice but to register the organization. I thought it was so witty and at the same time it showed such a resolve. They got back to me within ten minutes and said: "Action Group for Democracy. Any objections?" I was defeated on this one. Some of them were collecting money—and not only in America. Even before I left Nigeria, there was a group professionals, doctors, engineers, pharmacists, journalists between the ages of 25 to 45, some of whom have researched the resources that exist in the Yoruba part of the country. I was impressed by their industry. They had identified the minerals that could be explored. On one occasion they invited me, and said: "We have always admired you, and we will always give you support. But today we have not invited you to talk about how to terminate this dictatorship. We have made up our mind. We have not invited you to ask your opinion. We want to tell you what we want to do and we want to ask you whether you can help us. "We have examined our history; we have looked at the treachery of our leaders. We have asked you because you are not one of the traitors. But we feel that you are wasting your energy, and we do not want to be wasted. You have described your generation as the wasted generation. We are determined not to waste ourselves, and we are sure that you are wasting yourself because you continue to believe in a certain chimera called "Nigeria" ... We don't. This is our program. If it dovetails with yours, fine. But this is the platform on which we stand. We want nothing less than a Yoruba state. Our minds are made up. However long it takes we will hold on to this vision. We do not believe in Nigeria." And they showed me why the Yoruba nation should stand alone. I just sat amazed while I was being lectured for over an hour. And they said:

"O. K. this is our program. How can you help us—if you want to?" And that movement is gaining ground all the time.

U: An interesting rider on this. A few years ago I met a Yoruba Oba, a man of rare integrity. He told me that a certain mineral had been found on his territory. But he said: "I have no intention to do anything about it because if I do, some Northerner will get the contract. Maybe some businessman from Lagos will get the subcontract. But this town will get nothing out of it. All that will happen is that they will destroy our environment. Let it stay there..."

W: That's right. That is the mood right now. That is precisely the kind of language those young men are using. And in the recent constitutional agenda, even the women amongst them, say: "We only went there to let them know we want a Yoruba state. There are similar movements in different areas. And what we are witnessing is a phase of "into your tents Israeli." That is the expression we use when we want to translate the Yoruba expression "Let each person cling to his or her mother's breasts," It is essentially the political reaction of the prevailing sense of race humiliation.

U: It is a potentially dangerous situation. Who could have thought ten years ago that we would witness the rise of violent Hindu chauvinism in India. The Yoruba people certainly must reassert their cultural identity but we must hope that they will not lose sight of the essential values of their culture in the process. But when you think of the sixties, which we have been talking about as if they are the golden era, I'm sure that most people, certainly the intellectuals accepted the concept of Nigeria.

W: We certainly tried to make it work.

U: There was a lot of good will. People worked to give this a go! But somehow these so-called leaders frittered it away. They have sold out this idealism. Nigeria has just become the personal property of a few. In the sixties I was amazed by the optimism of Southerners who told me, "Look, with the spread of modern education we shall see the rise of a new elite in the North. A generation will think more like us. They will be less conservative, more liberal, more open to the world, and we will grow together." You may remember that in the last numbers of *Black Orpheus*

I published quite a few stories from North Africa. I tried to encourage this optimism by showing people that there was this other, liberal and open minded aspects of Islam. And up to a point I think you can say it's happening. Look at the last election. There was a definite breaking down of cultural and religious borders.

W: I was coming to that. Yes.

U: The Emir of Kano, he is a modern statesman. Nobody could accuse him of being a mediaeval potentate. Some change has actually taken place, but these people are not having their say in the North.

W: Absolutely not. There's still a clique, and I emphasize it in my forthcoming book. But to come back to the election, I have videos of Abiola's campaign. I have not seen such ecstasy on the faces of people, not since the time of Awolowo. You want to see those videos! You want to compare them to that of Tofa campaigning in the same state, his own state. And you will see that on the one hand there is total absolute rapture at the reception of this man. On the other side, duty and support, yes, but nothing compared to the reception that Abiola received. And all that bullshit that Northerners weren't ready for a Yoruba? It was exploded totally...

U: I suppose it is the frustration over the annulment of this election that has produced those extreme Yoruba nationalists you cited.

W: Precisely. Their feeling is: "If the nation went this far, and if there is a self-interested clique so determined, ruthless and unpatriotic as to actually fritter away this galvanizing moment of the national feeling and good-will—well, in that case let's not waste any more energy on an ideal that those who are in a position of power are willing to nullify. It's incalculable what June 12th has done. June 12th, 1993 by the way, was the date of the freest and fairest general presidential election ever held in Nigeria. Chief Mashood Abiola, a Yoruba, won, but the fact that he is a Muslim who has assiduously and expensively cultivated and won the friendship and trust of the dominant Hausa-Fulani Muslim North did not stop him from being contemptuously brushed aside, and his election annulled.

U: But let me come to a last issue. Whatever happens politically, supposing even that the political problems can be resolved one way or the other, there still remains a cultural problem because for several decades Yoruba children have been educated away from their culture at school. They have been educated to actually despise their history, their religion. We saw sparks of cultural revival in the sixties. Duro Ladipo's and your own activities have jerked people out of this complacency, and made them rethink their history. There is a new awareness. Nevertheless we are faced today by a profiteering class of Yoruba entrepreneurs who are only too willing to exploit their own people. So, political autonomy in itself is not the answer. There is a cultural vacuum. I met a new generation of Yoruba academics who came to me and said: "I missed out on this important period of our history. I was too young to experience the ferment of the sixties. I have never seen a Duro Ladipo performance. I never knew the Mbari club." There is a deep sense of loss, of being cheated out of one's heritage. To an extent I find myself playing the role of an "informant", an eye witness, to this younger generation.

W: Yes, and we did not even touch on the role played by foreign interests; what I call the "Walkman Culture". When I was running the Cultural Centre at the University of Ife, you remember we ran a bar in the foyer of the theatre and we had the rotunda. I made a rule that there should be no foreign pop music played in the foyer of the theatre. I said: "The students have their own club. Let them play what they want, whatever is to their own taste, there. But I run this place. This is Ife. This is an Ife cultural centre. I will not have this kind of pop music played here." So we played *Juju* musicians like Orlando Owo, we played music from the East, that wonderful singer Njemanze, and we played Professor Majority. And I said, "If any students bring in records of Rock or Pop, I'll get them smashed because this is an opportunity for all you students who come here to enjoy indigenous culture as an option. This is the purpose of this place." But interestingly they kept bringing their pop music, and it was not until I actually grabbed one record and smashed it that the barman understood I was serious. Unfortunately for them, this was the one place on the campus where they could relax. It was the one place where the toilets worked, where they could get cheap snacks, see some shows at reduced tickets—whereas they were charging high prices in their own club. They were fleecing one another. Some of them gradually got interested in the music I played in the centre. But it is tragic that a whole generation had been lost... They often asked, "What sort of music is this? This is square stuff." And I said: "Your father is square."

U: But this is something that went wrong very early on. Do you remember the "Universal Free Education Scheme" introduced by S.O. Awokoya in the then Western Region in 1956? He was one of my best friends, but I quarreled with him continuously over that issue. People in those days had a blind faith in that magic thing called "education" that was supposed to solve all the problems of society. Nobody thought of what the purpose of education was. What are we educating our children to become? What will they learn about their own society, their history, and the philosophy of the Yoruba? Where will their identity lie when they have passed through that education? Will they have learned anything at all about the other cultural groups in Nigeria with whom they will have to cooperate in forming a nation? If the education is merely job orientated, if all it does is to enable you to earn more money than those who did not go through that system successfully, are you not training a class of egoistical exploiters? If you don't know what the impact of this type of education will be on society, why pursue it? Nobody, literally nobody, would listen to me then. Only in the seventies Prof Babs Fafunwa started his experiment in Yoruba education at Ife. In six selected schools he introduced Yoruba as the language of instruction, right through Primary School from class I to class VI. He argued correctly that to impose English as a language of instruction too early would alienate them from their society and that it was not even an efficient way of teaching them English. He carried out this experiment with great enthusiasm and with considerable success, but of course nothing came out of it in the end. It was never adopted as general policy of education.

W: Yes, and what did he do to himself? After he became Federal Minister of Education, he declared publicly that he must no longer be called Babs Fafunwa, that he was now Aliu Fafunwa.

U: Was that the price he paid for becoming a minister?

W: That's right. When a senior person gives an example like that, of opportunism, which denies your own origin, how can people then take his project of promoting the Yoruba language seriously? It affects it, whether you like it or not. You cannot objectivate what you are doing and separate yourself from it by example. Your behavior seems intended to make you acceptable to a section of the country that happens to be distributing the goodies at the moment. You abandon a name by which you have been known for decades, Babs for Babatunde, and you publish it in all the papers that you want to be called Aliu.

U: You know, last night Al Imfeld said something to me that is quite relevant to this issue. You know that Al Imfeld is a cousin of the famous rebel Catholic theologian Hans Kung?

W: Oh, really? I didn't know that.

U: He told me that he once said to Hans Kung: "I am aware of all your ecumenical meetings and get-togethers and conferences and services... I do appreciate that you want to break down the differences between the different churches, and you are stretching out a hand towards Judaism and Islam. But at no time ever have you considered African religion as a religion." Now if you look at the Yoruba people themselves, all these younger people we have talked about, who has developed a new pride in Yoruba language and history and identity? And when it comes to religion...

W: They shy away.

U: Yes. And it amounts to a form of schizophrenia. If you are really going to have this Yoruba revival that you are talking about, regardless of which political framework it will take place in, sooner or later they will have to face the issue of Yoruba religion squarely. And I am not thinking of the Yoruba theologians, like Dr Idowu, who pick elements from Yoruba religion and create some kind of construction that will make it valid from a Christian point of view, while all those elements that do not fit the Christian world view will be declared a subsequent degeneration of the original "true" essence of Yoruba religion. That doesn't help. What has to be done is to show that Yoruba religion had some universal human values which are as valid today as they were a hundred years ago, and that there are elements of this religion that are superior to the so-called "universal" religions. For example, its tolerance, but apart from you, nobody has stood up and said this.

W: Well I have met some people of my own persuasion. You know at Houston Texas they have this huge festival every year which features one country. And this year it was the whole of West Africa. And there was a Yoruba there who stood up and said: "You cannot simply separate

171

Yoruba religion from the Yoruba world view and from all that you call Yoruba civilization."

U: It has been a taboo subject.

W: Yes, and you know, I take every opportunity to push it. I say: "Look you people with your big, so-called universal religions. All you have is a history of bloodthirstiness. You cannot find a single example of any Yoruba religion waging a war on its own behalf. There is no Orisa community that has ever gone aggressively proselytizing. In spite of this total lack of aggressiveness it penetrated and infiltrated other religions and has created whole new viable systems of values in Cuba and Brazil. There is at least one lesson to the world which divides itself into two or three religions to the neglect of every other viable system of values." I do agree, of course, that there has been a lot of superficial, sometimes ambiguous flirtation with African values, particularly in America—like *Kwanza*. They have set up their own African-American New Year Festival and it has become a big thing, thoroughly commercialized like Christmas. They send out Kwanza cards and they have a festival that mimics certain African Harvest ceremonies. They start preparing long in advance. They have write ups, they light candles, and they wear *Akwete,* colorful cloth woven in Igbo country.

U: That reminds me of Mr. Amu. Do you remember that charming musician in Accra who performed baroque music on *atentebem*, Ghanaian bamboo flute? For his daughter's wedding he invented an "African wedding cake". It was made of *fufu*. You cut it with a knife and it contained pepper stew. But what was the point?

W: Precisely. There is already a traditional form of wedding in that kind of society. So why use the cake symbolism? But you are right about the reluctance of African Americans to focus on a recognizable and still existing African symbols that still have meaning for a contemporary person in America. They don't use those; they substitute.

U: There are many things that you could use. Many Yoruba rituals have a universal meaning; they cut across all cultural boundaries. Tunji was very lucky because when he was born in Papua New Guinea there was a Yoruba doctor, Doctor Lucas, who was there on a WHO mission. He held a proper Yoruba naming ceremony for him—with pepper, honey and all the rest of it. And for us it was a great deal more meaningful than baptism and it had an equally powerful appeal for all the New Guinean friends who were present. One thing which everybody loved was that, instead of the parents dictatorially imposing a name on the child, every friend could confer his own chosen name on the child. So you teach the child from the beginning that he will be different things to different people in life, and that he is part of a larger community; that his parents are not the only ones who take responsibility for him, and that his own responsibilities extend far beyond his nuclear family.

W: And we don't need a priest to do it. Anybody can do it, and you can use whatever foodstuff is available. You can adapt and even add new meanings because the main point of the symbolisms is the grounding of the child.

U: And giving him a taste of what life has in store for him.

W: Giving him a little bit of bitter and a little bit of sweet. I myself have performed many naming ceremonies. In fact right now Olaokun, my son, is waiting for me to come and name his new born child. So he is also an example of this kind of sensibility—even though he grew up in England and married a white girl. But the passion with which he has integrated himself into the African community, both politically and culturally, is amazing...

U: But how will these values be imparted to a new generation? I find that my African friends in Germany face this problem. Their children grow up in an alien environment. It is natural for them to come home and expect to be served by their parents because that's what the children in their environment do. It takes a huge effort to teach them elementary rules of Yoruba behavior, of politeness and respect under the circumstances, not to mention to imparting essential values. How will children growing up in exile retain the subtleties of their language? How will they understand what *Orisa* is? Also, is a child in Lagos not as alienated from its culture as a Yoruba child growing up in America or Europe? Do we need to create institutions or some new form of education?

W: Something like this has been undertaken by a group in California. They call themselves the "League of Patriotic Nigerians." I went to give them a lecture to help them with their fundraising. They actually want to raise a structure which they call Nigerian House because they are acutely aware of the loss of this culture to their children. They have been exiled for a long time. They teach their children Yoruba or Igbo, as the case may be, at home. But they want to institutionalize this. They are going to make it open to Americans, too. So this is a tendency, and I doubt if it is going to be short lived, because there is a real need. And part of it arises from the fact that many children have been growing up accepting American values unquestioningly, and some parents have become so upset with it that they've decided to stem the loss. So I think all is not lost.

U: Sometimes one wants to despair. But the Yoruba people have demonstrated a remarkable sense of survival throughout their history. So that gives one hope that they will survive even this latest and most dangerous crisis.

Wole Soyinka
"IDENTITY"

U: Recently a famous commentator on African life and literature referred
to you as "the man between", and in his article he expounds that eternal
cliché of the African intellectual "between two worlds", between two languages, two cultures. But it seems to me that Europeans worry far more
about the "identity problems" of Africans than Africans themselves do. I
have known you now for over thirty years and you have never struck me
as somebody who is constantly aware of oscillating between two worlds.
Or have you ever thought of yourself as living in a situation of conflict?

W: It is a strange thing—that deeply ingrained attitude that certain commentators hold. And of course, it is a very Eurocentric thing. It does not
occur to me for instance to consider you, Ulli Beier, as a 'man between'.
It does not occur to me that you suffer from a conflict. You come to Yorubaland and you are immediately at home. You can sit in a Sango shrine
or follow the Agbegijo masqueraders, and you are just at home. And
there are some other Europeans like that. Susanne Wenger has stayed in
Osogbo for decades, and she has become a priestess of Obatala. It has
never occurred to me to consider her a 'woman between'. She is a deeply
spiritual person and an artist who creates where she has put down her
roots. I look at Gerd Meuer. He is at home one moment here and one
moment there. Right now he is in Addis Ababa. It has never occurred
to me that there is a problem or that there is something special about
anybody striving towards two or three, four or multiple worlds. It is a
very Eurocentric thing.

U: It's European, but it is especially German. In this country people still talk
about "die Bewaltigung der Vergangenheit", and they still wrestle with their

Nazi past. Even those who weren't even alive at the time torture themselves by examining their father's role in those years. There is a spate of books on that subject—very different kinds of books from your own reminiscences of your father. Germans have a problem with their identity because they are very theoretical people. They don't trust their gut reaction. They have to argue an issue to the end before they know how to react.

W: There is another aspect to this. I think that Europeans still marvel at the ex-colonial—somebody at the lower scale of civilization, as far as they are concerned—being able to respond in a very natural and intelligent way to another civilization. I think that this, lurching underneath it, is the notion.

U: Of course Europeans have long felt that they have to export their culture in order to lift other peoples to a higher level of civilization. In the early days of the University of Ibadan there was just this attitude. There was no curiosity about Nigeria at all. The notion that there could be some kind of exchange, some mutual enrichment was quite foreign to them. They used a formula to justify any absurdity in the curriculum which they imposed on African students. If you asked them why they thought it necessary to teach Anglo-Saxon in Ibadan at a time when no African language was taught and when there was not even a second European language, the answer was: "We have to maintain British standards." Africans were only acceptable to Europeans if they could perform on their terms and live up to "British standards." On the other hand I feel that certain kinds of early African literature have also contributed to this...

W: Indeed. I was going to refer to that. The early African intellectuals accepted this perspective themselves, and, as I wrote somewhere, enjoyed the "angst" which was created for them through the notion of having to transcend one culture and having to link up with a superior one. The early poetry...

U: Well, Senghor. He is certainly somebody who moves very smoothly between the cultures, but on the other hand he talks too much about it, doesn't he?

W: He wanted to intellectualize it. To create "problematique", then analyze and poetize it also because he used both approaches—the creative and the intellectual. Of course, he was a magnificent poet, and therefore his influence was more deleterious than, let us say, Mabel Imoukhuede. You know the kind of poetry we are talking about. But the interesting thing is that Mabel and others soon gave up on that line. There wasn't too much yardage.

U: No... Such notions were abandoned fairly quickly. But to come back to the European image of Wole Soyinka, "the man between," there are certain assumptions. Your British education, your high achievement in that culture and your exceptional command of the English language, these things now stand, allegedly, between you and your own culture. The English language separates you, so the legend goes, from Yoruba culture. It's like saying you've been converted; he who was a pagan and has now become a Muslim; he who was a Protestant has converted to Catholicism. You have given up one thing to attain another.

W: This is a problem that arises out of analytical attitudes. The very principle of analyzers is that an object or a subject is not interesting until you have created many analytical angles, and made the subject as complex as possible—never mind whether the various angles are interesting or not. Once you can create multiple approaches towards the understanding of a subject, then of course you can play games with the entire analytical nexus. And that applies very much when the subject is a writer or an intellectual or a creative person. The more complex you can make the subject, the more intriguing, and the greater the amount of conversation and discourse you can weave around it. I think that is exactly what happens. Whether their claim is true or not, people no longer bother about that because it is more interesting to propose, let us say, that because one has had a particular kind of education or because one has had a certain amount of success in operating within other cultural measures, something must have happened to that person. Some twist to his character, some uneasiness in the mind. And yet you have lots of people who leave their society completely and take up residence somewhere else—even in their formative years.

U: Joseph Conrad...

W: Yes, and nobody bothers about this alleged "problem".

U: Nobody asks: "What about his Polish soul?"

W: That's right. It's only when it gets to this ex-colonial... And unfortunately some of our own intellectuals who have their own axes to grind come out and say: "He is a success only because he had danced to their cultural tune." Some of them are even more overt—cruder about it: "Oh yes, he is completely alienated... They love him because his opinions coincide with theirs."

U: The Nobel Prize controversy...

W: That's right. You should never get the Nobel Prize. That's the ultimate proof!

U: That you're a traitor to your culture.

W: But some of these people who write these things... They can't stand in their own societies the way I can go back to my village and be immediately recognized and absorbed... They cannot. The contrast would be too shaming for them. So it's a myth that has been created for different kinds of motivations. Then common interest makes them all speak with one voice.

U: Maybe this is cynical of me. But you said that people create complicated arguments for their own sakes. But is it not also a case of people creating an academic career for themselves—creating a "subject"?

W: Of course, that's right.

U: Think of the Professor of English at the University of Ibadan who once said: "Wole Soyinka teaching English literature? Over my dead body! Only an Englishman can teach English literature." And that other gentleman who proclaimed: "If we were to teach the works of Wole Soyinka in the University of Ibadan, who are we going to drop, Milton or Shakespeare?" Now both of them are the big African literature experts!

W: They have to "find new angles" to replace the original resistance.

U: So they can talk endlessly about the agony of Wole "between two worlds." I've said that many times, there is so much attention being paid to the sociology of the writer... And not to his writing!

W: Aha! So it is high time we paid some attention to the sociology of the critic. That is important, and when you look into the sociology of the critic or analyst, you'll find self-interest, opportunism, often intellectual dishonesty. You will find phantasizing over and above the level of a fiction writer. You'll find the polemicist's tendency which has to be fulfilled, and it does not matter what the subject is. Before you come down to mundane issues like, "Is he or she married?, white or black?, or from another race?" I mean all those various things that are foisted on the artist, it's about time we directed them at the critics themselves! And I am telling you—the results! I have done it in one or two instances. The results are fascinating. For example, digging into the sociology of one of those people whom I call Neo-Tarzanists, I found that he fled Biafra during the war, and he's now suffering from that immense guilt complex. He resents the adulation I received from his compatriots for the role I played in that war while he was "busy collecting money for the Biafran cause"—though much of the money never arrived in Biafra! Little things like that. So it's about time we examined them and see what they eat, what they drink, what sort of clothes they wear, whom they move with, whose approbation they seek, what sort of conferences they go to, and in what circuit of conferences they are constantly to be found. It's about time we turned this blade around. The results will be most fascinating...

U: I think this should be applied on the widest basis. When this research scheme on "Problems of Identity" in Africa first started in Bayreuth a decade ago, I said, "If you think you are entitled to go into any part of Africa to solve their identity problems, at *least* you should have a parallel scheme whereby African scholars are entitled to come here to solve your identity problems because, in my mind, you have the bigger problem!"

W: The scholars who are into "what makes the African tick", the sociologists and the literary sociologists far outnumber and outweigh the creative material that is coming out of Africa today.

U: Easily!

W: I think it's about time we moved in and studied the identity problems of the European scholars!

U: Another thing is this compartmentalized thinking. When that Professor of English literature said: "Wole Soyinka can't teach English literature", the implication was "Wole ought not to teach English literature", just as there are still people who feel that someone like Akin Euba ought not to play Mozart. People want to protect their cultural preserves. No African could be sensitive enough to really understand *our* classical music. And when they say "classical", they take it for granted that they talk about European tradition; that no other culture can have produced a classical form of its own. A famous "ethnomusicologist" in Berlin issued a series of LP's on African and Asian music under the title "musical source material"—as if entire cultures had merely evolved to provide "source material" for his scholarly work. In the same way African literature is merely "source material" for some of the scholars. They may not even enjoy reading it.

W: They're using it for their careers.

U: A related issue concerns the English language. Some commentators, both European and African, have argued that using English as a vehicle for creative work is a sign of elitism—an argument that has been used especially against you. It's curious, but in a different context, those same people talk about "World Culture" and the "Global Village" and all that, and yet they want you to write in a language that will drastically limit your readership to a very local audience. I suspect when travelling around the world to their different conferences these same people are quite grateful to find that English is spoken almost everywhere.

W   I know. It is very curious. It's a non-existent debate that falls into two parts. Let's take the language aspect first. You will find that the African critics who are making this complaint are not making it in their own language. One would expect their commitment to be so total that they would turn their back on English and French altogether and write in, say, Efik, and declare: "Anybody who can read me, good! Anybody who can't: let him read Wole Soyinka." For me, that would be the first mark of integrity. If that is missing, it is difficult to take them seriously. The other thing is this. Am I, Yoruba speaking Wole Soyinka, to be cut off from Chinua Achebe, Taban Lo Lyong, Ngugi Wa Thiong'o and Dennis

Brutus? If South African writers followed this precept and wrote in their own languages, am I to be cut off from the political struggle in South Africa? It's an argument I have never really understood. I come now to the second part. I too, lament that in Africa, which I regard as my larger community, we don't have a language that binds us all together outside the European languages, the colonial languages. After all, even the European language fragments. I have to study Portuguese to read Dos Santos. I study French to read Senghor. I'm on record as having seriously promoted the use of Swahili. In the inaugural congress of the Union of Writers of the African People we took the decision that we should set up a cooperative publishing house, and undertake the mammoth task of translating all new works—all new works, to begin with—into Kiswahili. And we encouraged all African writers to reserve their rights to this cooperative publishing venture. I haven't seen any practical steps taken by the people who had been screaming their heads off about African languages. For me the two things go side by side. We should all admit that we need a single literature—which makes economic sense. We also asked that all schools eliminate one useless subject and substitute Kiswahili in order to build up a generation of Kiswahili speakers. The two ideas coincide, and I see no problem in this at all. I want to continue writing in English and, more importantly, reading in English the works of my fellow Africans and—of course—the literature of the entire English speaking world. I insist on keeping the facility to do this. Many people oversimplify the word criticism. They don't understand that criticism also means exposition—exposition of the work in all of it robustness... They feel simply that they have not engaged in literary criticism unless they are "criticizing"

U: In the sense of "finding fault"...

W: Precisely. They have to be negative. They make a fetish of it. And ultimately, which is nauseating, they profit from it. And they communicate this in the very language they condemn. How ridiculous is that! But this contradiction never occurs to them.

U: Even Europeans have talked about elitism along the lines of "More people can understand *Death and the King's Horseman* in New York than in Nigeria", which is not true at all. In fact from the reports I read, the people of New York were quite baffled by the play. They couldn't penetrate it at all.

W: Yes. That is true.

U: I don't think that any critic has the right to prescribe a particular language to a writer anymore than he can prescribe the contents of a book or the mood or the intellectual level on which the ideas are to be developed. The irony is that those who constantly nag Wole Soyinka about his 'elitism' forget that though you may have written some rather cerebral stuff, you have also operated on a very popular level. I can't think of another African writer who produced anything as popular as *Unlimited Liability Company*. In this LP album you even had to use Pidgin English to communicate.

W: I've used Pidgin, Yoruba, mime, song and dance. I feel a total—if you like—elitist indifference to those kinds of critics. I consider them quite ignorant. When I read a statement like "Nobody reads Wole Soyinka outside Nigeria", I ask myself, "What are these people talking about?" If they said: "This particular work is not read in Nigeria", we could begin to discuss that. But when they make a statement like "…Wole Soyinka is far more popular for his political position than for his creative work," I don't know what they are talking about. Unfortunately some of them are Nigerians!

U: Most of them!

W: We do our political sketches, and take them to the market place!

U: *Before the Blackout!*

W: Yes, you remember! *Before the Blackout!* from the sixties. And again, during the last civilian regime, with all the scandals going on, we took the theatre to the Museum Kitchen at Onikan in Lagos and moved from there to the street in front of the House of Assembly. We did a series of sketches there, quickly jumped into our vehicles and ran away before the police could catch us. There are various ways of communicating a work to the public. I use all of them, including, as you remarked, an LP record. We are bringing out a video shortly which has emerged from the latest equivalent of *Before the Blackout!*. We call it *Before the Deluge*. This came out of a theatre workshop in Abeokuta as well as the sketches we performed in public places. I reach the public in a way—and I am not being immodest—that few people do. Yet I am the one who gets all this nonsense about "Nobody reads Wole Soyinka even in his own country."

U: I remember some very potent poems of yours appearing in Nigerian newspapers—for example, the one about the pathetic death of a Yoruba Oba during the 1966 crisis in the West. Everybody would have understood that. Of course, I too may find some of your poems baffling—but few things could be more popular than "Telephone Conversation."

W: Of course there are always works that are more accessible than others.

U: Again this brings up the alleged identity conflict! There are two Wole Soyinkas, so the theory goes: one is the lofty intellectual who despises his readers; the other is the political agitator, the gang leader who doesn't mind throwing out the occasional doggerel rhyme—another simplification, another variant of the "man between". They don't seem to see that different situations provoke or require different responses from the writer.

W: Yes, I believe that the armory of creativity is so vast that one would be a fool not to select whatever corresponds to the theme one wishes to express at the moment.

U: I think we have agreed that most Nigerians cope fairly effortlessly with the alleged conflict between their own culture and the Western values that have been imposed on them. They don't worry about it and there is no intellectual equivalent to the *negritude* writers. But at the same time there has been little interaction between the various cultures in Nigeria. What attempts have been made to find common denominators between, say, Igbo, Yoruba, Efik and Angas? Do people consider it irrelevant or even undesirable? Remember what we tried to do in Duro Ladipo's play *Moremi*? Because the play deals with the conflict between the Ile-Ife aboriginal population and some Igbo raiders, I recruited a group of Agbor dancers for the production. So Duro had two languages, two musical traditions and two dance styles at his disposal, and I think these enriched his play enormously and the final scene was spectacular. The Yoruba *dundun* drums were played simultaneously with the Igbo slit gongs and horns. Duro made all the musicians orientate themselves towards a strong simple beat that was played by Rufus Ogundele on a huge conga drum. It was a very successful piece of "fusion music" even though we did not know the term in those days. I rather hoped it would lead others to develop this idea further, but it wasn't taken up. What a missed opportunity! Imagine a Nigerian orchestra, involving *dundun, bata, bembe,* slit gongs, xylophones from the Plateau, horns from Ekiti and Igbo country and *kakaki* trumpets from the North. You could create sounds that would make a European symphony orchestra sound grey!

W: It's interesting you should say that. Just yesterday when we were rehearsing the poetry with Okuta Percussion, and Tunji played that Indian gatham, my mind went straight to the Igbo pot drum. And you are right. There has not been that fusion of music. Even in a choir like Stephen Rhodes Voices...you'll find that they make a point of including at least some songs from other parts of Nigeria in their repertoire. But it's done on an itemized level, not integrated. I have always felt the need for this myself. Remember that I brought the Atilogu dancers from the East when I produced *A Dance of the Forest* for Nigerian independence? And since then most of my productions have integrated, wherever possible, a wide range of music. My mind goes instantly to whatever is available within my entire cultural milieu... When I made *Unlimited Liability Company* one side—and that is acknowledged on the cover—was

U: Was based on Njemanze!

W: Yes. I have always had this idea of cross fertilization, but the composers, the real composers, don't seem to use it.

U: There has also been an unfortunate influence, I think. The various States "Art Councils" in Nigeria have promoted a kind of folklore.

W: That's right. You know after the oil boom, there came a time when culture became culture with capital "C", and folklore became folklore with a capital "F" for 'Folklorism! There was money for the states to set up individual Arts Councils and all those national competitions were organized. Each state went its own way with a sense of creative rivalry. This has affected and impoverished the range of creative possibilities.

U: There was another very negative aspect to those Arts Council competitions. It's an absurdity to have a group of Sango priests who are performing *Sango Pipe* compete against *Alarinjo* singing *Iwi* or *Babalawo* chanting *Odu*. What criterion is there to judge it? And usually it involved the humiliation of the performers—some pompous cultural bureaucrat herding them on stage, and after ten minutes saying, "Okay. That's enough! Obatala priests next please."

W: It's still going on.

U: And then the crude attempts to "choreograph" what, to the people concerned, is a ritual—not a theatrical performance! I suspect that the unfortunate model for all these developments was Keita Fodeba's Ballets Africaines.

W: Oh yes, the beginning of African folklore cut to European taste. But at least they moved on from there, whereas there has been—from the videos I have seen of the "National Troupe"—no such evolution in Nigeria. I gather that there has been no mandate for it to get a modern choreographer and produce a synthesis. It's been a question of simply gathering troupes from different areas, and each doing their own thing. There has been, shall I say, a lack of progressive cultural policy. But the answer never lies in government policies. For example, Peter Badejo went to the North, to Ahmadou Bello University, and created a really marvelous form of choreography. He was able to utilize material from all over Nigeria with very impressive results. From small beginnings he went there to take a diploma, and he has proved himself an imaginative choreographer. Recently he did the choreography for *Death and the King's Horseman* in Manchester. Nigeria is very rich and there are many idioms of creativity which really beg to be welded together. For me it is not a principle. It's just that the material is there. The possibility is there. Why isn't it used?!

U: Some Nigerians have come to think that there are incompatible elements in the various cultures. This belief has expressed itself in a great deal of political strife, even in violence and civil war—thirty years after independence! Have we come any nearer to any Nigerian identity or have we moved further away from it? Has Nigeria been no more than a colonial conception? What does it mean to be a Nigerian today?

W: That is a question which has been given very high profile in recent times. Consequent on the civil war, consequent on the rise of Islamic assertion which has taken its toll on the Nigerian psyche, with sudden

185

violent clashes eating into the university system, with fundamentalists organizing themselves and laying down the law for the rest of the society, the question, I am afraid, is on everybody's mind and lips. It is a very real problem, and it demands that a national debate should take place on the national question because certain parts of the country feel that other sections are dictating *their* idea of Nigeria, not a national concept, but simply *their* own attempt to impose what they consider the ethics of *their* locale—whether it's religion or whatever. Certainly it is a very large question. What form it will take, I don't know.

U: The only hope for the country to become a genuinely organic unit is for it to be allowed to grow isn't it? You cannot prescribe national unity, it can only evolve.

W: Yes, that is correct.

U: Is it not then the creative people who...

W: Oh, no, I don't accept any extra burden for creative people. It is as much the responsibility of the politicians, the bureaucrats because we are talking, after all, about quite prosaic things like the resentment of certain states over the apportionment of revenue. That kind of thing is listed as part and parcel of the need to discuss the national identity. It is being suggested that certain areas are being consistently privileged over and above others. But, you see, when the writer comes in and tells the truth about a situation like this, he is then charged with fanning ethnic tensions. In other words, he can add to the problem while he thinks he is trying to reduce it. It all depends. There is a joint responsibility. The artists can't be expected to take a leading role in it.

U: Well, of course, if it comes to solving such issues, the artist is only another citizen. But I was in fact referring to something quite different. How does the image of Nigeria evolve? Who defines Nigerian identity? Does it not happen through the kind of creative activity of creative artists such as Peter Badejo whose success you have just described?

W: I am afraid it is romantic to think that fifty or a hundred Peter Badejos are going to create that national fusion. There was a former student of mine, Jimmy Sodimu, a marvelous actor, who was caught in the recent Kano riots. He was one of those who went independent and formed their own little troupes. He was in the North doing a one man show using an interpreter. His interpreter was beheaded right next to him, and he himself received severe machete cuts. Are you ever going to persuade that person to go on any 'cultural fusion' mission—ever again in his life? No way!

U: This happened recently?

W: Recently. This was the very latest riot that was triggered by that German evangelist. There are lots and lots of cases like that, and everybody knows somebody who has been traumatized as a result... Now people are asking: "Does it mean that I cannot go anywhere in this country, on whatever mission, without fear?" In Bauch somebody was driving a delivery truck. He'd done so for donkey's years around that town. When the riot started that driver was taken out of his lorry, the vehicle was set on fire, and he was burnt. There we had just an ordinary worker, a driver who happened to be driving a truck load of beer and delivering it to all the shops. This is no problem for the artist. The artist will create his own work and fulfill his mission, but it's on a different level...

U: Is it a situation, then, of which we can't know where it is going?

W: No, I cannot. I believe that successive governments have underrated this question. Take even people like myself who always assumed that we had a nation; or at least, as you rightly said, that if things were just left to follow a progressive course, that a nation would evolve. There is a debate going on about all this. Since the whole debate began I've found myself cornered several times. Whenever I give a lecture, somebody is bound to get up and say: "Excuse me, Professor Soyinka, what do you say to the national question?" And I would pretend not to know what he is talking about. I know damn well what he is talking about; but I also know that whatever I say can be taken the wrong way. So I would say something like this: "Listen, I can be in Enugu or in Kano or in Jos or wherever. As long as I have my typewriter with me, that's where my nation is at the moment." But I know that's not satisfactory and the questioner is not satisfied. He wants Wole Soyinka to pronounce, and from the way he asks the question I know what he wants me to say. And he will be satisfied with nothing less than what he wants me to say... Whatever I say can also be misunderstood. The next day there'd be twenty headlines and as many twists in the newspapers. Words I could not debate would be put in my mouth. So now I simply say: "Listen, if you see me afterwards we can sit down and talk." I am not going to be drawn into that debate in public because I know what will happen.

U: But beyond this issue of the "national question" there is also that natural sense of obligation that a person like you has towards Africa at large...

W: Precisely. I keep reminding people that I have a very large constituency which extends well beyond the Nigerian borders. I tend to see even Nigerian problems in the context of my vision of Africa. This has been with me for a long time—ever since my student days when I was so focused on South Africa that my early play dealt with apartheid. And even now in practical terms, if I get an invitation from Angola or Cap Verde, the passion with which my presence is solicited is much stronger than what I could get from Nigeria... So I make an extra special effort to fulfill those requests whenever I can. This also creates extra problems for me. Sometimes when I'm away, some new event—something that has outraged public—happens. Within a few days people begin to think and say openly: Oh yes, Wole Soyinka has stopped speaking. He doesn't comment any more. He doesn't criticize the government." The expecta-tion is that I should be in Nigeria for 365 days a year giving running commentary on the government's activities. It's an absurd expectation, of course. So I ask these people: "What did you do? What exactly did you do?" Very often, it's not even the case that I do nothing. It's just that by the time I arrive from overseas things have quieted down or are no longer news, no longer on the front page anyway. Still, and when necessary, I move to act in a quiet, strong and often successful way. But it doesn't hit the papers, and the next thing is I get flak from these lazy, idle, comfort-able armchair critics whose mission in life is...to point the finger and say "Oh, Wole Soyinka's no longer doing anything, he's saying nothing."

U: Not unlike those literary critics.

W: Yes, they don't even know what else I've written and how it's been received, but they will say: Yes, Soyinka is elitist now; he's removed from "the people." It's boring. It's one huge bore. They don't even know that they've said it all before, and that they've been proved wrong. It makes no difference.

U: There is a whole level of society that expects you and—maybe Tai Solarin—to take on the burden of pulling the government to heel, and to constantly serve as the consciousness of the nation. Mind you, I remember very well the time of the first real crisis we went through, the time of the massacres that preceded the civil war. Who else was speaking then? The fact is that everybody remained silent, and that was the most frightening aspect of it. There is no country in the world that does not experience violent convulsions—as parts of Europe do now. But when everybody is suddenly on the winning side...?!

W: Yes, it was one of the worst periods—the exhibition of collective compromise! Acquiescence! A kind of surrender and moving from surrender to aggressive association with the side that inflicted a very serious wound on the national psyche...

U: Do you think that a lot of politicians still blame colonialism for the country's problems and for their own short-comings?

W: No, not the politicians, but the intellectual commentators. They still do that to some extent, but that has been diminished over the years—as they have seen the capacity for economic deprivation. They finally could no longer close their eyes to internal oppression in their own societies.

U: What about the new debate on compensation for slavery? Isn't that a revival of the argument that colonialism is solely responsible for what's gone wrong in Africa? Of course I am fully aware that colonialism hasn't ceased to exist after independence. On the contrary! The exploitation of Africa by the West is far worse now than it has ever been.

W: Oh yes! But on the other hand foreign firms could not exploit Africa without the cooperation of some Africans. That's why, say in Nigeria, we have all those industrial white elephants, those vast factories that produce next to nothing. It's huge! Bottomless-stomached white elephants! Yes, they're all over the place! Nevertheless, I find the reparations theme very fascinating. First of all, it's such a wild idea! That I find attractive. Also it could have a concrete result. If, for instance, the whole industrial world, the former colonial powers, the former slaving powers suddenly say: "OK. We forgive all your debts. That's your reparation. From now on we are entering a new relationship. We wipe the past clean and establish a totally new economic relationship. We are going to be strict, and it's going to be a *quid pro quo*... You sell, we pay—in order to get what you're selling." It's a curious thing, but a wild idea like this might just work...

U: Maybe that's the way to finally get rid of these eternally strangulating loans.

W: Thank you. For that reason I don't dismiss it outright. But I agree. It's a debatable notion, a very controversial notion.

U: Well, to begin with, you can't just isolate the trans-Atlantic slave trade as the West's one big crime. What about the Aztecs, or the Incas, or the Australian Aboriginals? The West would have to compensate the whole world, and if that's carried out, there would be nothing left of the West! Although that might not be a bad thing, it is simply not feasible!

W: And then how to work it out? It's very complex.

U: And in fairness to the West you have to admit that they have had no monopoly on genocide! What about Idi Amin! Bokassa! What about the long catalogue of atrocities carried out by Africans against Africans?

W: Oh yes! And then we would have to talk about the Arab slave trade which was every bit as atrocious as the European one. I have always said that there must be no double standards! No double standards! If we're going to have reparations, it's a very dangerous, two-edged weapon. But if it can be handled in such a way that the West will get tired of the noise say: "OK. We forgive your debts; go away! Now we're starting all over again. It's a new relationship" That would be a very interesting development.

U: An utopia!

W: But a fascinating exercise!

Sophie Oluwole
"THE MAKING OF A PHILOSOPHER"

U: There are not many people who have tried to study and define Yoruba philosophy. This is surprising because you might say that those of us who study the art, the literature, the religion of the Yoruba people are studying various manifestations, symptoms perhaps, of the basic Yoruba interpretation of life. And yet philosophy was introduced rather late into Nigerian universities and most Nigerian philosophers seem more interested in Greek or British philosophy than in African philosophy. I am curious therefore to hear from you how you became interested in the subject and what problems you faced on the long road towards becoming a leading authority in Yoruba philosophy. First tell me something about your background.

S: Well, I was born in Igbara-Oke, a town that lies on the border between Ilesha and Ondo.

U: I know the place well. In the fifties and early sixties it was a favorite stop-over for truck drivers on the way to Benin City. The road side restaurants sold the best pounded yam and the best bush meat... I enjoyed many wonderful meals there.

S: Yes, that is true. Unfortunately our people lost that trade when the shorter Lagos-Benin road was built further south. Nowadays that market has almost disappeared.

U: What did your father do?

Photo courtesy of Sophie Oluwole

S: He was a trader. He first went down to Lagos in 1910, buying clothes. Then, in 1912, he established his trade in Igbara-Oke and he would walk to Onitsha...

U: ...walk all the way to Onitsha?

S: Yes, in those days there were no trucks. Traders used to trek with a group
      of carriers. So for many years he would walk between Igbara-Oke and
      Onitsha which was even then the largest market in West Africa. My
      mother was a trader in Igbara-Oke. She was also a dyer and a weaver. She
      must be close to a hundred years old now because her first child was born
      in 1918. She had eight children altogether. Four of them died... I am her
      last born. My mother was a very short woman. That's why she married
      rather late. She still looked like a child when everyone in her age group
      was getting married. She told me that she married about four years later
      than her peers.

U: Did you still know your grandparents?

S: Yes, my grandfather came from Benin. My father was born in Igbara-Oke,
      but my grandfather came from Benin in about 1850. He was already a
      married man then, with at least five wives. He had been a high ranking
      official in the Oba's palace in Benin. Igbara-Oke was part of the Benin
      Kingdom then; in fact it belonged to the Oba's mother because the Oba
      divided the Kingdom among members of the family. So when there were
      reports that Ogedengbe was raiding Igbara-Oke...

U: You mean Ogedengbe, the famous Ijesa warrior?

S: Yes ... and so it became necessary to send somebody to keep watch...;
      somebody to act as a kind of 'Resident' or 'Governor', and look after the
      interests of the Oba. In those days the Chief of Igbara-Oke could not
      make any decision without consulting my grandfather.

U: What about your father's mother. Was she a Yoruba woman?

S: No. As a matter of fact, she was the daughter of another Benin 'Gover-
      nor' who resided in Ogotun, a few kilometers away. Ogotun was also
      under the protection of the Oba of Benin... My father married the
      daughter of a man who accompanied my grandfather from Benin. That
      man, my grandfather, married a Yoruba woman. So only my maternal
      grandmother was Yoruba, and I am actually an Edo woman except that I
      was born and bred in Igbara-Oke.

U: Did your father speak Yoruba or Edo?

S: My father grew up speaking Yoruba, but he made sure that he went back to Benin to learn Edo. My mother could not really speak Edo. She was a very shy woman. She understood Edo, but she could not speak it.

U: Did you consider yourself Yoruba or Edo as a child? Or didn't you really think about that?

S: I did. I thought of myself as an Edo girl because throughout my primary school years the Oba of Benin would stop in Igbara-Oke whenever he travelled to Ibadan. You remember that Benin was part of the Western Region of Nigeria then, and the Oba of Benin had to attend the House of Chiefs in Ibadan. So whenever he travelled on that road, he'd send a message some days ahead to my father, and as from seven o'clock in the morning all the Edo people in Igbara-Oke would wait on the road side, drumming and dancing, with a banner, saying: "Welcome, Oba of Benin!" There were about ten Edo families in the town and the local people referred to us as *Ado Igbara*.

U: *Ado* meaning *Edo*?

S: Yes, that's how they pronounced it. And even the local people would come and gather on that day, because we had different drumming and different dancing ... Many of them were interested or curious enough to forego their jobs, and enjoy the Edo community's festivity.

U: Were you singing in Edo?

S: No, we were singing in Yoruba. From his car, the Oba would wave, hold a brief talk with my father, and then drive away. He did not stop in Igbara-Oke on the way back to Benin. Only once did he appear mysteriously on his way from Ibadan... I remember that night well, though I was still a small girl. We were sitting in our house and we suddenly saw the Oba. I was frightened because I had never seen him leave his car, and he was totally unexpected. My father immediately took him into his private room, and told us to keep away. What happened, apparently, was that there had been an accident involving the Oba's car about five kilometers away from Igbara-Oke. So the Oba found his way to our house to seek help...

U: Was that Akenzua II?

S: Yes, it was Akenzua II. My father then arranged for a mechanic to go to the site of the accident and repair the car. He found the driver in a great state of desperation, having searched in vain for the Oba. Naturally he was relieved to see the Oba, but as soon as he got back to Benin he resigned his position! Anyway, as a small girl, and although I never learned the language, I always referred to myself an Edo girl. Of course I understood a little, but I could not speak it. My sisters speak Edo very well and so does my only brother, a famous journalist with the *Daily Times* in Lagos. He has now retired and he lives in Benin. You know him. His name is Ebenezer Williams.

U: What names were you given by your parents? What does the initial "B" stand for? Is it a Yoruba name or a Bini name?

S: It is Yoruba. Bosede means "Born on Sunday." And I was also named Olayemi, which is Yoruba again, meaning "Dignity befits/becomes me" or "I feel comfortable with dignity."

U: And how did you get Sophie? It is unusual in Yoruba country.

S: My parents didn't think of such a name, of course. But we had a headmaster who was also a friend of the family. I suppose he came to the house often because there were several beautiful young girls, and he was unmarried. I was very tiny then. He liked me, and he gave me biscuits. I followed him everywhere, and I ended up living with him at the age of eight. When I started school and was to be baptized, he told my father to name me Sophia. My father didn't even know what the name meant. But the headmaster chose it because he thought that I was a clever girl. It is funny, but many years later my supervisor for my PhD thesis at the University of Ibadan said: "Why should you call yourself Sophia just because you have decided to become a philosopher?" And I said to him: "I was given that name long before I knew what it meant." I remember we used to spell it with an 'f' like the capital of Bulgaria.

U: What kind of naming ceremony would you have had? Was it like the Yoruba one where you give the baby various things to taste—kolanut to teach him that life can be bitter, pepper to teach him that life can hurt, and honey to teach him that sweetness often follows pain?

S: It would have been similar, only some of the items would have been different. For example, in Benin we hardly conduct any rituals without including coconut or snails among the offerings. Snails symbolize peace and harmony. It moves slowly. It is soft. It doesn't fight, it doesn't harm people. And when you break the shell there is that beautiful bluish water. There used to be abundance of snails in Benin. In the olden days, when you cooked food and the meat was not enough, you would just go behind the house and pick a dozen snails. They were everywhere. But today they're gone, and Bini people buy them from their Yoruba neighbors.

U: So you were not given any Edo names?

S: No, but my siblings were... Before my time there was some nostalgia—an urge to go back to Benin, and even my father's grandchildren were given Edo names, all of them. At that time he would have loved to return to Benin. For one thing, he was not fully accepted in Igbara-Oke perhaps because he reminded them of the 'colonial' rule of Benin. There was an incident that nearly forced even my father to leave Igbara-Oke. My brother attended Government College Ibadan, as you know. During the first term he identified himself as a Benin boy, and that was enough to get Igbara-Oke angry and complaining. "Why should he call himself a Benin boy? Was he not born and bred in Igbara-Oke? And his father as well?"

U: I gather that your parents were both Christians.

S: Yes, they were Anglicans. My father was baptized in 1912, and my mother in 1915—just before they got married. In fact you could say that Igbara-Oke had become a Christian town by those dates.

U: That means, I suppose, that you grew up without knowing anything about Yoruba religion.

S: Not quite true. In our compound we had my grandfather's Olokun shrine. All the traditional dances were still performed for him annually, and all the devotees of other Orisa would come and celebrate with us. For us children it was very, very interesting, and in the evening when nobody was watching, we would imitate the Olorisa. We would dramatize the ritual with all the songs and dances. But my father, a Christian, was always discouraging us. He was always cautioning us not to go and watch 'pagan' ceremonies. As Christians we were supposed to stay clear of all that. To him it was like worshipping the 'devil'. But we would always sneak out whenever there was an Orisa ceremony, and lie about our whereabouts when asked. One morning during our prayer session my father let us know that he knew we had been lying. He added that he was tired of warning us, and he was not going speak to us about attending 'pagan' ceremonies anymore. But he had just one more thing to say, namely, that we should all remember that on the day of judgment, God would select his own children while the devil would also select his. Some of us would claim that we're God's children, but the devil would say: "No, you are mine." Then there would be an argument. God would say: "They are my children" and the devil would say: "They belong to me." And then the devil would have to prove his case, and this is how: "Do you know that each time you are watching the Olorisa the devil is there with his camera, taking the picture of all the worshippers? So on judgment day, all the devil will have to do is to bring out his pictures. When they have identified you on the photographs, you will be asked if the ceremony you attended was for God or for the devil. And since you mustn't lie, you will have to confess that it was for the devil." From that day on, we never went to see another Orisa ceremony, and for years afterwards I was so afraid. And at night I wondered how I could capture those photographs from the devil because although I had stopped going to the ceremonies, what of the pictures he had already taken?

U: Did you go to school in Igbara-Oke?

S: Yes, I finished my primary school. Standard VI. Then I went to Ile-Ife to attend what was known as 'Girls School'. It was only a two-year course, but it was so intensive that you could come out with a Class IV certificate. In those days the full secondary school was six years, but you could leave with a Class IV certificate and find a job fairly easily. Or you could go back to school and work for your Class VI certificate. I went on to Women Training College in Ilesha. It had been set up by the British on the eve of Nigerian independence, and it was wholly financed by the British government. 13 out of our 15 teachers were Brits, and every single thing we used in that school was imported from Britain—biros, paper, even our uniforms! Everything! After my training I began to teach first in Ogotun, and later on in Ibadan.

U: But your teaching career didn't last long. When did you go to university?

S: When I went to Moscow in 1963

U: You went to Moscow to study philosophy?

S: No, no. My husband got a scholarship and I went with him. I wanted to study economics, but I would have had to do a year of preparatory classes—mainly in Russian... But after one year, my husband decided to leave the Soviet Union, so I never had a chance to do the do the intended course...

U: Why did he decide to leave? The life style? Politics?

S: He found the language too hard. He wasn't a language man. As for me, I picked it up quickly...

U: What was life like in Moscow? On the campus? Did you have Russian friends?

S: We lived in what they called "Cheriomushky"—a whole house full of foreign students. Maybe I was biased coming from a completely free country, but I found everything terribly regimented. You could not, for instance, freely listen to the BBC. If you wanted to visit somebody you had to deposit your passport with the porter. You had to tell him which room you were going, and whom you were going to see. They recorded the time you left and the time you returned. Another issue was food. Rice was rare. Sometimes you'd see people queuing in front of a supermarket because it had been announced that rice was going to be available. After three or four hours someone would come out and ask why we were waiting. When we said we were waiting to by rice we'd be told there was no rice. Just like that, and we'd disperse without saying anything... In 1964 I went to the Studienkolleg in Cologne, and my husband went to the United States to continue his studies. I didn't have A-levels so I couldn't enter a German university directly. I was required to do another preparatory year. It was more or less like what I had to do in Moscow, except that this time I studied German. I did well, but I didn't enter a German university although I had been offered a full scholarship to study philology. I went instead to join my husband in the US. But after three months I decided to return home to be with my children. I already had three children then. But before leaving I made sure I gained admission to the University of Lagos.

U: You went on a long Odyssey abroad that in the end didn't get you anywhere. But I suppose that it was all to the good. If you had stuck it out overseas and completed one of those courses you would never have become a philosopher.

S: That's right. And when I got to Lagos I was still not thinking about philosophy. I had been admitted for BA Education and my main subject was to be English. But in those days the University was very relaxed about things. As long as you had a letter of admission you could go around and shop for subjects and majors. You could study in any department as long as the department was willing to take you. I did not really want to get back into teaching. I first decided to do English, but some of the students said to me: "Madam, you better be careful. If you want to do English you may never end up with a degree from this university." The reason, I was told, was that Wole Soyinka was their lecturer and he had passed only two students that year! So I ran away. I didn't want to waste my time because I already had three children to consider. I continued searching for the subjects. I had 0-levels in history and geography, and I needed a third subject. Philosophy was the only department that was willing to take me because it was the only department that did not require prerequisites. The way things worked was that you could start your degree by studying three subjects. After the first year you could drop one subject, and declare yourself a 'Combined Honors student, studying two subjects. Or if you did very well in one subject, you could declare yourself a 'Single Honors' student. I had intended to drop philosophy. But at the end of the first year my worst subject was history. I discovered that I didn't have the retentive memory of an historian. So I dropped history and decided I would try to aim for a Single Honors in geography. If you could score more than 60% in one subject, you would be allowed to do Single Honors in that subject. At the end of the second year I qualified to do geography, but I also qualified to do philosophy. I got 62 % in geography and 64 % in philosophy, and I found it difficult to make a choice. Geography was willing to take me, but at that stage I had already discovered my love for philosophy. The problem, however, was that the philosophy department was understaffed, and therefore could not accept a Single Honors student. The good news was that a new lecturer was expected shortly. I decided to run two Single Honors courses concurrently, knowing that I would choose philosophy in the end. So as soon as the new lecturer arrived in the Philosophy Department I dropped geography. It became very embarrassing because the geography professor said: "But she is my student!"

U: So you got into philosophy almost by accident. Or was it Esu blocking all the other roads on which you attempted to travel until you hit upon the right one? What finally attracted you to philosophy?

S: It was my nature. I found it so easy. I wasn't good at learning facts, but I have an analytical mind; I could look at issues critically. I could take a sentence and tear it to pieces. So I was comfortable...

U: What kind of philosophy did they teach you at the University of Lagos? I suppose it wasn't African philosophy.

S: No, no. During the first year we did Greek philosophy starting with Thales and down to Plato and Aristotle. The second year we did British philosophy—Hume, Locke, Hobbes—all of them. In the final year we did British philosophy again with the one exception our English head could not ignore, Immanuel Kant. That was the only German philosopher we studied. I came out top of the class, Second Class Upper Division, which was the best you could hope for in any Honors Subject in those days.

U: What could you do with a philosophy degree in Nigeria then?

S: I had to get a teaching job. I asked to be posted to Igbara-Oke because I hadn't been home for many years, and I wanted to spend time with my parents who were getting old. I taught geography and history in the local High School. But then a telegram came from my head of Department in Lagos asking me to come and see him. He showed me an advertisement in the *Daily Times* asking students who had graduated with an Upper Second Honors degree to apply for a scholarship. I hadn't seen this ad at home, and it was now past the dead line. But Mr. A.G. Elgood spoke to the registrar, and he agreed to accept my late application. Four months later I became a university scholar. That was in 1972. As a graduate assistant in those days I became a senior staff member of the university immediately. Unfortunately Mr. Elgood who had been so nice to me left, and I had to wait for a new supervisor before I could register for my Masters Degree. Fortunately Dr. J.B. Danquah Jr. joined the staff and he supervised my MA. My topic was "Transformational Grammar and Philosophical Analysis."

U: You will have to explain to a layman like me what that means.

S: There was this Noam Chomsky who tried to prove that grammar and philosophical analysis were identical. He broke away from traditional grammar and created a new grammar which he called 'Transformational Grammar'. He said that in a language there is a surface structure that does not actually give you the true meaning of a sentence; the true meaning is the deep structure. So Chomsky claimed that trying to distinguish between the grammatical form and the logical form of a sentence was really a philosophical process. For him grammar and philosophical analysis are the same thing, if it is properly done. I wanted to refute that. That was the focus of my thesis. Up to a point Chomsky is right. But when it comes to metaphysical issues the grammarian has nothing to say. For example take the word 'shadow'. For Chomsky it is something you can analyze. Shadow is a noun. It refers to an object. But the point is this: Is shadow a physical object or is it abstract? You can see shadow, but it is not a concrete object. So what is the true nature of shadow? Let's talk about another example: The mind. What is the mind? Physical? Non-physical? Spiritual? Here, you are really talking metaphysics. That is not grammar. So I tried to show that we might actually start from identical notes because the philosopher actually talks of the grammatical forms as being misleading. Gilbert Ryle, for example, has shown that some grammatical forms are systematically misleading as to their true meaning. He once wrote a paper called "Systematically Misleading Expressions", but his most popular work was *The Concept of the Mind* in which he tried to show that we may try to say something but the intention is different from the meaning received by somebody else. For example, if I say: "Punctuality is worthy of praise", you may mistakenly take it that 'Punctuality' is the name of a person. I finished my Masters in 1974. But I had to wait a long time for my PhD because there was nobody to supervise. In 1976 a new Head, Prof. G. Chatallian, arrived from the United States. He came with all the arrogance of a typical foreigner. He told us that he intended to make the Philosophy Department of the University of Lagos the best in the world. Apparently the way he thought to achieve that was to remove all African lecturers from the department. He said this publicly, and in the first year he sacked Dr. Danquah. And when Dr. Danquah left, he held a staff meeting and said to us (all Nigerians) that we shouldn't be too happy because actually his recommendation to the University had been that we should all be sacked! But the University had said that he could not sack all of us at the same time; that he should do the sacking one faculty at a time. He said the next one on the list was Dr. Idoniboye, the most senior member of faculty. I was the most junior, but I just had to ask him: "Why are you sacking us? Is it because we lack competence?" And the answer was: "No. There are many competent people in the world, but I want the best." Then I asked: "Who determines who is the best?" He said he was the one—by virtue of his position. Then I said that if I were the head of the department, I would say that he was incompetent. He said I should wait until I became the head of department before I could do so. I asked him what he expected us to do when we lost our jobs as we were all married with children. He said we should not worry because he would give us all letters of recommendation to the new State Universities that were emerging everywhere in those days. Then I said: "Yes, that is a good one. I can just imagine what you are going to write: "Mrs. Oluwole was so good that I fired her!" It became a big tussle and I had to go to the people in authority. And this was the man who was to supervise my PhD! I had first wanted to write on witchcraft and he said I would need somebody who could read Yoruba. I went to Wande Abimbola and enlisted his support. Then I handed in my proposal to Prof. Chatallian. A year later he called me and said that I ought to have noticed that he had not been looking at my papers. I said: "Yes, but why?" He said that I was too rude! And he said that was why he felt he was not going to look at my papers.

U: What? All because of that earlier incident?

S: No. There was something every day! We were always coming up against each other. For example, there was a time when we were going to reorganize the syllabus. Prof. Chatallian said he was going to teach a course on the philosophy of non-violence. I said I was going to teach the philosophy of violence. He objected, saying: "Nigeria does not need violence." I said: "Who determines that? And secondly, you are a philosopher. You are not supposed to be dogmatic. We should give the students the option to choose. I have nothing against your teaching the philosophy of non-violence, but you must allow me to teach the philosophy of violence. He said there is nothing like that. I went to my office and picked out a book entitled *The Philosophy of Violence.* So we were always having conflicts. There came a time that when I greeted him, he would not answer. But I continued to greet him. It's a subtle way of being rude. After a while he became uncomfortable. He called me to the office and said: "Mrs. Oluwole, why are you so stubborn?" I said: "What do you mean?" He said: "For the past six weeks you have been greeting me. Have you noticed that I've refused to answer you? Then I said: "Oh, I am sorry. I haven't noticed that you have not been answering me." His response was: "1 am telling you now that I will not answer because you are being rude. So you should stop greeting me." I said: "That is interfering with my personal freedom. I give you the option to answer or not to answer when I greet you. But it is my decision whether I want to greet you or not. I am not asking you to answer." The next day he answered me. The problem was that he was the only person in the department who could supervise my PhD because he was the only professor. So I had to look elsewhere. I went to Ibadan, and Dr. Bodunrin told me that he would accept me. So I registered to do "The Rational Basis of Yoruba Ethics." But he said there was no way I could do a PhD on anything relating to African philosophy under his supervision. So I was forced to look for a new topic. I looked at the work of Professor R. M. Hare who had a strange theory that was similar to Kant's—though he claimed that there was no similarity. Well, his theory was that if you take some moral terms, and examine how they function in human language, and then examine the logic of their function, you will have two principles of understanding which will now serve as logical principles. These principles will then define the language of morals. This was the thesis of his first book, *The Language of Morals.* His next book was *Freedom and Reason.* The actual thesis of the book was that every human being would prefer to do as he pleases, but reason tells us there should be consensus. But then how do you reconcile freedom and reason?

I called my own thesis *Meta-Ethics and the Golden Rule.* My argument was that all formulations of moral principles which—like Kant's—claim a position of universality, are formulations of the golden rule. The golden rule is usually defined as "do unto others what you want others to do unto you". People have always defined it as the supreme moral principle. But in my own analysis I tried to show that it was not a law, but merely an attempt to define morality. And once you view it like that, you don't have to use it to find out whether an action is right or wrong because it is actually not a canon of moral action; it is a definition of rational behavior. Morality to me is a discipline; it is something you can describe in vivid terms. When I think of salt, I think of its chemical properties. If I think of water, I am talking about an object. But whether or not my own personality as a subject comes into it—that is another matter. At least my aim is to look at water and to know *what* it is. But when you talk about morality you have to assume the existence of at least two human beings and their relationship. So it is purely a classifying definition; I am not giving a law. I am not telling you how to behave. I'm merely telling you that morality is about human actions and human relations. And if you want to study human relations, in most cases the golden rule will fall into place. So that was my PhD thesis in 1984.

U: I heard you got into conflict with your supervisor at Ibadan also.

S: Well, it had a lot to do with Prof. Bodunrin, even outside my thesis. I had started the Philosophy Students Association of Nigeria in Lagos, and I was its first president. The Association had spread to all the universities that taught philosophy, and we organized an annual Philosophy Week. So I had frequent meetings with Prof. Bodunrin for discussions on this and that. But we hardly ever agreed on anything. Even when he was supervising my thesis, he could see that I was unhappy because I couldn't openly voice my opinions. In the end I felt as if I was writing *his* thesis, not mine. So when I had the oral examination he was there with Prof. Wiredu of Ghana and Professor Sodipo. When they had finished examining me I had to go out so that they could discuss my performance. After about 45 minutes I was invited back into the hall, and my supervisor said: "Well, congratulations, Mrs. Oluwole. You have done very well, and I think we will now give you the authority to say all the nonsense you have been wanting to say because with a PhD people will have to take you seriously."

U: Well, I guess the man was honest at least. But now that you have told me how you cut your path through the university jungle to obtain your PhD, I want to know how you got interested in Yoruba philosophy, and how you finally devoted yourself to the study of it after so many detours and side issues.

S: It was Dr. Danquah who first got me interested in African philosophy. But he was onto that Egyptology thing, trying to trace or affirm the African origin of Egyptian religion.

U: Another detour!

S: Yes. Although his father had written *The Akan Concept of God*, he had not actually stressed that point. The grand old man was not interested in proving to the West that Thales had borrowed the concept of God or mathematics or whatever from Egypt.

U: It is still fashionable. Cheikh Anta Diop and so many others still claim that there was a West African civilization from which the Greeks derived their ideas.

S: Yes, but I had a feeling right from the start that if it is true that the Greeks came and stole African philosophy, what happened to the Africans and their thought? You can steal my ideas, but you can't steal the brain from my head. Forget the borrowings. I don't mind what they took. But do we have anything left *today* that I can show? So my first concern was to find records of Yoruba thought. I went to the Yoruba Department and asked them whether I could have access to some record of pre-colonial Yoruba thought. There was an Egba poet called Sobo Arobiodu. I had heard about him even as a small girl, and my father would often quote his poems and his proverbs. I was excited to find that Prof. S.A. Babalola and Moses Lijadu had recorded him, and that I could listen to this material. But I was disappointed to discover that he had become a Christian and was talking about Jesus! He was hardly a Yoruba thinker! But the Yoruba Department had no other records predating him. So I decided to look into Odu Ifa, Ifa texts. To be honest, I had no hope of finding 'philosophy' there. But at least I knew that these texts predated Christianity. At first I found it difficult to read it properly; the language is not the common everyday language, and I had no training in that level of the Yoruba language. It took me hours to figure out the first lines! But when I had worked out the meaning of the first poem, I was thoroughly surprised to see that there was nothing religious or supernatural! It was a purely secular argument! There was a verse, for example, about the relationship between an adult and a child.

U: Ifa uses the famous imagery which shows us that the arm of a child may be too short to reach the shelf under the rafters, but the hand of the adult is too large to fit into the neck of the (storage) gourd.

S: That's right. So it explains with simple logic that adults and children are interdependent; that none is superior to the other, and that each has his own value.

U: Which is a philosophical statement...

S: Yes, but I realized immediately that I would have an uphill task. If I called Ifa philosophy, I would encounter a lot of criticism. People would say that oral literature did not qualify as philosophy because there is no author. They would say it was not a vehicle for philosophy. There was this notion that there is no room for criticism or argument in oral traditions and poetry, and as such, oral traditions cannot be treated as intellectual source material. There was also the view that although Africans sometimes say things that were philosophical, they did not have a tradition of philosophy. Some of the views were not even as articulate, but they were strongly held anyway. They simply say: "Philosophy is scientific, and Africans are not scientific." I was able to use Ifa to debunk all that. The more I looked at Ifa the more I saw that all those things which they claimed could not be found in African thought are there. In Ifa we find arguments, we find criticism; Ifa is open, and you can do a lot with the system.

U: They will probably tell us that Africans had no system!

S: I was corning to that. Do you know the work of Allan Wood? He was a young man who wanted to write on the development of Bertrand Russell's philosophy. But he died young... He had only written about ten pages or so, but this beginning was a masterpiece. And Russell himself later included them in his own book, *My Philosophical Development*. Allan Wood showed that Russell had a good understanding of the way the Western mind worked. He knew that they were lovers of systems; that they liked to create systems. But the only system they like is the hypothetical deductive one; that is, you start from basic axioms, and then go deductively to arrive at conclusions. They believe that anybody who cannot show that a conclusion is derived deductively from basic axioms is not capable of a philosophical inquiry. That is a widespread belief in the West, but Russell also said it was a fiction of the mind; that thinking does not have to start with an axiom and end with a proposition. He believes that we cannot demand that our axioms be accepted as certainties. But philosophers who have been brought up in a Western System don't realize that they have been trapped. They always start by asking for "the facts." When you put up a piece of oral tradition they ask, "What are the facts?" Can you move from premise one to two? You must prove things logically and draw your conclusion from the premise." Well, this is an approach that is fine for mathematics, but it is not even adequate for even science. Scientific theorems are not absolute. No fact of experience logically entails a theory. Sentences that express causal relationships do not have to be logically related to one another. David Hume actually taught us that in science there is no logical relationship. When we say "Fire causes heat", heat is not logically deduced from fire. It is just a matter of experience. Regardless of the validity or otherwise of the Western approach, I wish to maintain that the validity of African philosophy does not ever have to rest on the West's formulae. In other words, even if the Western approach were valid, African philosophy does not have to be based on the West's deductive systems.

U: Now tell me one thing. Are you still the only one trying to establish Yoruba thought as a philosophy? Or are there others working in this field? Do you still come up against a lot of opposition?

S: There are now quite a number of lecturers and students who want to establish African philosophy. But the fundamental difference is: what is the basis for their claims? If you look at my book *Witchcraft, Reincarnation and the God-Head,* my claims are based on what people are saying in the street. How they describe a witch or what reincarnation means to them. But one must always be very careful because we can never be sure what recent ideas—for example Christian ideas—have influenced people's thinking. People are sometimes not even aware of such influences. For example, there is a current belief among Yoruba theologians that you cannot become an ancestor unless you have lived a good life. Prof. Awolalu at Ibadan said so in his book. My concern is with the sense in which he is using the word ancestor. You see, in the Yoruba conception your father and your mother are your ancestors. Once you have lived to an old age you become an ancestor. And when you have problems you can always go and pray to your ancestors. The conception of a holy life has nothing to do with it. Whatever one's father was in his earthly life—an armed robber or whatever—he is still one's father. I cannot imagine that a Yoruba will say, "My father died in prison, therefore I will pray to another man's 'holy' father. These theologians are confusing ancestors with sainthood. But to declare that you cannot be deified unless you are a saint is a distortion of the facts. Was Ogun the best man in the world?

U: None of the Orisa could be described as 'holy'. On the contrary, they were all too human. Some were violent, all committed serious faults during their earthly existence before their metamorphosis.

S: Exactly. So where did this idea of 'holiness' come from if not from an imposition of Christian ideas on Yoruba thought? But even the opposite can happen. Perhaps another good example is the argument that arose when the government considered cremating corpses in Lagos due of the shortage of land. The first people to protest were the bishops. They said cremation was against the Bible. I had to go on television with some of them and ask to see "Just where it says in the Bible that cremation is an offence. I am not denying it, but where is it written?" The argument was that when you cremate the dead, you are destroying God's handwork. My answer to that was: "Who is destroying God's handwork? Is it God who allows me to die, or is it the one who burns my dead body? After all, we are not talking about burning a living person. So if I die, and you bury me, am I not being destroyed?" I tried to let them see that the problem with the Lagos bishops was that they were imposing their Yoruba beliefs on Christianity. As an African, I cannot allow my father to be burnt, and this is simply because I know I must pray to him. What I am saying is that when you have a source that is dependable because it records what people said a long time ago, then we are on a much firmer ground on which to base a claim of an authentic African philosophy which predates colonial education. Ifa is the most ancient and reliable source we have. I have found that many times the Ifa verses contradict what we have been accepting as Yoruba belief. For example, we often assume that the Yoruba associate age with wisdom. The Ifa oracle states very clearly that a young boy can at times be wise. So it is not the prerogative of the elders to be the only wise ones in the society. Then there is the popular belief that masqueraders are ancestors who have returned. This worried me, and I wondered if my people could be so stupid as not to know that there were human beings beneath the masks! It was a relief to find that the Ifa oracle tells a very elaborate story about the origin of the *Egungun* masquerade, which makes it very clear that it is human beings wearing the masks.

U: I think that the myth of the naivety of the Yoruba women and children who are terrorized by the masks is a missionary invention. Yoruba women have always known that the masks have human carriers though of course, during the ritual the performer may become the ancestor as the ancestor may speak through him. Similarly the Orisa can speak through the priest who is possessed by him. Yoruba people have a great sensibility for the powers of the supernatural, but they are certainly not naive.

S: An ancient proverb says: "A masquerader dies during the day, and the news is hidden from his family. But even though we're supposed to believe he's a heavenly being, his parents will demand to see their son at the end of the day."

U: That is right. The Yoruba are very sophisticated people. They are neither hoodwinked nor intimidated by a fraudulent class of priests as the missionaries used to claim. The Yoruba are not fundamentalists; they understand the meaning of symbols, and they have a great deal of commonsense.

S: Yes. There is another proverb which says: "If you are being chased by a masquerade, keep running. Just as human beings get exhausted, so too, do those heavenly beings." What I am trying to say is that there are a lot of people working on African philosophy. But what they sometimes do is to take some western concepts—God, society, woman and what not— and then seek the equivalents in Yoruba thought. They go into various customs and proverbs and look for a way of justifying the existence of these in African thought.

U: Archdeacon Lucas and Dr. Idowu come to mind.

S: Well, I don't mind them. But my own approach is different. I say let us examine what is in Ifa. Let us see what the oracle says, let us look at the style, and let us look at the methodology. Let us look at the philosophy. I want to look at the aims of the traditional intellectual Yoruba artists and the intricacies of the Yoruba language. I want to look at the forms. It is both natural and tempting, because of our training, to apply Western principles and yardstick in our study of African philosophy. But if you

209

do that, you are not going on a journey of discovery; you are going on a journey of invention. But I don't want to *invent*. I want to *discover* African philosophy.

Richard Olaniyan

"THE PROCESS OF REDISCOVERY"

U: I know that you were born in Osogbo. What is the name of your compound?

RO: My compound is Ile Onisigidi.

U: A dangerous name! How did your people acquire it?

RO: Our compound used to be known as Ile Abiawe. Alawe indicates that the ancestor for which the compound was named was born during the time of fasting. But Onisigidi dates back to the time of Ibadan imperialism. This was when our great grandparents placed a *sigidi*, a mud figure that is endowed with magical powers, in front of the compound, just by the compound gate. As you know, *sigidi* is believed to be capable of destroying one's enemy—sometimes by causing bad dreams and thus disturbing the enemy's sleep. The *sigidi* in front of our compound is said to have chased off the arrogant agents of the Olubadan of Ibadan—hence the new name, Ile Onisigidi.

U: Are you referring to the time of the Fulani wars when the Ibadan army set up its camp outside Osogbo?

RO: Even much later than that. The Ibadan saw themselves as the rulers of territories like Osogbo, Ede, Ido Osun, Ofatedo and so on.

U: The Ibadan filled the power vacuum that had arisen after the decline of the ancient capital of Oyo. After the destruction of Oyo by the Fulani it was the Ibadan army that held the Fulani Jihad at bay. Twice they defeated the cavalry from the North, just outside Osogbo. So naturally

Photo courtesy of Richard Olaniyan

they claimed a leadership position. Even today the Olubadan must confirm the installation of the Timi of Ede.

RO: Yes, but they became very arrogant. The Olubadan—Oba and the military ruler of the city of Ibadan—and some other senior chiefs from

Ibadan would send their agents to Osogbo to carry out all kinds of rapacious activities. They could plunder our farms and even take our wives with impunity. So my people made a *sigidi* and placed it in front of the compound. It had only one hand. Behind the *sigidi*, there was a fence of mats. One evening, some strong young men, equipped with *atori* (whips), took up position behind the fence, and when the Ibadan agents passed by our compound on their way to the palace, they were whipped by the *sigidi*! The attack was so effective that they never dared to pass our compound again, and soon they stopped coming to Osogbo altogether. And indeed today, when passing by our compound on the way to the Ataoja's palace, every band of drummers, including the ones accompanying a Quarter Chief, must acknowledge our compound by reciting: *O d'Onisigidi, kan'se. O d'Onisigidi, kan'se, kan'se, kan'se...* (You've reached the Onisigidi compound. Stamp your feet, stamp your feet).

U: Both your parents were Moslems. Did you see Orisa ceremonies in your compound when you were a child, or had all that disappeared?

RO: I saw Obatala festivals. I liked to participate in the propitiation rites because I liked to eat the *moimoi*, ground black-eye bean paste. We had Egungun. Several of my uncles were blacksmiths, so of course, we had Ogun. We still have a couple of blacksmiths in the compound now, but they have become Moslems. So they employ somebody non-Moslems to perform the annual dog sacrifice. I have never told you this before, but when I was six or seven years old, I tried to become a professional drummer! There was an elderly man in our compound who played the *gangan*. I apprenticed myself to him and learned to play the accompanying rhythms on the *gudugudu*. My teacher wasn't a very successful drummer. He certainly wasn't a crowd puller, and he didn't have a band of his own. He was a solo performer who appeared at religious festivals uninvited and earned himself a few shillings by playing the *oriki* of the Orisa to whose ceremony he had invited himself. I remember following him to Adigun, one of the sacred spots of the Osun River, where barren women went to pray for children. My mother used to go to that spot before she became a Moslem. Looking back on it now, I wonder how serious a drummer I was. I was probably more interested in the different kinds of food that we could have during the religious ceremonies. At that time I was particularly fond of *adigun*, mashed yam with palm oil, a favorite dish with Yoruba children. This is also known as the favorite dish of Tortoise, the hero of

213

Yoruba folktales. I was often easily distracted, and due to that, I would miss my beat and my teacher would knock me on the head!

U: Did your parents become Moslems when they were grownups?

RO: Yes. My father lived in Ghana as a trader when he was a young man. When the going got rough he returned to Ososgbo and became a farmer. He remained a farmer until his death in 1986. My mother became a Moslem after she married my father. She was an *iyan*, pounded yam, seller. She prepared *iyan* with the help of my sister and various other female relatives. Then she wrapped the balls in leaves and sent the girls out to sell them along Station Road. They went out at about 12 o'clock, and returned around four in the afternoon.

U: Who bought the pounded yam?

RO: It was bought by families who had prepared their own soup at home, but saved themselves work by purchasing my mother's *iyan*. There were hardly any restaurants in those days.

U: Did you grow up in one of those large traditional Yoruba compounds?

RO: Yes, I did! It was a large mud compound built around an open courtyard. The mud figure of Esu stood at the entrance and in the centre of the courtyard there was a big stone called *Ayale* which had the power to ward off evil. In the evening elderly people would sit with the children around *Ayale* and tell stories, especially on moonlit nights.

U: Story telling forms part of the education of every Yoruba child. But thinking back on the experience now, did you see it as education or as entertainment at the time?

RO: As a child I thought of it as pure entertainment. We had to sing, clap and sometimes dance! But there is no doubt that even without realizing it, we received a lot of cultural education in the process.

U: What kind of ideas and values were transmitted?

RO: Values of good and bad, the relationships between all things—living or otherwise; the roles of the gods in the universe as well as those of animals

214

and man in the ecosystem. We learned the names of trees, leaves and animals; we learned about rivers, and even the histories of different communities formed part of the stories.

U: Would you hear anything about the history of the Osogbo?

RO: The story teller could relate the role played by Osun as the protector of the children, for example.

U: There is one thing that is remarkable about Yoruba stories. Very often the evil doer is also the hero! I grew up on Grimm's Fairy Tales. In that European tradition good always triumphs over evil in the end. But in Yoruba stories *Ijapa,* Tortoise, is one who cheats everybody, he is mean, he is greedy, he can be cruel, but usually he gets away with it. Why is he so popular? Why is the villain the hero?

RO: I suppose *Ijapa* is popular because he has the courage to confront the most difficult situations; he challenges much stronger opponents; he uses his wit to get out of his troubles; he is a survivor! We sympathize with the underdog! It may also have to do with another characteristic of Yoruba society, namely the tendency to sympathize with the one who is guilty or is in trouble. People always intercede on behalf of the guilty one.

R: It's moderation.

U: Moderation forbids you to feel superior or self-righteous. Even an offender is somebody; he is somebody's child, and as such, he has human rights and deserves sympathy.

RO: There is sympathy for the weaker one. And people often enjoy it when the weaker one has the last laugh.

U: What other ways, apart from storytelling, were there to influence the behavior of the children? It seemed to me that in those days Yoruba families did not regiment their children in the way Europeans did a generation or two ago.

RO: The compound played several roles. The compound was a place of security. It provided security for men, women and children. Small children were never without protection. If the mother left to go to the farm or to fetch water, there would always be plenty of older women around to look after them, and they became an educational resource. Mostly it was the grandmothers who educated the children because they were always there. They taught them how to behave, how to run errands, how to be polite to older people, how to eat, what to say and what not to say. A whole gamut of cultural transmission took place without anybody being aware of it.

U: The education process was not so formal.

RO: That is what I mean...

U: How many children were there in your compound?

RO: At any time 25-30.

U: So you would have plenty of role models around while growing up. In the nuclear family the relationship between adults and children is rather tenser.

RO: Another learning process arose from the children's natural curiosity. We were very curious about everything the adults were doing and saying. So we were learning every minute of the day.

U: Yes, because you were *allowed* to listen. You were not sent out of the room when adults discussed a 'delicate' subject.

RO: We also have a way of controlling a child just by looking at him. It hurts you more than any other form of punishment; more than whipping! If your father gave you one of those looks particularly in public—it really hurts! When I have done it to my own boy, he has later come and begged me never to do so again; that in the future I should flog him rather than give him *that* look...

U: Another interesting device that Yoruba culture offers is that any conflict between parents and children will be settled—in public. In fact whatever conflict there is—you always bring people to plead... Whatever happened...

RO: And you have to forgive. I think that Yoruba are fond of keeping harmony and peace in their society rather than conflict, animosity or tension. I don't think they can endure crisis for very long. They are willing to make sacrifices in order to reestablish peace and harmony in their society...

U: Which means you don't exploit your advantage to the last...

RO: For if you do, you create disharmony; you prolong conflicts. I believe that ancient Yoruba society was a society without winners or losers; without victors or vanquished. We also have a saying: 'If you don't forget the quarrels of yesterday, you won't have anybody to play with today." They also say: "You don't fight to the end." You fight, yes, but never with the intention of killing or destroying the other person. You have made your point and that is enough.

U: The remarkable tolerance that Yoruba have shown in political or religious situations may ultimately spring from such everyday situations.

RO: I think you are right. If one creates pockets of animosity, one disrupts the harmony of the entire community. And creativity and resourcefulness—in fact all the positive human virtues—thrive much better in a settled, harmonious community. The Yoruba did not want their energies dissipated with less important things.

U: How could you find the concentration to worship your Orisa if you desecrated your life with too many petty quarrels? In the fifties I knew many Olorisa—many priests of Sango and Erinle. Theses priests had set themselves very clear priorities in life. They had limited objectives, but they pursued those with great intensity. Then there is also the institution of sacred kingship. You must have seen Oba Adenle in office. He was the first literate Oba in Osogbo and the first Christian one. He found no difficulty in accepting the fact that the religion of his people must also be his religion. He would go to the mosque, to all the different churches and he would celebrate all the Orisa—Osun, Sango, Ogun, the Ifa festival, the ancestral masquerades...

RO: It is a role the Oba accepts freely and willingly; he has to commit himself not only to the community of the living, but also to the community of the ancestors. That is very important. They are not physically with us, but they are part and parcel of us. The Oba' s palace is the *orimu*—the source of the community. That is why he is not only the political head, but also the spiritual and cultural head. He is the embodiment of tradition.

U: All these values were somehow transmitted to you during your childhood, even though your father was a Moslem. Did he send you to the Koran school?

RO: He did not, but I was curious myself. When I was a small boy I spent my time helping my father on the farm. But I had a younger cousin who went to the Koran school, and whenever we were going to the farm together he would recite his verses from the Koran to practice, and I would memorize them. I had no idea what it all meant, but I was fascinated by the sound and rhythm of the poetry. At the time, even my cousin had no idea what he was reciting.

U: I am surprised that your father allowed you to go to a Catholic School.

RO: He didn't. I got there by sheer accident. It began on the Empire Day celebration of 1946. My father and I were going to the farm. I had never heard of Empire Day and had never seen such a collection of school children, well dressed, marching in their starched uniform! I begged my father to let me stop and watch a little while. But after about five minutes, he tapped me on the head and said: 'Let's go.' I started weeping and wept all the way to the farm. Something happened to me on that day. I think I had almost come to a decision that whatever it was these children were doing, I wanted to be part of it. On the farm I met an older cousin who helped my father. He was someone I could confide in. I told him what I had seen. He explained Empire Day to me, and said that one had to go to school to be part of it. He was sympathetic, but he didn't know what he could do about it.

In those days my father used to send us to town in turns to pay his contribution to the farmer's savings club. In December 1946 it was my cousin's turn, but I begged him quietly to let me go instead. This was the time when children had to register to be admitted to school. When I got home I told my mother that my father had sent me home to attend school. My mother, being a very kind woman and always obedient to her husband, bought me a school uniform, a slate and chalk and off I went. Meanwhile my father wondered why I had not returned to the farm, and he came home to look for me. That was on Friday evening. Whether he didn't know that I was enrolled, or whether he pretended not to know, I will never find out. But he said nothing over the weekend. On Monday morning he woke me up very early and said: 'Come and carry the basket to the farm.' Of course I started crying and it was then that my mother realized that I had lied to her. Unfortunately my father believed that she had been conniving with me. This made me sad because I was wholly responsible. My mother said to me: "Forget the money I spent on your uniform. Go to the farm with your father." So I went with him, but after a while, having overcome his initial anger, my father gave me a knock on the head and said: "You *alakori,* blockhead, run back to your mother." I ran home as fast as I could... And that was how I became a school boy.

U: And did you manage to retain your romantic vision of school or was it shattered by reality?

RO: Of course, there was only one Empire Day, and I had to wait a whole year for it! But going to school, we were immediately faced with all kinds of challenges that excited me—learning the letters and learning the numbers. I was entering a strange and incomprehensible world, but I was anxious to compete with all those other children. Right from the start I began to take first position in class, and I became the pride of my mother and father, though my father wouldn't talk about it. Even in later years when I was at the University he would seldom show publicly that he was pleased with me. But when I went and told him that I had been promoted to become a professor, he looked puzzled for a while, and then he asked: "How many of you in Osogbo?" At that time there were only three of us who had reached that position. Then he said: "You can see why I am proud of you."

U: Did you find, at any time, that what you were taught at school was conflicting with the values you had absorbed at home?

RO: I don't think so. I was too young. I had not developed any special liking for the farm. My awareness about life and social responsibility really started at school. I just fell in love with schooling, with my new friends, the teachers, the bell, the singing... So many exciting things. The school became my world, my playground, too. This is where the football field was. My life became inseparable from the school.

U: How did you become a Christian? Was it conversion, gentle pressure, enticement?

RO: School and church were inseparable in my mind. Catechism classes seemed like an extension of school. We were encouraged to attend, even though we were Moslems. I could not let my father know that I attended these classes, but my mother knew. Finally, when I graduated from Standard VI, I decided to take my baptism and confirmation. I didn't tell my father formally, but he heard about it in the mosque, and he was very upset. People had challenged him. I told him that I had not taken the decision to ridicule his religion, and that if his friends were complaining, they should invite me to the mosque and I would answer their questions myself. Then my father said: "That is exactly what I will to do." But of course nobody ever invited me.

U: So that's how you became Richard. What were you before?

RO: I was called Rabiu. I retained the 'R'.

U: Where did you go after completing your primary school?

RO: I first became a pupil teacher in 1955.

U: Of course, that was the time when S.O. Awokoya introduced Free Primary Education in Western Nigeria.

RO: That's right. There was a sudden need for teachers. The students in my class were seven or eight years. I was about 13 years old.

U: Did you have any problems with discipline, being so young?

RO: None at all. Children were highly motivated in those days. They wanted to learn and the teacher was a highly respected figure in the community. I then went on to St. Peter's Teacher Training College in Akure. It was run by Christian Brothers from Canada. They encouraged me to sit for the GCE and eventually they helped me to get a four year scholarship to Regis College in Denver, Colorado. My original intention had been to study economics, but when I saw that mathematics was a requirement for that course, I switched to history.

U: Why economics?

RO: It was a popular subject in Nigeria at the time. I did not expect to get a scholarship, so I had intended to do economics as an external student of the University of London.

U: What type of history did you study in Denver?

RO: At first European and American history; later European diplomacy and African history of the 19th and 20th century.

U: Colonial exploration, independence movements?

RO: Yes, and Development later at Washington from 1965 to 1969 when I was at Georgetown University.

U: You spent nine years studying in the United States. How many times did you go home during that period?

RO: Not once!

U: Didn't you get home sick?

RO: Yeeees, once in a while; but I had the privilege of knowing a family who recorded my voice on small discs, and sent them home to my father. He would then go to his letter writer friend who helped him to send me frequent letters. I was also a good letter writer myself, and I corresponded with many friends in Osogbo. So I always got the news from home.

U: Did you find it hard to adjust to American living conditions?

RO: Not at all. I was made to feel very much at home. In the first two years I shared a room with a fellow student. Later I had my own room.

U: What did you miss most about Nigeria?

RO: The food! During my four years as an undergraduate I had no opportunity at all to eat Yoruba food. When I got to Washington a friend from

221

the Midwest invited me to his home and he cooked for me. The very same day I learned to cook.

U: How could he get the necessary ingredients in those days?

RO: Of course, we could not get any yams, and if we could, we wouldn't have been able to pound them, anyway. But if you mix potato powder with semolina you get a reasonable substitute for pounded yam. And you could substitute tinned spinach for *efo*.

U: So it was very much a substitute?

R: Very much so, but it was a good substitute and it helped me to feel at home in Washington. Also I must be thankful to the Americans in Denver because they accepted me as one of their own. The families, church groups, individuals; everybody looked after me.

U: When you returned after nine years, did you have a problem re-adjusting, or did you find the country hadn't changed all that much?

R: Well, there had been the civil war. Also the University at Ife had been established. But in Osogbo I could still recognize the landmarks; life had not changed all that much. The pace of life was still the same.

U: The drastic change began to happen just after your return—the oil boom, the *nouveau riche*... I believe that when you joined the staff of the History Department at Ife, you first taught European history. How did you get into Yoruba history?

RO: I discovered that I had no access to primary sources for my research in European History, so I decided to turn to Yoruba history where I could at least make use of oral traditions. But there is also something about studying the history of other people that forces you to master and understand their social and political institutions. When necessary you can always adapt the skills you acquired in that process to mastering and understanding your own culture. You begin to discover that your own people have devised their own ways and means of coping with life and its challenges; that they have their own organizations and institutions that are comparable to the Europeans'. In my study of European history

I had been particularly fascinated with diplomacy, and in looking at the Yoruba, I saw that they had a well established diplomatic tradition which played an important part in their relationships with neighboring people.

U: So after a long absence from home you go through a process of rediscovery...

RO: That is very true. I can give you an example. While I was in the US I built up a very good collection of classical music because I had the privilege of being allowed to make copies from the library of Georgetown University, and I made full use of it. I thought that when I would go back to Nigeria I would have the best collection of classical music on any University campus. But one day a family friend visited me in Washington, and I thought he would be happy to listen to classical music. I put on the first tape there was no reaction. When I put on the second one he asked: "Do you have any music?" That jolted me. So I had to go out and look for African recordings the very next day. I found that this music fascinated my friend more than *my* classical collection! From then on, I started to order African music from New York and Los Angeles. Since coming home I have almost abandoned classical music altogether. I listen to Gregorian chants occasionally. They are peaceful, they can affect you spiritual, and personally I've found them helpful. But I think you are right. When we return home we all go through a process of rediscovery. Some go all the way and abandon all the 'foreign' things altogether, but others, like myself, can still find a peaceful coexistence between the two cultures. While I was in the US I remained conscious of my background and of the world I would return to eventually. That allowed me to immerse myself in the foreign culture and to enjoy every minute of it. But I never abandoned myself to it. I was always conscious of what I was doing.

U: You never felt tempted to remain in the US—like so many other Nigerians?

RO: There was no reason for wanting to stay. In those days there was an exciting life waiting for me back home. The universities were functioning, the economy was strong, and the educational system was vigorous. And there were opportunities to interact internationally through conferences.

U: When you were a child you decided to become a Catholic—behind your father's back. The Catholic church has looked after you very well, providing you with a scholarship to the US and thus launching your academic career. But growing up and seeing the church becoming less and less relevant to life in the West, taking many antiquated stands that make it irrelevant to current world issues—did that not make you critical? Above all, when you returned to Nigeria, did you not find that the Catholic Church was not just preaching a religion, but that it was also imposing a foreign culture? To put it unkindly: was the Church wittingly or unwittingly an instrument of colonialism?

RO: I think that the Catholic church here is now becoming aware that you cannot promote Christianity outside the cultural context of the people. This does not mean that they encourage syncretism, but there are many cultural practices which in no way conflict with the teaching of the Church, for example, drumming and dancing in the church. The liturgy is becoming Africanized. We have discovered that we can enjoy the worship more when we play our own music. You can go to a Catholic village church now and think you are in an *Aladura*, Pentecostal, congregation. The *Aladura* churches were perhaps the first churches to introduce drumming, dancing, trances and faith healing into their rituals...

U: So far the Catholics have remained rigid on issues like polygamy and celibacy.

RO: Polygamy and celibacy are central to the teaching of the church.

U: But the African Churches argue correctly that the Bible does not speak about polygamy. Jesus never mentioned it—so it could not have been important to him. Is this objection to polygamy merely a European cultural prejudice?

RO: It is true that for a long time people who had more than one wife were not fully accepted into the church. They could not receive the sacraments. But on the other hand many of those who embraced Christianity sincerely found a way of doing away with many of their wives and remaining with only one. I have known people who, once they decided to become full Catholics—that is, receive the holy communion—work out a compromise whereby they engage in sexual relations with only one of their wives—although they still maintain a polygamous household.

U: I see from your answers that your loyalty to the Church is still unshaken.

RO: In the US my interest in the church lapsed a little, but since my return, I have become an active member again. In fact I am the *Baba Egbe*, the lay chairman, of the Parish Council.

U: In spite of all this you have remained very much a Yoruba. Your attitude to death for example, to ancestors, your capacity for extrasensory perception, all these seem to have deep roots in Yoruba culture.

RO: I don't know what you are referring to...

U: Well, the fact for example that you buried your father in your compound, not on a cemetery.

RO: Oh yes. Before I went on Sabbatical to the US in 1978 I decide to make some arrangement for my father's burial should he die while I was overseas. So I selected an area quite near his building, and 1 left him money to develop it. I did not tell my father what I had in mind, but I think he knew. He went ahead and did a better, more beautiful job than I could have done. When he died, that's where he 'slept', that is to say, he was buried in that space.

U: I remember you telling me that your father knew precisely when he was going to die.

RO: Yes, that is true. In retrospect I now understand that he was giving me an indication that the time had come for him to leave us. Three months before he died he asked me to bring him water from Ife. He claimed that he preferred the taste of it—though it all came from the same piped water system. But now I believe that he merely wanted to see me more often. I fulfilled his wishes, but during the last two weeks before his death I kept delaying my trip to Osogbo. I had the water stored in the booth of my car when he died. He also gave other indications to the women in the house. Whenever he asked them for something he would add, "Give me what I ask for as there may not be another opportunity." Or he would say: "When I die I will be resting in the arms of my child." They didn't take that seriously and they joked: "Don't die now because we haven't got the money to bury you." Then he replied: "Don't worry. When I am ready to go, you will all have plenty of money. Your trades will be booming."

225

Shortly before his death he told my sister to visit him in four days time because he wanted her to run an errand for him. But he did not disclose the nature of the errand. My sister first went to Lagos to attend a naming ceremony, and my father worried that she might not make it back in time. So he invited one of his nieces to visit him on the same day. His niece misunderstood him, and arrived a day earlier. But he scolded her and told her to go back to work, and return on the following day.

In the meantime my sister had a very frightening dream in Lagos. In that dream some of the deceased members of our family gathered to honor my father. They were rejoicing and celebrating as if my father had received a chieftaincy title. Very early in the morning she rushed back to Osogbo. My father was so happy to see her that he said: "You are my true daughter." He asked her to prepare *eko ogi,* corn palp, for him. He took only about six spoons and said that was enough. Then he slept. My sister said that as he was lying on the bed she noticed a complete transformation. His face suddenly looked radiant! She had never seen him like that before, and she called in a girl from the kitchen. The girl was equally amazed. At 2 o'clock my father woke up. It was time for the Moslem 2 o'clock prayer. My father said, "God is great" three or four times. My sister was curious and she asked him, "Why are you saying this?" "Isn't it true that God is great?", he asked in response. My sister noticed that his hands and feet were wet as if he had performed the Moslem ablution. At two thirty he took a deep breath and he started to talk about forgiveness. If there was anybody he had wronged in his life, he asked for their forgiveness because nobody could go through and entire life time without offending somebody. My sister grew more worried. Then again he repeated: "God is great." At about 3 o'clock he took another deep breath and asked my sister to prepare *amala,* dough made of yam flour. My sister was annoyed. Hadn't she just given him *ogi eko,* a short while ago? But my father said, "Whatever I ask, do it for you may not have another opportunity." Just as the *amala* was about to be served, my father asked my sister to sit closer to him, and that he wanted to rest in her arms. At a quarter to 4 o'clock he took another deep breath and died.

My sister was very happy and proud that she had been able to witness that moment. Then she did something one would generally not expect a woman to do in a Yoruba compound, namely, she bathed his body and dressed him up before she announced to everybody that her father had died. In the meantime she sent the girl from the kitchen to Ife to give me the news. She arrived at about 7 a.m. and I was just taking my bath.

Meanwhile in Ife, another strange thing happened. When I heard someone knock at the door I announced that I wanted to be the one to open the door, though usually I would send someone else to do so. To make it even stranger, I was taking a bath when I heard the knocking, and yet, I insisted on being the one to open the door—though the bathroom was in fact quite far away. Anyway, I rushed out in my bath towel and when the girl saw me she started to cry, saying that my father had died. I shouted "Hallelujah! Hallelujah!" I was so happy for my father. He had gone to rest and he deserved it because he had lived a fulfilled life. He had lived to see his children succeed and his grandchildren grow. He was proud of us all, and he was always delighted when I visited him. We could sit together for hours without anybody knowing that I was in the compound. He was my best friend.

U: This is an emotional reaction you could not easily find in Europe. Rationally we can tell ourselves that we should be happy when our father dies, but our immediate instinctive reaction would not be to shout "Hallelujah". Maybe we are too concerned with ourselves at that moment?

RO: In my own case I was really happy, hence the spontaneous reaction. I knew he had been transformed to go into another world to meet his other relations—his father, his mother, his wife. And I hoped that he would be able to carry some messages too, that he would tell my mother some of the things she had not been able to experience on earth. She died in 1961, 42 days after my departure from home!

U: This strong awareness of the ancestors, the interaction between the living and the dead maybe is as a result of having grown up with Egungun...

RO: Yes. The Yoruba believe in retaining contact with the dead through ritual and prayer. They invoke the spirit of the father and the mother. And when they offer prayers, especially for the community, they invoke the ancestors.

U: Who are buried in the compounds...

RO: Not just anywhere in the compound! In the bedrooms—where people live and sleep; even Christians still ask to be buried in their home. They would feel symbolically cut off from their family if they were buried in the church yard.

U: Now what about your father's prediction, that when he died there would be plenty of money in the family to bury him?

RO: It was like a miracle. I was poor when he died; in fact so penniless that I had to borrow five naira from my mother-in-law to buy petrol. I borrowed it in my wife's name because I was a little ashamed. That was at 8 o'clock in the morning. By midday, I was 3000 naira the richer! When I heard of my father's death I didn't know where to turn. But people were so kind to me; they offered me help and reminded me of that well known axiom which says "You don't save money for funerary purposes!" The first person I met was Professor Akinjogbin and when I told him of my father's death he said, "Congratulations!" and before I could even ask he offered me some money. By noon I had enough money. When I reached Osogbo I found people celebrating everywhere—killing goats, cows etc. etc. Even people I had never met came to greet me, telling me that they had come to celebrate my father's funeral. I couldn't believe it. My father's was the kind of death many would wish for!

U: I suppose you couldn't have come home for your mother's funeral because you had only just arrived in the States. That must have been hard to bear.

RO: Yes, it was hard. When she died my father could not write to me himself. So he went to the principal of the high school. The principal was very close to me. He was the man who had been responsible for my scholarship and trip to the United States. I received the letter one morning at 10 o'clock just as I was just about to enter a science lecture. My roommate, a New Yorker called Roger, was with me. The moment I held the letter in my hand, I said, "My mother has died." Roger couldn't believe it because I hadn't opened the letter. He said: "If you seriously believe that your mother has died, how can you calmly go into a lecture without opening the letter?" I said that I thought that's what my mother would want me to do. She would have said something like "Having lost me, don't fail your exam as well!" So I went into the classroom. I could concentrate on the lesson, but Roger could not. He was terribly restless. He kept asking me to open the letter. I handed it to him but he said he couldn't open it himself. So in the end and to have my peace I opened it and the first sentence read: "Your good mother is dead." It was very hard, but I was sustained by my belief that my mother would be proud if I obtained my degree. But of course, at night I would hide under the blankets and cry, making sure that my roommate, Roger, did not notice.

U: You spent the first six years of your life in a traditional Yoruba compound absorbing some very basic and deep Yoruba attitudes to life. And in spite of receiving a foreign education, embracing an alien religion and living abroad for almost a decade, you have remained solidly rooted in your culture in several ways. But it seems to me that a new generation is growing up who do not have that advantage and who might find themselves thoroughly disorientated. You rightly remarked that between 1961 and 1970, the time you spent abroad, Osogbo had not changed drastically. It may have grown bigger, but essentially the pace of life had remained the same and the social stability had remained fairly intact. The real change, I would like to suggest, came later during the oil boom that made some people extremely rich and others extremely poor. Now in the nineties we see Yoruba society sadly divided. On the one hand there are whole villages that have lost their land. On the other hand there is a class of excessively rich landlords who have amassed vast fortunes, sometimes by dubious means. They are aware of the fact that they have alienated themselves from their own society because they build themselves huge concrete mansions surrounded by heavy ugly walls and guarded by security men. These houses look like bunkers rather than private residences. So the coolness, the harmony and the tolerance you have previously mentioned as core characteristics of traditional Yoruba life have gone out of it. We now have a brutalization of society. There is oppression, exhortation and confrontation. Can a true Yoruba identity survive under such circumstances?

RO: I think it is inevitable that these kinds of people will be with us because they have been part of the process of modernizing the economy. There will always be industrialists, traders, public relations gurus, middle men and indeed exploiters. But traditional Yoruba culture will continue to survive because no amount of money can transform every Yoruba village into a Lagos or Kaduna. I also believe that water always finds its own level. People will find their form of happiness, and they will express this happiness within the means that are at their disposal. I also believe that people will embrace religion in order to find peace and meaning within this chaotic modern world.

U: I believe that this is so. But haven't the religions also become part of this so-called modernization process? In traditional Yoruba culture rivalry between different Orisa houses was unknown. They practiced "ecumenical" ideas long before anybody had coined a word for it. But nowadays Christian sects fight each other, and in spite of all declarations to the contrary the antagonism between Muslims and Christians is increasing!

RO: Nevertheless I think that our religious leaders are aware of this. There is now a definite policy in the Catholic church to study Islam, to understand Islam and to stretch out a hand of brotherly love to Moslems. I still believe that in the end the fundamentalists in all the camps will not prevail. I believe that we will go through a new age of realism, and that gradually we can achieve once again the harmony, tolerance and the balance that our forefathers achieved in their own society.

Ulli Beier talks to Femi Bodunrin
"ICONOGRAPHY OF ORDER AND DISORDER"

F: Please permit me to borrow *Iconography of order and disorder*—Hans Witte's subtitle to his study on Ifa and Esu—as a tentative guide for our discussion. Permit me further to give a brief description of the sort of 'order' that I have in mind, hoping that would lead us to its twin concept, 'disorder'. The kind of 'order' that I have in mind resembles the one depicted by R.H. Stone in his book, *In Africa's Forest and Jungle: or Six Years among the Yorubans* (1899). The passage that I would like to cite has also been quoted by Robert Farris Thompson in *Flash of the Spirit: African and Afro-American Art and Philosophy* which was published in 1983. Thompson introduces the passage as follows: "One bright morning in the middle of the nineteenth century, a young American missionary, R. H. Stone, ascended a lofty granite boulder and looked down upon the Yoruba city of Abeokuta [and from there] he wrote:

> What I saw disabused my mind of the many errors in regard to Africa. The city extends along the Ogun for nearly six miles and has a population approximately 200,000... Instead of being lazy, naked savages, living, on the spontaneous productions of the earth, they were dressed and were industrious... [They made] everything that their physical comfort required. The men were builders, blacksmiths, iron-smelters, carpenters, calabash-carvers, weavers, basket-makers, hat makers, traders, barbers, tanners, tailors, farmers, and workers in leather and morocco...they made

razors, swords, knives, hoes, billhooks, axes, arrowheads, stirrups...women...most diligently follow the pursuits which custom has allotted to them. They spin, weave, trade, cook, and dye cotton fabrics. They also make soap, dyes, palm oil, nut-oil, all the native earth ware, and many other things used in the country.

Stone's observation of the city of Abeokuta seethed with creative activity which belies the condescending Western image of "primitive Africa". Was this the sort of setting that you found in Yoruba cities and towns when you arrived there in Yorubaland in the 1950s?

U:　...I found a very similar situation, and all the crafts Stone listed were still very active. Yoruba towns were industrious and they were bursting with activities. In Osogbo I lived opposite a blacksmith's workshop. All day long half a dozen craftsmen were busy producing hoes cutlasses and other farm tools. They were even forging the pellets for shot guns by hand! They tended to beat in a steady rhythm, like musicians creating a "groove." From time to time they interrupted their work for a brief spell to recite *Orisa* on what you might call a "talking anvil." When that happened you knew that some important person was walking down Ibokun Road. Looking down into the Abolubode compound from my back verandah, I could see a woman weaving *aso oke* on a vertical loom. Within five minutes walk I came to an *alaro's* compound with huge dying pots standing in an open courtyard. Yarn, *kiijipa,* and *adire*, tie-dye fabric were hanging up to dry in the sun. There were many *alaro* and many *aladire* in Osogbo, and the cloth market was a feast for the eye. A large variety of *aso oke* and *adire* was on sale. A specialty of Osogbo women weavers was the heavy beddings—a kind of large toga in stripes of different shades of indigo—woven, of course, from thick handspun cotton. I still have some of these cloths in my possession. After forty years they have neither faded nor worn thin! *Adire eleko* was so common that you thought nothing of cutting up the most refined *ibadadun* to make yourself a shirt or *yepe*, traditional trousers.

　　Intellectually one knew, even then, that these crafts could not survive the onslaught of Western industrial products. But you could not really imagine such a situation because these arts were so well-established and so alive. There was leather work and refined embroidery; there was even a brass caster, Jinadu Oladepo, who lived down the road from me.

Only the great Yoruba tradition of woodcarving had ceased to exist because Oba and chiefs no longer commissioned carved pillars, and the Olorisa were too poor to commission *ere*. Many of the old carvers had become carpenters, and they now made wonderfully inventive and elaborate chairs, a new art form, for the Oba! Another new art form was cement sculpture—lions, elephants, and occasionally, soldiers placed on the balconies or arched gates of Brazilian houses. In many respects Osogbo, Ede, Hobu, Ifon, Erin-Osun were fairly traditional towns. Of course there were inroads into the culture. Each town had its motor park with its noise and, if you like, "vulgarity". There were also new professionals—tout, *mekaniki* (mechanics) and vulcanisers. The motor parks had their own culture. The tail boards of lorries were usually painted with proverbs and images. *Iwalewa* could often be seen at the back of a truck! In those days the truck drivers would cleverly manipulate their motor horns, rubber balls at the end of a shiny trumpet-shaped horn, for example, in order to address potential customers. They could actually "talk" on these new instruments and inform people that they were about to depart for Lagos or Ibadan. Often enough, when I lived in Ede in 1952, they woke me up at three or four o'clock in the morning. People liked night travelling in those days because the roads were absolutely safe and one could reach Lagos in time for a full day's business activity. To cater to the travelers, clusters of restaurants grew around the motor parks—a modern development because in traditional towns there was obviously no need for a restaurant. But these little restaurants were wonderful places to eat pounded yam with superbly cooked *egusi* or okro and bush meat. The restaurateurs, all women, competed with one another. You sat in a simple wooden shack made typically of wood and covered with corrugated iron sheets. The tables, in those days, were scrubbed until the wood became white and exposed its markings. The women entrepreneurs would also sell palm wine or, if you preferred, they sent out for "Star" beer. Some motor parks had a nationwide reputation for the quality of their cuisine and the availability of bush meat. Travelling to Benin or further east I would invariably stop at Igbara-Oke for a meal. Even architecturally Yoruba towns in the fifties would not have been all that different from the Abeokuta that the reverend R.H. Stone saw. He might even have seen a fair sprinkling of Brazilians houses co-existing harmoniously into the townscape of sprawling mud compounds.

F: Many people have talked about these Brazilian buildings. Could you please tell me the genesis of these Brazilian buildings?

U: A Yoruba town used to be a maze of large rectangular mud compounds. The size of these compounds depended on the terrain. In the landscape of Oyo province they tended to be huge. In the hilly areas of Ekiti, they were more compact. These mud buildings had virtually no windows to the outside. Facing inwards the doors of the different rooms would open onto a wide verandah. Short square mud pillars supported the roof that gave ample shade to the people working in this space. In the palaces of Oba or Chiefs the low roof would be supported by carved, wooden pillars. In the palace of Old Oyo the pillars in the Alaafin's palace were made of brass. What a sight that must have been!

The rooms were mostly sleeping rooms. Social life and activities took place on the verandah. That's where people would sit and eat. That's where a woman might have her upright loom against the wall. Some of the slightly larger rooms might serve as shrines. The shrines of Yoruba Orisa were extremely modest: a mud bench served as the altar; there were some pots with sacred water; a calabash containing kola nuts; maybe a couple of wooden carvings, and sometimes a carved door. The shrines were no bigger than was necessary for three or four priests to officiate in it. The bulk of the worshippers would sit in the verandah, and when it came to dancing they would step out into the open courtyard or onto a space in front of the house.

The mud walls were repaired with a mud slip after every rainy season and then polished with a stone, so that the red laterite facade would shine like marble. In the fifties the majority of houses in Osogbo were still of this traditional type. Only the thatched roofs had been replaced by corrugated iron. In most Yoruba towns the council had made this a law due to the danger of fire. Undoubtedly, pressure was also exercised because some British firms made a lot of money selling this highly unsuitable material in Nigeria. The roofs were quite beautiful to look at once they were rusty—almost the color of laterite, and Yoruba builders created attractive roofs with little gables jutting out, and with decorative cut shapes along the corners. But of course, they made the houses uncomfortably hot. Many of these beautiful mud compounds soon fell into disrepair in the late fifties as they became increasingly neglected. Deep cracks in the walls and the parallel building layers were exposed to the eye. It was apparent that the owners were saving money for cement to build *peteesi*, and considered it a waste of time to work on the old buildings. *Petesi* was neo-Yoruba for an "upstairs" house, a country version of the so-called Brazilian mansion. Brazilian architecture was introduced by liberated slaves from Brazil in the middle of the 19th century. Brazil had experienced a number of slave revolts in the 1820s, and all the revolts had been organized by slaves of Hausa or, in any case, Muslim origin. In the early 1830s the Yoruba slaves also revolted, and the size and vehemence of the uprising alarmed the government. But it is noteworthy that there were twice as many slaves in Brazil as Portuguese "masters".

F: Oh, the sort of thing one reads about in the novels of Jorge Amado?

U: Yes. But remember also that slavery in Brazil was different from slavery in North America. It happened that slave owners gave some of their favorite slaves their freedom, settling them on a plot of land. Some slaves could save enough money to buy their freedom. When the uprising was finally put down, the ring leaders were killed, and the liberated slaves who had supported the revolt were repatriated to West Africa. Lome, Ilu Ajase (Porto Novo) and Lagos were the major sites for resettlement. These Brazilian Yoruba soon became the region's elite because they were literate and were competent in several modern crafts, such as building. They built beautiful houses with pillars, balustrades, balconies and archways, and often with heraldic lions demurely resting their paws on a shield, and sitting over the gate. Stucco decorations were imitated in cement. The centre of Lagos—the triangle between Broad Street, Martin Street and what later on became Nnamdi Azikwe—were full of such beautiful houses. The British administration destroyed most of these houses in 1959 in what was absurdly called the "Lagos slum clearance scheme", and they replaced it with a concrete jungle which set the stage for the home of permanent traffic jam that Lagos has since become. A few houses are still left to give an indication of the former charm. In Independence square Olaiya House is still standing and most fortunately, No. 10 Elias Street has been declared a national monument. It's a remarkable house with a cast iron revolving staircase inside, and with blue Delft tiles covering the walls of the first floor on the outside. The Dutch had occupied Salvador, the capital of the state of Bahia, for only two years but they left this tradition of blue tiles behind. Even some of the early mosques show the influence of that style! Upcountry it took a great deal longer for this new architecture to become fashionable. In the town of Erin-Osun, six kilometers from Osogbo, the first corrugated iron roof was constructed in 1924 and the first "upstairs" house was built in 1935. It is a small building erected in thick walls that taper inwards. It has few windows, but both the windows and the front door are surrounded by elaborate moldings carried out in cement. When I last saw it, it was painted in a pale pink. In those days people did not bother to apprentice themselves to a professional builder. They looked at the Lagos houses, and went home and copied it. I asked the builder of the Erin-Osun house who had taught him to do this. He laughed and said: *ogbon ori,* a blend of commonsense and astuteness.

The great days of Brazilian architecture were the forties. In Ikole Ekiti, one of the palace buildings was a five-storey in mud! It was incredible. As the style became fashionable upcountry it became more baroque and more extravagant. These buildings were full of fantasy, and the classical Brazilian sculpture, the demure heralding lions, evolved into a fantastic new form of cement sculpture—lions, elephants, soldiers, snake—in relief! The illiterate Yoruba builders used all these different style elements quite freely. They played with them. Osogbo still has some wonderful houses dating back to the forties. You may know Olaiya's house right next to the Oba's palace; a four-storey mansion! It is linked to the smaller buildings that are set further back from the road through a balcony supported on pillars. An amazing device! The cemented open space in front of these two buildings has been used for the last forty years as a second hand bottle market. Nobody had to go and teach these Africans about "recycling"!

These houses were built by an Ibadan man called Kadri. He also designed the house I rented, 41 Ibokun Road. But whereas the houses on King's market were built in brick, mine was built in stone by Kadri's, another self-taught builder. I went to visit him in Ibadan and he told me that once he decided to build himself a house, he simply went and watched the construction of the house he wished to replicate. I was also told that when he built 41 Ibokun Road, he would sit under a little shade tree in the black smith compound opposite, and draw with his finger in the sand. Then he would instruct his builders to put three windows here, and put the door there! There was no plan, but the statics of the house are perfect; no sinking foundations, no cracks in the wall, no leakages, no damp! The building became quite famous and variations on it were later constructed by Kadri in Ikirun, Okuku and elsewhere.

These Brazilian houses were prestige objects. People didn't really like living in them. Old people certainly did not like to live high off the ground! It seemed unnatural to them. They were status symbols of new bourgeoisie— cocoa fanners, transport magnates, contractors and so on. Of course, the traditional status holders Oba, Chiefs—had to compete. Still, if you compare these houses to the concrete monsters the *nouveau riche* of today are building for themselves, "Brazilian houses" were really modest. And they were works of art. Moreover, they seemed to grow organically out of the lower mud compounds, and they did not fight their surroundings. The builders were capable of producing new ideas, yet respecting what existed. At that time one could feel optimistic about Yoruba culture; it seemed capable of absorbing a wide range of foreign influences without giving up its identity. The Yoruba lifestyle was not destroyed by these wealthy traders in the forties. It was the lawyers and doctors and accountants who returned after years of study in the U.K. who built themselves "modern" bungalows—ugly concrete houses in splendid isolation, complete with hideous glass louvers and other obnoxious materials. These houses were simply antisocial; they were intended to emphasize the owners' elitist status. In fact they were sometimes were grouped in "housing estates" that aped the British General Residential Area." Like the colonial housing estates these were elitist ghettos. I was happy that, when I changed over from the English department to the Extra-Mural department, I could move out of the University campus, which was also a ghetto, and live in a town of my choice where I also could, to my delight, pick a beautiful Brazilian house. Since many of them were empty in those days, they were cheap to rent. You could have a beautiful two-storey mansion for 10 pounds a month and what is more, you could live right in the middle of town where all the life was, and where drummers would come past your house in procession virtually every day.

F: And what was ten pounds worth in terms of other things?

U: Quite a lot really. I remember that even in the early sixties a petrol station attendant might not earn more than two pounds a month. I gave some of the Osogbo artists three pounds per month, and they could eat well on that.

F: Considering the fact that you could get a meal for six pence! In a recent interview with Olu Obafemi, you observed how in 1956 at the first Pan

African Conference of African Writers and Artists, Richard Wright and Aime Cesaire clashed in their views over African culture, with the former perceiving African culture as riddled with superstition and thanking the ... "white man for destroying our culture..." Twenty years later in 1976 Soyinka, in his *Myth, Literature and the African World,* compared the colonial mentality of Samuel Ajayi Crowder, the first African to be ordained bishop, with that of the new African ideologues who were as ashamed as Wright of African culture. Are we at the threshold of the "disorder' for which one may blame the colonial domination?

U: Yes, you know that in the fifties and sixties many Nigerian academics and intellectuals thought of me as some kind of crank. Tony Enahoro once said to me, in front of the Ooni of Ife: "You with your African culture. There is no such thing! It's just medieval culture." I will not deny Tony Enahoro's many achievements, but the sad implication of his remark is that African culture is "backward"; that we must discard it, and "catch up" with the rest of the world. The Ooni of Ife, with whom I had had many interesting conversations on Yoruba culture, kept quiet. Once confronted with this kind of "progressive" jargon, few Yoruba people had the courage to stand up for their own conviction in those days. At a stage Tony Enahoro was the only African member of the "European Club" in Ibadan. There were others who aspired to becoming honorary whites. No wonder the man in the street began to call them *oyinbo dudu,* westernized Africans.

F: The *been-tos.*

U: Yes, the *been-tos* displayed British mannerisms and many of them became remote from their own society. Chief Awolowo himself spoke in derogatory terms about Yoruba culture in his book, *Awo.* He had no interest in Yoruba art or music, and he despised Yoruba religion. He would not even eat pepper! The *been-tos* created an "elitist" class in Yoruba society. You could say that is the beginning of the disorder you are talking about! In the 1950s I still experienced Yoruba towns as classless societies. Of course, they were highly structured—innumerable chiefs and priests all with specific duties and functions assigned to them. But titles were not passed on from father to son. They were open to competition. Perhaps most importantly, political power could not automatically be translated into wealth—as it happens today. The Oba was a man through whom a great deal of wealth circulated, but he was not meant to accumulate it. He was not even meant to build a house for himself or family while in office. Additionally, the Oba had almost unlimited social responsibilities. If a woman had triplets, he became automatically responsible for the upbringing of one of the children; if a woman could not find a husband, perhaps because she was unable to produce children, he would have to marry her; when a woman gave birth and there was neither husband or father or any close relative to bury the afterbirth, the Oba had to do it— which meant that he became the father of the child. In the fifties every Oba I knew—literate or not—had to spend much of his time farming in order to meet his social responsibilities. After all there was no religious ceremony to which he was not obliged to contribute food!

F: And all this did not fascinate the new African elites as something they wanted to carry on?

U: No. On the contrary there was this obsession with "progress" which I found really painful at the time because I could see where it would lead. The society was very well balanced at the time and it was also fairly well off. No one suffered real hardship. There was no poverty. With communal land ownership administered by the Oba, no one could go hungry. And the extended family, the compound, created a social security net that worked better than ours here...

F: The welfare state?

U: It works better than our welfare state on several grounds. First of all, in European society there are many people who fall through the "social security net." Even in this small provincial town, Bayreuth, we have an increasing number of beggars on the street. Secondly, the system is becoming absurdly expensive. I know a single, self-employed woman who has to pay 700 Marks a month for her health insurance. In the end you work your guts out just to pay insurance and tax. What it means is that you can't live a simple life any more. You spend an increasing proportion of your life dealing with bureaucracy. Thirdly, Western society considers old people useless. They are looked after in a home, maybe with a fair amount of comfort, but they are removed from families and they feel that they are a burden...

F: But even the former, I mean the "fair amount of comfort" has become a myth. My wife has worked in many of these homes in London, including the ones that are meant to cater for the *nouveau riche* of British society, and each time she went, she came back with tales of woes. The majority of these homes are now in private hands, and their owners have to cut back on staff and many other facilities so as to maximize profit etc. etc. etc.

U: Whereas in Yoruba society there were some tasks reserved for old women. For example, the collection of *elu*, indigo leaves, or the preparation of ashes for the *alaro*, professional dyers, were essential services which kept a typical old woman active and gainfully employed...

F: In other words, there was no real unemployment.

U: In Yoruba society everybody had something to contribute—however little, even children—and your dignity did not depend on the type of job you did. You would be respected as long as you did your work well—whatever it was.

F: You had your freedom, but with responsibility.

U: Exactly.

F: Many scholars have blamed the "collapse" of Yoruba traditional culture on the slave trade, civil wars, and modernization. Which among these experiential factors has done the most damage?

U: I don't think anybody could measure the share any of these three evils had in corrupting Yoruba society. The slave trade was certainly the beginning of the disintegration of Yoruba society and other West African societies for that matter. It is not just the brutality of European or Arab slave traders; it is above all the fact that there were enough Yoruba willing to hunt for slaves and sell slaves in order to supply the new "market"—though many Yoruba succumbed to this temptation under pressure. But the outcome was that the tolerance, the respect for human dignity and individuality were abandoned. The damage to the society must have been irreparable. You could say that there is a contemporary variant of the slave trade today. About a year ago one of Georgina's students from the Nike Centre was asked by a car dealer to drive a white Mercedes to a customer in Ede. On the road he was waylaid and the car was robbed. The young man went to the police to report the incident. And, you know the Yoruba custom, on serious business you don't go alone. So he picked up three friends at the gallery to accompany him. The police jailed all four of them and demanded a heavy ransom. This happens all the time nowadays. People are imprisoned for no good reason and their relatives or friends have to buy their freedom.

But let's go back to slavery. The slave raids as well as the inter-tribal wars, which Samuel Johnson describes so vividly, must have had an equally disastrous effect on Yoruba society—not merely because of the many deaths and the displacements and the suffering, but above all because of the loss of values. The brutalities of war often have to be jus-tified, and it is this "false morality", this "doublethink" that does more harm than the war itself. Let me give you an example. Johnson reports that the Olowu of Owu was captured by an Ibadan warrior when the city fell. The warrior carried the Olowu to Ibadan and delivered him to the Olubadan. The Olubadan, however, was horrified. How could he, and ordinary Baale keep a sacred Oba, a descendant of Oduduwa as a common prisoner in his palace? His traditional Yoruba world view was sufficiently intact for him to realize that this was sacrilege. He feared the curse of the Olowu, and devised a way to get out of the Ibadan palace as quickly as possible. He would have preferred to see the Oba dead rather than alive, but who would dare to lay hands on an Oba? In the end he came up with a ruse. He told the Olowu that he was too big an Oba to be held at Ibadan, and that the only Oba who could look after him was the Ooni of Ife. One of his chiefs was detailed to lead the Oba to Ife. An Hausa slave was told to accompany the two, but in fact, the Hausa slave was to kill the Olowu. In return he was promised his freedom. The arrangement was that that slave would always walk behind the Olowu, and as at an appointed place near a river, the chief would give a sign for the Hausa man to kill the Oba and throw the corpse in the river. The Hausa salve kept his side of the bargain, but was immediately killed by the chief who then prayed to the spirit of the Oba: "Kabiyesi, you see that I have avenged your death! Do not punish me for the crime that this worthless slave has committed." This, to me, is the symbol of a perver-sion of cultural values. People pay lip service to traditional values, while they have in fact succumbed to the uninhibited lure of power, violence or greed.

That said, I must also add that in spite of the disruptive effect of both the slave trade and the fratricidal wars on Yoruba society, the Yoruba people showed considerable resilience and surprising ability to restructure their society. When I first came into Yoruba land in 1950 there was a sense of order and stability. Many traditional Yoruba values were very much alive. Religious festivals were being celebrated with vigor. We have to acknowledge here the fact that the situation was helped by the *Pax Britannica*. It was not that the British really had the military force to suppress all the fighting, but the Yoruba kingdoms were probably tired of wars, and were glad to accept this unexpected arbitration.

Subsequently the British Colonial administration did not interfere very much with the daily lives of the citizens in Yorubaland, but instead they had brought the concept of "indirect rule" with them from India. Under this system they ruled through the existing chieftaincy structures, not because they had any real respect for Yoruba culture, but because it made it possible for them to rule the country with a minimum of personnel. In order to rule through the traditional rulers they had to leave all the traditional structures that propped up their authority intact. Thus, they could not interfere with the chieftaincy structure, the Ogboni society or any other aspect of Yoruba religion. Otherwise they would have undermined the Oba's authority. It is true that they outlawed the Sonponna cult, but it was a Nigerian doctor who spread the rumor that the Sonponna cult spread the disease in order to make money—a case of vicious libel! However, having banned the cult officially, they made little effort to effectively suppress it. In fact in the 1950s Sonponna shrines existed in all Yoruba cities. I was familiar with, and I attended the *ose* of Sonponna in Erin-Osun regularly while I was living in Ilobu

F: So the sort of thing Soyinka describes in *Death and the King's Horseman* is an isolated incident?

U: It was a major interference and a tragic one; but the district officer simply lacked the knowledge to realize the implications of his action. As far as he could see, he was trying to save a man's life.

F: So it was a case of ignorance rather than oppression.

U: Absolutely. But of course a lot of harm is done through ignorance. The late K.C. Murray used to point out that the Colonial Education Ordinance started with the sentence, "Education is an instrument of change." The implication is clear. Education was not a means of widening people's horizon. There was no attempt to build on what was there already. It was a matter of discarding everything you had, suspending any belief you ever held, disowning every kind of wisdom you ever held and embracing wholesale and without adaptation, somebody else's lifestyle. So it was the education system that deliberately helped to destroy the fabric of Yoruba society. Many of the school teachers and clerks who attended my extramural classes, and were also personal friends of mine, could not understand why I spent so much time with Sango worshippers. They could not see the beauty of the dances or the poetry of the music. They could not read the beauty in the faces of these magnificent people. They simply said: "Sango does not exist." And I said, "why not?" "Because you can't prove it." And I asked: "Can you prove the existence of the Christian God?" To them one was "superstition", the other, "truth". They measured both with a different yardstick.

F: In one case you're prepared to suspend disbelief. In the other you keep it intact.

U: Biblical mythology was taught as "fact". Yoruba mythology was denounced as some backward, heathenish, even evil superstition. I once spent a couple of months as a school inspector for the Education Department in Ondo province. It was a very revealing experience. Nobody among the teachers ever explained the difference between "truth" and "fact". Nobody ever attempted to find common ground between the religions. I told a class that the Yoruba people had their own version of the Biblical myth of "Paradise Lost." Every single child knew the Yoruba myth that said: "Once upon a time the sky was very low down, and when people were hungry they could simply cut off a piece of sky and eat it. For a long time everybody obeyed this rule, until one day a greedy woman cut off a huge piece of sky. She could not finish it, and even her husband and her children and all the relatives could not finish it. The entire village ate of this huge piece of sky. When they could not finish it, the woman had to throw the remains on the rubbish heap. The sky felt deeply hurt and removed itself from human reach. Since then, human beings must plant to eat." The teacher felt offended. He thought I was undermining his authority and putting funny ideas into the children's heads. The children, who had younger minds and were less prejudiced, responded with curiosity and enthusiasm. I pointed out that the Yoruba story in some respects compared favorably with the Biblical one. The basic idea of course, is the same: Once life was better and easier. Man was closer to God. But through man's own fault and disobedience, hardship was brought into life. The difference lies in the image of God. The Biblical God is all powerful, cantankerous and self-righteous. He is in fact taking revenge. In the Yoruba story, God is vulnerable; he can be hurt. The vice that has brought the misfortune upon mankind is not so much *disobedience* but *greed*. The story is perfectly applicable to Yoruba society today. It is above all greed that has created even greater distance to God and ultimately destroyed Yoruba society. Yoruba religion was designed to overcome this distance between man and god, and the Yoruba developed a technique of breaking this distance—if only for brief moments. Through trance the Sango worshipper could be united with Sango, and the Sonponna worshipper become one with Sonponna, and they could come back from this excursion into the supernatural world with renewed strength, understanding and wisdom.

It would have been easy to relate Christian mythology to Yoruba mythology: the creation of man; the flood; the sacrifice of the only son are all myth that are partly related to Yoruba traditions, but in each case the Yoruba God is less self-righteous, less perfect, more human than the Biblical one. It was sad for me to see how readily the Yoruba intellectuals succumbed to the cultural brainwashing of their European mentors. As I have described in a little essay called "In a Colonial University" the cultural arrogance of the British was extraordinary. The first professor of History at the University of Ibadan said: "There is no such thing as African history, only the history of the British in Africa." And everybody accepted it. Of course, we soon had people like Dike and Biobaku who proved him wrong, but when it came to Religion, people were inhibited. But I think that the most damaging influence on Yoruba culture is Western materialism which, I suppose, "modernism" mostly boils down to. Initially, people were dazzled by the opulence of the life style of people who returned from Europe—the lawyers and the doctors and the engineers... Their wealth isolated them from the community. I remember that when Dr. Dike became a lecturer in history at UI, he sent nine nephews and nieces to secondary schools! And even the first generation of politicians believed in circulating money. Many of them tried to upstage the local Oba by making bigger donations to the local school or church or sports club, demonstrating through lavish spending that they were the new elite, and that they had a legitimate role to play in the running of the community. Such politicians have become very rare nowadays—although M.K.O. Abiola is a notable exception!

F: One of the greatest damage that the elitist outlook you have just enumerated also did to the fabric of our society was that most of the people who became generals in the army were also the college drop-outs. So they more or less had a grudge against everybody because they were the ones who were not expected to do well...

U: I can't judge that. I have met some very intelligent ones too—for example, the former foreign minister Joe Garba, whom I found most impressive. I had the opportunity of meeting him, when I went to thank him for a donation by the Nigerian Government to the Institute of Papua New Guinea Studies in 1976. During his term of office Nigeria was held in very high esteem in Africa and throughout the world. Similarly one can say that the present military governor of Osun state is far superior in both intelligence and integrity to the civilian governor who preceded him. But the problem I see in the army is this: You can't have a national army before you have a nation. How strong is the Nigerian identity? I believe that at the time of independence most intellectuals believed in the ideal of Nigeria, but over the years this belief has been weakened. A succession of coups and counter-coups, the Biafran war, and the disaster in Ogoni country have eroded the belief in Nigeria. When Nigeria was on the brink of civil war in 1967 the position of the British was that Nigeria's unity must be preserved, "because it is a big market." Is that all it's meant to be? This type of attitude, if anything, has given rise to a new form of nationalism and separatism in many countries. So if you don't have a concept of Nigeria, then to whom is that army going to be loyal? Is it not going to be divided on ethnic lines? And is that surprising? What effort has been made in Nigerian schools to teach people about their country? A Yoruba child can go through primary and secondary school without learning anything at all about his or her own culture, let alone other people's cultures. How much does a Yoruba child learn about Igbo? Does a Yoruba school teacher or doctor or engineer know what an Ikenga is? Does he understand the concept of "*chi*"? Does he understand what the building of an "Mbari House" means to the community in terms of its identity and in terms of harnessing its creative energy and so on?

245

In 1966 we brought the Agbor dancers and musicians to Osogbo to participate in the performance of Duro Ladipo's *Moremi*. We had a Yoruba and an Igbo orchestra on stage, we had two different styles of dancing and singing and in the end we integrated everything into an organic whole. That happened at a time when the NNDP plastered Yoruba towns with anti-Igbo posters which were so aggressive in tone that they reminded me of anti-Semitism in Germany in 1933. It was in some way Duro's greatest performance, and it was so successful in Osogbo, Ibadan and Lagos that I expected a whole spate of future plays to make use of different musical traditions and integrate them into an orchestra, but it never happened. Everybody remained in his corner because the education they had received did not prepare them for any multicultural thinking.

F: According to Robert Farris Thompson, it is believed that Ifa encompasses the whole of the wisdom of the ancestors, the whole of the deities, and thus safeguards...everything that is considered memorable in Yoruba culture throughout the ages. Do you see the total absence of this all encompassing wisdom in the syllabi of colonial and neocolonial educational systems as the primary factor accounting for the precarious African present?

U: Yes! Ifa is a great source of wisdom and something against which our modern wisdom can be measured. It could indeed fulfill the same role in Yoruba society that the bible fulfils in Europe. Not many people in Germany or England *really* know the Bible, but everyone knows and sometimes lives by certain ideas that are in the bible. People justify their general conduct and set moral standards with the help of certain catch phrases like "love your neighbor as yourself." I only have a very superficial knowledge of Ifa, but even from the little I have learned from Timi Laoye or Wande Abimbola, I have adopted certain lines that have clarified ideas in my mind and actually serve as guidelines for my life. For example, anybody who encounter beauty without recognizing it diminishes himself. I think anyone who lives by that saying will be immune to the corruption of materialism. But nobody wants to know about Ifa, or Sango, and their complementary poetic forms—*Sango pipe* or *ijala* or *ewi* because they are associated with "paganism".

At the core of the disaster is the missionary concept of "conversion". In order to become a Christian you must publicly *denounce* every aspect of your forefather's culture, wisdom and religion. In the old days this even involved public burning of images. The problem with this situation is that you cannot in actual fact wipe out the past or your personal experience. You cannot eradicate them from your mind; you can only suppress them. Sigmund Freud, the founder of modern psychiatry, proved that most neuroses can be traced to suppressed memories—particularly early childhood memories. And unless you bring these back from the patient's subconscious to his consciousness, he will not be able to cope with his situation, his neurosis.

Every culture in the world is multicultural. This is because conquering peoples usually absorb much of the culture of the aboriginal inhabitants. Babylonian culture was superimposed on the culture of Sumer and Akkad. The Assyrians in turn conquered the Babylonians, but at the same time they picked up many of the cultural achievements of the vanquished, their writing for example. The Yoruba people and most other African societies respected the people they superseded politically, and invariably, they absorbed aboriginal cultures, and integrated them into their own. Only the monotheistic religions refused to tolerate any other ideas, other wisdoms and other aesthetic concepts besides their own. This purism must warp the mind of converts, giving them all kinds of inhibitions—even an inferiority complex. How can you feel confident if you have actually been taught to despise your ancestors?

Some Europeans have seen me as a convert—a European "gone native", as the phrase used to be. In their eyes that meant I'm a human being who has dropped all his standards, and has gone "to seed"; I have become mentally derelict. I was the object of much European prejudice in the fifties. That didn't bother me, but it was sad that there were even a few Africans who felt the same! But for me the Yoruba experience in particular was not a case of exchanging one set of values for another. It was a case of widening my horizon, of having a new yardstick to evaluate my own culture; of being more sensitive. I learned what was really relevant in my own background to my life as well as what was not. I became a better judge of classical European music after having been exposed to the experience of Yoruba music. I still listen to Bach and Beethoven passionately, but also more critically. I am more aware of what is mere technical perfection and routine, and what is organic and alive. In Africa you learn what spontaneity is, what improvisation is, and you become more sensitive to the weaknesses in many European performances.

247

I believe that Yoruba religion is much more flexible than the monotheistic religions with their claims of absolute universal truth. And this has affected every aspect of Yoruba life. Take the position of women, for example. In Christianity and Islam women are defined as inferior to men and treated as such. In spite of the strong feminist movements in Europe deep Christian prejudice towards women has not been eradicated in people's minds—although the law has made them equal. Among the Yoruba society by comparison, both men and women have monopolies on certain professions. Men are drummers, wood carvers, and brass casters. They are weavers, but can only use a certain type of loom. Women hold monopolies on pottery, indigo dying, batik, tie-dye, and weaving on the vertical loom. They are also in charge of oil and soap production. In the worship of the different Orisa women can hold the most senior positions. Men basically run the government, but women have strong representation through the Iyalode and they can exercise various veto powers. Women dominate the market, which gives them financial independence from their husbands. On the whole their position was infinitely stronger than the position of European women up to the Second World War.

In spite of these formal divisions between men and women, and these clearly demarcated spheres of influence, the male and female roles are not as rigidly defined in Yoruba society as in Europe. The sex of many Orisa is changeable. Oduduwa is sometimes the creator of the earth, a male god who descended from heaven, and sometimes he appears as mother earth herself! Esu, the ever changing, ever paradoxical deity can surprisingly appear as a woman. Even Sango, the most masculine, extrovert, boisterous of all the gods is worshipped as a woman—wife of Jakuta in Ketu and other Western Yoruba towns. The fiery priests of the thunder god wear a woman's hairstyle, an earring and their dance costume resembles a woman's wrapper. Similarly the priestesses of Sango adopt certain male mannerisms. For example, they prostrate to the Orisa like men, rather than kneel, like women. You were speaking about Richard Wright earlier on. You have read his book, *Black Power.* It's a book about his experience in Ghana, but it also shows his total misunderstanding of Ghana. It's the most revealing thing—some of the ways which he looked at Africa.

F: From the Western perspective...

U: Yes. Emotionally he could not accept the fact that he was thinking in totally Western categories, and that he harbored the average American's prejudices. That is why he found it hard to adjust. To give you a typical anecdote, he went to a nightclub where he saw men dancing together, and even holding hands. He refused to believe that these men were not homosexuals; he could not understand that the relationships between the sexes are more flexible in West Africa, and that there is not even a word for homosexuality in West African languages. Like a colonialist he imposed his own categories on a foreign culture.

F: Compartmentalization.

U: Compartmentalization! If you put one step across it, you've already labeled it as something, and you're almost forced into a way of life. This can't happen in Yoruba.

F: And it is absolutely staggering what you said earlier on about intelligent school teachers uttering these self-deconstructive statements. It conjures the same image for me because I read Wright's *Native Son*—which I still think is one of the most wonderful books ever written—before stumbling on extracts of his other book that you've just mentioned in Jacob Drachler's *Black Homeland/Black Diaspora,* and I thought how can a man of such sensibility think like this?

U: Look, I used *Native Son* and *Black Boy* in my Extramural classes. It was because I taught him so successfully that I was waiting to meet him in person in Paris. But once I met him, we couldn't get on for five minutes. There was no way in which he could see anything positive, or useful, or good or intelligent in anything African. He just felt that it ought to be wiped out! He thought, "I'm black, I'm coming to my home", and he therefore assumed that he was going to have an instinctive understanding. So he was more prejudiced because he couldn't even contemplate the possibility of a prejudice, you see?

F: Reflecting on similarities and parallels between Japan and Africa, and praising the former for having learnt so much from its turbulent past, in a recent article, poet and academic Niyi Osundare surmises that the apparent technological ingenuity of the Japanese people underscores a view of the world that is authentically Japanese in nature. How much of the rush to be accepted universally, without acquiring a relative expertise in the ABC of their cultural mooring, has blurred the worldview of the emergent socio-cultural and political elites in Africa?

U: This is a very relevant question. The Japanese—with all the mastery of Western technology—still show a great deal of respect for their tradition. They have been helped greatly by the fact that they have never succumbed in any large numbers to Western missionaries. Until today, their traditional religions, Shintoism and Buddhism, are intact. All their great theatre traditions—No, Kabuki and Bunraku—are still immensely popular with the Japanese public. The government continues honoring its great actors, artists and craftsmen by declaring them "living national treasures." This assures them a life free of material worries, and they can devote their entire time to perfecting their art. Can you imagine a Nigerian government conferring a comparable honor on the leader of a troupe of traditional masqueraders? Has the Kwaghir masquerade in Tiv ever received any real support from the government? Look at Atanda Oyeyemi, the head of the Alarinjo group from Erin-Osun. It is the only Alarinjo company surviving in Osun state, and that is due to the giant effort of this one man who trained his family relentlessly in the arts of singing, dancing, acrobatics and theatre. Yet he was jailed three times by his relatives in an effort to force him to become a Muslim and give up his profession. The only support he received came from overseas—not from their nation.

The Japanese have been unusually successful in mastering Western technologies and even Western culture. The prominence of Japanese performers in classical European music is because they are educated to become Japanese first. With all their Westernization they could not dream of making English the language of instruction in their schools. Yoruba educationists have underestimated the potential of their language. You are right in talking about "the rush to be accepted internationally." A typical case in hand is the late S. O. Awokoya, the first minister of education in Western Nigeria. He was a very brilliant man and the first Yoruba friend I ever had! I had met a Nigerian student in London (Tommy Ogbe) who told me to contact Awokoya on arrival in Nigeria. I did so and he came one day and picked me up to spend a weekend at Molusi College in Ijebu-Igbo, where he was principal. I had my first Yoruba meal in his house. He showed me that he had worked out a complete Yoruba vocabulary for the study of Chemistry. He explained that the Yoruba language had the capacity of creating new words out of clusters of nouns, very much like German, and he gave me the German example, hydrogen had been translated by German scholars in *Wasserstof,* which is made up of *Wasser,* water and *Stof,* matter. I saw a lot of Awokoya in my early years, and I enjoyed his company and his brilliant mind. But when he became Minister of Education he did not implement his ideas. Chemistry was being studied in English and so were Physics and Mathematics, History and Geography! He had demonstrated the capacity of Yoruba to go through a process of modernization, but he lacked the conviction or the political clout to implement his idea. I remember telling him about the introduction of Hebrew as the official language of Israel. Long before the state of Israel was created, the nationalists in Palestine in the early 1930s rejected both German and Yiddish or English as possible official languages. They were not deterred by the fact that Hebrew had not been a spoken language for 2000 years. They worked on this fossilized language until it became a modem tool in which you could study atomic physics if you wished. It required a certain fanaticism—even violence—to get it accepted!

In Nigeria educators were overawed by the English language. In 1956 Awokoya introduced the famous free universal education scheme. ("First in Africa" as the Action Group proclaimed it). I said to him: "You are embarking on a very dangerous project. You have a school system devised by the British and it has been set up to alienate children from their society. As you can see it has already created a deep rift within Yoruba society. Should you not first give some thought to the *context* of education before you subject everybody to it? Nobody has asked the vital questions about what kind of citizen is desirable, and how to go about educating him towards this end; what must he know about his own language, history, religion; and what must he know about his own people, their diversity and the concept of the nation state." Awokoya's answer was that "The rift in Yoruba society has come about because the educated class consider themselves superior to the illiterates. Once *everybody* can read and write there will be nothing special about it anymore." It was a good argument on the surface. Besides he believed that a reform of the school syllabus could come later. In retrospect I wonder whether he was not under pressure from his party, the Action Group, because at that time, you couldn't get much political mileage out of any agenda to reform the school syllabus. That kind of thing was a quiet revolution. And in this case Awolowo, the party leader, would not have believed in Yoruba Studies in local schools. The prevailing attitude was that the way for Africans to become equal to Europeans was to become *like* them. George Orwell understood this whole syndrome when he said in his novel, *1984*, "You become what you fight". Conversely, the introduction of free universal education gave the Action Group the image of being the most progressive party in Nigeria; of "forging ahead" and turning the Western Region into the first modem state in Africa—whereas everybody else was lagging behind and remained "backward"! Needless to say it didn't work like this. The Free Universal Education scheme merely served to ingrain British education further, and it invariably lowered the standard of education. It was one thing to build thousands "of new classrooms within two years"—a fantastic achievement, no doubt, but it was not possible to train sufficient teachers in that short a time. The massive introduction of "Pupil Teachers"—standard VI leavers who received a 6-week crash course—meant that standards dropped disastrously. Standard VI leavers had earlier on been employable as junior clerks or sanitary inspectors, but the graduates of the Free Universal Education system were no longer employable because their literacy skills were quite limited. But being "literate" also meant that most of these them no longer wanted to work on the farm, so the drift into the cities began—with untold negative developments. Four decades later, one can still observe another disturbing development in the big cities, particularly Lagos. What is happening to the Yoruba language? If you listen to taxi drivers or touts or "area boys", is that still Yoruba? They speak it so fast that the tone levels are somehow flattened, and the rhythm of the language is lost. Yoruba used to be called the "missing link between music and speech", but the music seems to have gone out of the language altogether. There are not many people left who still have that sonorous quality in their speech or can still take their time over it. Chief Muraina Oyelami, a well-known musician and artist, is one.

F: And that supports your point about modernization having done the greatest damage. First, we were encouraged not to speak the language the way an *ara-oko*, the bush type, would speak it. Then in school we were punished for speaking it at all.

U: That's criminal! This is one of the things that contributed towards the twisting of people's minds. On the other hand you must admit that there are quite a number of people who survived it all. Look at people like Biodun Jeyifo or Kole Omotoso, or Sophie Oluwole or Wole Soyinka.

They had to go through all this, but they refused to be alienated from their culture, while still availing themselves of the opportunities that the foreign language and the foreign education provided. Wole Soyinka must be the most international figure among African intellectuals, yet who but a Yoruba could have written *Death and the King's Horseman?*

F: Yes, and none but a Yoruba could have translated *Ogboju Ode Ninu Igbo Irunmole.*

U: Exactly. In spite of his very wide horizon Wole has remained a thoroughly Yoruba person. In a way you could say that I went a similar way—except in the opposite direction. My background was THOROUGHLY EUROPEAN, highly "civilized", but also very middle class, and a bit stifling. It was the experience of Yoruba society that widened my horizon, gave me an international perspective, and offered me an entirely new angle from which to view my own culture. Even when I had virtually no opportunity to speak my language, the German language, I kept reading it. In all those years, I kept reading German poetry and drama. I even translated several radio plays by Günther Eich for WNBS, Western Nigeria Broadcasting Services, and they were produced in English by Segun Olusola. We produced a radio play, *Der Doppelganger* by Friedrich Durrenmatt, in Yoruba with the Duro Ladipo Company. I adopted two other Durrenmatt radio plays, *Evening in Latre autumn* and *Conversation at Night,* for the stage. They both starred Segun Olusola and Segun Sofowote, and they became part of the repertoire of Theatre Express. I have always believed that cultural boundaries are there to be crossed and that any culture that tries to seal itself hermeneutically from the rest of the world will quickly become stale.

F: We've already described someone like Soyinka as a giant, someone who has been described by other commentators as a barometer for measuring the intellectual climate of not just his generation, but of succeeding ones as well. But don't you think that even such a complex writer didn't escape the sort of mental flights that you've been talking about? The pages of *Myth, Literature and the African World,* for example, are filled with his attempt to supply a scientific equivalent for almost everything African or Yoruba.

U: But then, if you read his conversation with me about Orisa ("Orisa Liberates the Mind"), he no longer takes that point of view; in fact he very much leaves the mystery intact! But in general terms, I think you are right. Those who try to come to terms with Yoruba thinking often try to justify it in terms of European equivalents. Science is still the ultimate symbol of "progress".

F: But do we really need that?

U: Well, we don't. I am convinced that mankind doesn't. The scientific revolution has a momentum of its own and nobody knows how to stop it. Yet fewer and fewer people believe in its blessings. The great medical achievements are proving to be a gigantic failure. I can say from my own personal experience that malaria has become a far more dangerous disease and far more difficult to cure than it was forty-five years ago when I first had to grapple with it. Things are out of control. We cannot stop Shell from causing environmental pollution in Nigeria, just as we failed to stop Conzinc Riotinto from totally ruining the environment of the island of Bougainville. Some people think that science has helped to lengthen the life span of human beings and will be able to lengthen it further. But is that desirable? Once the quality of life has been destroyed, what is the point of prolonging the agony? And in any case, how many changes, how many bitter experiences, and how many disappointments can we endure?

The quality of life does not depend on technology. I have lived amongst people in Papua New Guinea whose technology was minimal, yet their life was rich, their social organization wise--having created societies without hierarchies. Status had to be constantly *earned* through courage, diplomacy, and above all through rhetoric and poetry. Wars had been ritualized into tournaments, with grand displays of finely carved arrows and shields, feathers and body painting. After the first death, the warring parties retired in order to allow for funeral rites to take place and hostilities did not resume until months or years later. The people were completely self reliant; "trade" was a means of keeping friendly relations with neighbors rather than a method of making "profit". People's lives were guided by mythology, poetry, dance and song. Life had its cruelties and hardships, but nothing was as barbaric as the kinds of wars that Western technology has made possible and our progressive scientists are still perfecting.

F: In Cuba, Brazil and among other New World Yoruba, the cult of Roman Catholic saints were not merely introduced, but their attributes were learnt, and series of parallelism linking Christian figures and powers to the forces of ancient Yoruba deities, The smallpox deity, Sanponna, for example, was equated with saint Lazarus because of the latter's wounds as illustrated in chromolithographs; the Virgin Mary was equated with the sweet and gentle aspects of the multifaceted goddess of the river, Osun; and Sango, the Yoruba god of thunder, was equated with Saint Barbara etc. etc. Why has such a relative reorganization or syncretization of traditional religion with the imperial religions eluded the Yoruba in the homeland?

U: Conditions in Brazil were unique. African slaves outnumbered the white population two to one! They therefore constituted a potential threat to the "masters". Plantation owners encouraged their slaves to hold traditional dances after Church on Sundays so that they would retain loyalty to their respective "nations". It was hoped that in this way the slaves would not unite. The policy was successful. Some of the early slave revolts were staged by Hausa slaves, but the biggest and most dangerous of all in the early 1830s was a Yoruba revolt in which the Hausa slaves did not participate. But it was this policy that gave the slaves the opportunity to practice their traditional religion—even though they often did so in disguise to satisfy the Church. For example, the Yoruba would always have the statue of a Saint placed at the door of the *condomble,* and if a pastor came to ask what they were doing they could say: "We are praying to Saint Peter", when in fact they were worshipping Ogun. So the famous Brazilian syncretism started as a form of camouflage, and the identification between Saint and Orisa was on the most superficial level. Saint Peter was identified with Ogun because he cut off a soldier's ear! Saint Barbara was identified with Sango because she is symbolized by a tower of alternating red and white bricks similar to Sango's necklace of alternating red and white beads. Yemoja, goddess of the ocean, was identified more logically with the Virgin Mary in her specific role as protectress of sailors. Yoruba slaves had carried their belief system to the new world *intact.* Since they did not become literate in Portuguese for some time, they saw Catholic Saints like some additional Orisa to be incorporated into their pantheon, or the manifestations of existing ones. In the same way in which they could recognize Obatala, Orisa Ogiyan and Ajagemo as different manifestations of the same Orisa, they now embraced Catholicism on their own terms. It should be noted that the Catholic Church has always had the policy of allowing elements of traditional religion to be absorbed into Christianity; the Christmas tree and Easter eggs are ancient pagan rituals absorbed and trivialized by the Church. With the Olorisa in Brazil, however, the policy backfired; the Yoruba would not allow their traditions to be trivialized. There was a famous incident to corroborate this. According to Verger, one day the Yoruba led a candlelight procession along the bay of Copacabana in Rio de Janeiro, and when they reached a certain sacred spot they turned to the sea to offer a sacrifice to Yemoja. The Church, which by now had become worried about the persistence of "pagan" rituals, decided to stage a counter procession. When the Christians arrived at the beach carrying the image of the Virgin Mary, the Yoruba turned around happily saying, "The Virgin has come to greet Yemoja". They prayed to the Virgin, then faced the sea, and continued their ritual unperturbed.

Another interesting thing that happened in Brazil is that while Yoruba religion absorbed elements of Catholicism, other African religions identified with Yoruba. I once hit upon a ritual in Bahia which I could not interpret. It was conducted in a language I had never heard before. When I asked them about the Orisa whom they were worshipping, they said: "This is Ogun Angola".

Yoruba religion has such a prestige in Brazil that other African religions now identify with it. In the meantime, you can also find many white people worshipping in the condomble, and unlike Nigeria, the Orisa holds a strong appeal to people from all walks of life. I encountered police officers, even lawyers in the candomble; and of course, many artists and writers feel drawn to it. In Brazil a successful balance was achieved between Yoruba values and a more modern life style. In Nigeria on the other hand, I had to watch the painful process of disintegration of the culture. The educational system managed to create a rift between the Olorisa and the "educated" Christians, not to speak of the Muslims. On top of it all we experienced the oil boom and all the corruption it brought in its wake. I witnessed a generation of priests who were aware that they would be the last exponents of a great and noble way of life. Nevertheless they carried the burden of that huge responsibility without compromise

At the core of any Orisa ritual was the trance. For the ritual to be concluded successfully, the Orisa must be present amongst the worshippers. And the only way in which he can manifest his presence is to "mount" somebody's head. During the weekly *ose,* worship, on Jakuta day, Sango would mount anyone of those present. The worshippers dance in a circle to a monotonous *bata* rhythm. Suddenly a slight tremor goes through the body of one of the women; her eyes are glazed, and she is gently led aside into a cool recess of the shrine where she will rest until the ceremony is over. Then the senior priests will gather around her and she will prophesy. The Orisa's manifestation is so discreet in such a case that a stranger happening on such a scene does not usually realize the drama that is played out in front of his eyes. There are other situations, however; when the god manifests himself in a spectacular manner. During the annual *ebo,* sacrifice, in front of the Oba's palace Sango will manifest himself in his full force, and only a powerful priest who has been subtly prepared can carry the weight of such a manifestation on his head. He has to *be* Sango in public! He must walk like Sango, roar like Sango, speak like Sango and dance like Sango. He is wild, fierce, awesome, yet again gentle and witty; he is a great performer who entertains the public not only with demonstrations of supernatural strength, but also with humorous conjuring tricks and a sleight of hand!

F: Every culture perceives the world ultimately through its mythological allusions. As someone who has been associated with Yoruba culture for such a long time, how would you describe the mythological pantheon (pre)suppositions of the Yoruba?

U: A major difference between the Yoruba world view and the monotheistic religions is that Yoruba does not insist on a declaration of *faith,* whereas in Christianity faith has become the ultimate virtue. In the medieval play, *Everyman,* a successful rich man is suddenly confronted by death. Having led a ruthless life, he doesn't know how to confront his creator. He begs his friends to accompany him and plead for him, but they all desert him. He asks his good deeds to go with him, but they are too weak to make the journey. In the end he is saved by his faith alone. In some fundamentalist Christian religions and in Islam the ultimate evil is to *renege* on your faith, and doing so is punishable by death. In Yoruba, this notion does not exist. A Christian may find himself morally obliged to *believe* something that his reason tells him is wrong. Yoruba people don't draw this rigid line between physical reality and the mind. An Obatala priest in Ilobu was taunted by his grandson: "…The teacher said Obatala does not exist." Whereupon the old man answered: "Only that for which we have no name does not exist." Reality is not a set of scientific data; it is the interpretation we impose upon the world in order to make sense out of it. This reality is flexible, changing, and it exists in the context of other parallel realities. The Christian single-mindedness appears naive, if not slightly absurd, from a Yoruba point of view. Hence the Yoruba term for a Christian is *onigbagbo*—someone who has faith or someone who worships faith.

F: The question that I would like to attach to that is, which among the many orisa exercise the most fundamental influence in every, or any, area of experience or entity, and what are the fundamental dichotomies in their functions—either within the cultural framework or body of mythological presuppositions?

U: Strictly speaking this question makes no sense in Yoruba terms because for every human being it is an individual's *own Orisa* who will exercise the most profound influence on his or her life. An Obatala worshipper is not normally concerned with the power of Sango or Ogun. It is the relationship he can create between himself and Obatala that will shape his life. That is not all. There are different manifestations of Obatala, namely, Orisanla, Orisa Ogiyan, Ajagemo and so on. The devotees of these manifestations of Orisa Obatala are all closely related. They regard one another as one, and they attend each other's festivals, but they emphasize different aspects of the Obatala's personality, and these aspects—from the Olorisa's point of view—are not interchangeable! On the other hand there is a philosophical framework within which the personal interactions between Orisa and man take place. And here we have a body of mythology that is widely shared—even though different variants of the same myth may be told in different cult groups.

There is a body of shared knowledge that informs people's attitudes to the world. There is the well-known myth about Oduduwa, the creator of the land. Oduduwa descended to create the land because at the beginning there was only water. He carried a snail shell full of earth, some pieces of iron, and a cock. He placed the iron on the water, poured the earth over it, and instructed the cock to scatter the earth. As the cock scratched and scattered the earth, a solid substance formed and the earth was born. Oduduwa called the sixteen major Orisa from heaven. The Orisa arrived and settled on the newly formed earth which they called

Ile Ife. This holy city, according to the Yoruba and the meaning of the name, was the birth place of the earth.

The political significance of this myth is that Oduduwa is the creator and therefore the owner of the earth. Therefore every Oba owes allegiance to his descendant, the Ooni of Ife. But there is a second, equally well known myth about Oduduwa. Here he is represented as a brave leader who led his people across the river Niger, subdued the aboriginal population in the Ife area, and forced them to settle within the walls of the city of Ife, the town he founded. What's of note here is that unlike the oriental despotic rulers who tended to wipe out the descendants of a defeated king—to the last baby—Oduduwa integrated the conquered people by giving their king a chieftaincy title within the hierarchy of Ife. This whole episode is commemorated annually in the Edi festival in Ife. During this festival the original owners of the land are recognized and paid homage to before the status-quo is restored and the Ooni, descendant of Oduduwa, rules for another year.

To the European mind these two myths are contradictory, and an historian might be tempted to say that if one is the true story the other must be wrong. But it is this very capacity of the Yoruba mind to accept these two apparently contradictory accounts as alternative truths that enables them to also recognize the conquered culture as of equal worth. Therefore they could accommodate the coexistence of these cultures within the walls of the same city, and Ile Ife emerged as the first multicultural city! And it is not hard to see why Muslims and Christians—or even different Muslim sects or different Christian sects—cannot easily live harmoniously together. The very fact that each claims to be the sole custodian of the truth makes coexistence extremely difficult. On the other hand, the Yoruba, who liken God to a swarm of bees, or a conglomeration of many Orisa who represent specific aspects of the divinity, makes a harmonious society *imperative* because society as a whole cannot exist unless all segments of the community—including all the different groups of Olorisa—put their insight, wisdom and the ritual *techniques* together for the benefit of the community. But there is another aspect to that story. Oduduwa did not descend from Heaven *alone*. In fact the mission to create the land had been entrusted to his senior brother Obatala, and Oduduwa was only accompanying him. But on the way Obatala drank too much palm wine and fell asleep. Oduduwa usurped his brother's responsibility, and performed the duty that led to the creation of the earth. This leads us to another very important element, namely even gods are human. They have virtues and vices. They are strong and weak. They are generous and vindictive, loveable and fearsome—all at the same time. In their imperfection the Orisa are merely a reflection of the world as it is. This divine fallibility features prominently in the second creation myth. Here Obatala creates human beings out of clay, not in a single act of creation but continuously. Here again in the middle of his task the Orisa got drunk on palm wine and as a result he created albinos, hunchbacks, and various kinds of impaired people—including lunatics. Unlike the Biblical god who is perfect, and invents the devil to explain imperfection, Obatala takes full responsibility for *all* his creations, perfect or otherwise, and encourages a very tolerant attitude towards all. If Obatala is responsible for deformed people then we must respect his spirit in them and we must pay them a certain respect. In Obatala shrines special positions are given to albinos and hunchbacks, and in all lunatics are treated with extreme respect and tolerance in Yoruba society. As long as a person is not violent, he has the *right* to wander about naked, to let his hair grow into dreadlocks and to sleep on the market place. Everyone has a moral obligation to feed such people or clothe them—if they accept clothes. In the early sixties, I knew a couple, a man and a woman, who wandered about together, and eventually had a child who was born in the market place where they lived. When the child was about six years old Duro Ladipo went to them and said, "Look, I think it would be better for your child if you allowed me to bring her up for you." The child subsequently grew up in Duro's home, led a normal life, married and had children.

F: Incredible!

U: As the French artist, Jean Dubouffet, once said, "Lunacy is the extreme form of individualism." One could say that Yoruba people feel that way, too. There is a modern trend in Europe to open up psychiatric hospitals and send the patients back into the community, but people in Europe find it hard to deal with the mentally ill. They have neither the tolerance nor the patience.

F: You were saying that every Orisa embodies one aspect of a specific way of looking at the world?

U: There is a story that explains the multiplicity of the Orisa. At the beginning there was only one Orisa. He is depicted in this myth as an old man who lived under a steep cliff. He had one servant who secretly hated him. One day when Orisa returned home in the evening, the servant hid himself on top of the cliff from where he had a clear view of Orisa. As soon as Orisa entered the hut, the servant rolled a huge boulder which crushed the hut and Orisa into hundreds of splinters which scattered throughout the world. Orunmila, the first Ifa priest, collected as many pieces as he could find, put them into a calabash which he deposited at a shrine in Ife. This he called it Orisanla, the big Orisa. But many of the splinters are still in trees and rocks and rivers and animals and human beings. So there is some spark of the divine essence everywhere—even within ourselves! But we have to discover it and try to be in harmony with it because it is not like the Biblical concept where there is "God" on one side and the world on the other; or "God" telling man to make the earth and everything in it his subject. So it follows that the Yoruba saw themselves as part of a divine environment. They believed in balance—balance between gods and men, between animals and men, between plants and men. It would not have occurred to them to cut down huge stretches of forest to create plantation. Their farms, even in the fifties were small patches that were integrated into the forest. It is only since they have lost their religion that the Yoruba began to destroy their environment.

It is a curious thing that many intellectual Yoruba, even those who try to come to terms with their culture, still can't face the "stigma" of polytheism. They dodge the question, or they concoct a scientific myth according to which the Yoruba were good monotheists, but somewhere along the line they degenerated into Orisa worship; or else they try to see the Orisa as a mere mediator between god and men, as something separate from, and essentially different from god. The Yoruba world view is more subtle than that. The only who has really understood that was a Muslim friend of mine from Bamako, Mallam Hampate Ba. He was a very pious Muslim. People at home revered him as a saintly man. He was also a scholar of Fulani and Bambara religion. When he met the old Magba Sango at Ilobu, he was so impressed by her personality that he remark, "When people talk to me about polytheism, I tell them that Allah has 99 names, and how do you know that each name is not the name of another god?"

But let's return to the concept of the scattering of the divine essence. Since every person has some of this divine spark within him, it is his duty to identify the nature of it. Unless you know who you are and what your human potential is, you cannot establish the right relationship with an

Orisa. In other words, you can only worship the Orisa that befits you, not just any divinity. The myth of *akunleyan* and the "garden of *ori*" explains this concept. Before you enter this world you are led into the "garden of *ori*, heads, literally, or destinies metaphorically. You pick your own 'head', your destiny, and this is what you bring down with you from heaven. This is what you have to live with. But this is not to be confused with a fatalistic world view. On the contrary, what you bring down from heaven is your capital, and you must make it work. Your *ori* sets your limitations; it determines your potential. You must make sure that you develop this potential to the fullest. To enable you to do so you must identify *your* Orisa—the one that is congenial to you; the one whose personality is closest to your own because only with that Orisa will you be able to achieve the interaction and harmony that will enable you to develop your potential to its fullest extent.

Yoruba religion and Yoruba philosophy place the utmost importance on the development of individuality—there is no regimentation in this culture even though you have to develop your personality within a certain framework. You have to work at yourself all the time; you have to work at your relationship with the Orisa continuously and relentlessly. It is a religion that places a lot of responsibility on the individual. This is why, contrary to the prejudice that was long held by Yoruba scholars, Yoruba art was anything but anonymous. We have since learned to distinguish easily between the styles of say Bamgboye, Areogun and Olowe of Ise. And even within the work of a single artist you always find some unique pieces! Some little joke, some quirk of the imagination which the artist produced only once. That is why when you look at the vast collections of Yoruba art that are found in Europe and America, there are always pieces which you can't classify because they don't seem to fit any of the laid down criteria. The Yoruba were too flexible for that. They wouldn't allow their imagination to be regimented.

F: Would you like to talk about the Orisa that attracted you most?

U: I think I felt most comfortable with Sango.

F: Why?

U: I don't really know. Many of my friends were Sango priests. I felt immensely comfortable with them. I had Sango friends in Ede, in Osogbo, Ilobu, Ifon,

Ara, Otan, Okuku and Ila Orangun. There was a huge circuit of Sango shrines and we constantly travelled from one festival to the other. I felt attracted to Bandele of Otan, that fiery dancer, and to the Magba Sango in Ilobu, a very old woman of great beauty and passion. I also had very close relationships with the Erinle priests of Ilobu and with the Sonponna priests of Erin. Sango is a colorful god. I liked his sense of humor, his playfulness, his generosity. His anger was not to be taken too seriously, after all when there is thunder it is only very rarely that lightening actually strikes. Sango is a grand Orisa, and undoubtedly one of the most lovable.

F: The Sonponna cult is something that literally strikes terror into the hearts of people. Why is that so? Is it evil—as many Christians would say?

U.   That is a total misunderstanding—if not a deliberate distortion. To justify their domination of others, Westerners have always looked for evidence of "evil" in foreign cultures. The Yoruba, as we have said before, conceive of the divine essence as something infinitely complex. So no individual—and not even an ancient hierarchy of priests—can grasp it all; people can only understand aspects of it. And according to the nature of our *ori*, we can become specialists in dealing with certain aspects of supernatural powers. For example, the Egungun, masqueraders, are specialists in communicating with the dead. Sango worshippers know how to communicate with another aspect of the divine essence. It is naive to say "Sango is the god of thunder." Of course, thunder is one of his symbols, but it does not describe him. To understand the complexity of his being, we must listen to his *oriki* instead of transferring the shallow terminology of latter day Greek mythology to this Yoruba Orisa. Sonponna has to do with suffering, and the Sonponna priests can teach you how to live and cope with suffering. ... You don't simply fight the disease, even though the Sonponna priests have treatments. You are made to see that the Orisa has something to tell you, that he wants to draw you into his orbit, and that he uses this harsh method to let you know. You will lead a much more meaningful and purposeful life once you have understood the message and drawn the consequences. If you read the *oriki* of Sonponna or Obaluaye or Alajire—the various manifestations of the god—you will find a lot of tenderness in them. Such tenderness could never be engendered by a cult that consists of exploitative charlatans—as some missionaries claimed. These vicious tales are absurd. First of all, if they were true, why were the Sonponna priests not rich? They were as poor as all other Olorisa because material wealth didn't even enter it! Secondly, look at the faces of the Sonponna priests I photographed in the 1950s. How do they get such sad, wise, compassionate faces? You don't put on a face like a mask. Your face is the result of your life; it is the result of your spiritual life. It cannot lie. Again, it was the personalities of the people that attracted me to Sonponna. Their *ose* was not boisterous and witty like Jakuta, the weekly Sango ceremony. But I found the people very moving. Sonponna is a very beautiful, poetic Orisa.

Orisa worship is not about good and evil in the Christian sense. Nor is it about following rules and regulations and commandments. It is about fulfilling yourself. About living out your *ori*, about becoming what you are meant to become. Only closeness to the Orisa can help you do this.

F: According to Hans Witte, in contrast to the Orisa and earth spirits who attract worshippers on the basis of family tradition, profession, special vocation, Orunmila and Esu are venerated by every traditional Yoruba. The cosmic system would fall apart without the integrating activity of the Ifa and the trickster. What is so extraordinary about these two deities?

U: Each Orisa has a very distinct historical personality, and an Orisa's cult is particularly virile in places where this connection is strong. There are some religious institutions, though, that cut across Yorubaland, and they even play a politically unifying role. The Ogboni society is one of these. If you are an Ogboni you can go to any town in Yorubaland, go to the *lledi*, make yourself known through a series of passwords, participate in their rituals, and contribute to all their deliberations. The Ogboni society has been used, historically, as a peacemaker between warring parties because this cult cuts across national boundaries. One of the binding principles is that all Yoruba people live on the earth and they must take care not to offend the earth spirit. The Ogboni therefore have a lot of political influence beyond the walls of their own city.

In a very different way Ifa transcends all boundaries. Information about one's Orisa is *absorbed* from childhood, and you learn your Orisa's *oriki* simply by hearing the drummers or chanters at the big festivals; you are not made to sit down and learn a catechism. Ifa on the other hand is a code of knowledge that had to be learned and interpreted by professionals. It was not written and not fixed; new *Odu* were always invented and added. The study took at least seven years, and a real Babalawo would extend his knowledge at every major festival when he heard other great priests recite their versions of the *Odu*. Ifa created a structure, a framework in which the wild and the ever changing interaction between different Orisa and conflicting mythologies could take place. It imposed some kind of order onto the multifaceted world view of the Yoruba, but you must not think of the rigidity of European or Middle Eastern belief systems when you hear the word "order." For example, when you come to an Ifa priest, Babalawo, with a problem there is no clear cut answer, and he does not consult a law book. There are numbers of *Odu*, Ifa verses, that he can quote and interpret...to grasp and address ... his client's problem.

Now to your question about order and disorder, Esu has always been called the principle of disorder. Superficially that is true. But remember there is a new branch of physics, chaos research, which is based on the assumption that what we perceive as chaos is simply a different kind of order. Now take the myth I recited before about Orisanla being crushed by his servant. Here somebody creates chaos—or apparently so. But when I tell you that the servant was really Esu in disguise as is said in some versions of this myth, then there is an entirely different significance to it. It becomes a case of divine intervention, and what looks like chaos is in reality a new kind of order. Instead of a single monolithic god we now have divine substance spread throughout the world, and present in everyone and every object. We have a new world order in which god and the world are inseparable and interwoven.

And this is the function of Esu. He creates a new order by challenging the old. The Yoruba have always understood that routine is the death of creativity and that complacency is the death of a spiritually alert life. Therefore Esu systematically upsets our plans, provokes us with the unexpected and keeps us wide awake. Esu reminds us every minute of the day that we cannot take anything for granted, that we have to live responsibly all the time, and that we must work at our relationships with gods and men. If you look at modern life in Europe, you can see that our thinking is dominated and shaped by the media, by advertising, commerce and politics, our youngsters often turn into zombies, and their concentration span shorter and shorter. I feel that we badly need Esu in the modern world. We badly need the intervention of the trickster god!

F: People just get into set-patterns, and do the same thing over and over. But to revisit the site of the origin of this disorder, we have established that the Christians had little difficulties in translating Esu as the Biblical equivalent of the devil. It was done by a Yoruba man apparently...

U: Of course, yes.

F: Well, my question is, if Ifa, as we are often told, consists of the sacred texts of the Yoruba people as does the Bible for Christians, and Esu is the path to Ifa, could one say that the literal translation of Esu as the biblical equivalent of Satan or devil is more than an accident? That the translation was, in fact, meant to sound the death-knell of this view of the world?

U: I am convinced it was a deliberate attempt to discredit, to demonize Yoruba religion. The Church has a long history of that. They have done the same thing in Europe. They have a real difficulty in grasping the complexity of Yoruba culture. In Christianity there is this rigid division of the world into good and evil. They could never understand a concept like *aje*, witch, for example. *Aje* represents the magical power of women, particularly of the powerful female spirits whom even the Orisa must fear. But their power is not necessarily evil. It can equally be creative. There was the concept that an old woman could become vehicles for destructive magic forces, and she could quite unwittingly at times be responsible for the death of children in the compound. It was usually the Egungun, masqueraders, who could identify such a person. But she was not killed—unlike in medieval Europe where "witches" were burnt alive. Yoruba society was content to identify the destructive force and through exposure render it impotent. It was not a question of crime and punishment, but rather a question of the restoration of balance and social harmony.

F: I am aware of your disdain for theory and cultural theorists, and I would not like to bore you with too much of what they say. Nevertheless, going back over the years could you explain why you adopted one in particular, among your fascinating pseudonyms, I mean the controversial Obotunde Ijimere—which raised a disturbing association with the signifying monkey or trickster figure even though you were using the pseudonym while writing *The Imprisonment of Obatala,* a tragedy?

U: That has been talked about a lot. The name was picked on the spur of the moment, as a joke, really. But if you were to put an interpretation onto it with hindsight, I would say Ijimere is not a common monkey jumping from branch to branch. He's a wise animal whom some Yoruba compare him to a Babalawo. I certainly would not want to claim wisdom for myself, but I was fascinated by this creature. He waits for you on the road and looks you straight in the eye, and challenges you. When a little tribe of Ijimere crosses the road, the big male will stare at your car until they have moved to safety. I have always been fond of Ijimere and we have had several of them in the house.

F: If I could use that analogy to latch on to the tragic story—*The Imprisonment of Obatala*—do you feel that epistemologically speaking, the abiding metaphor of Yoruba philosophy or mythology reposes on tragedy rather than comedy?

U: This is difficult to answer because you are now imposing foreign criteria on the culture. It is true that every Orisa lived a tragic life; that it was disappointment with the world, disillusionment with the small-mindedness of human beings that made them remove themselves to another sphere where they could really become themselves. Either through suicide, like Sango, or through a metamorphosis, like Otin, but the transformation of a human being into a river or a rock is merely a mythological metaphor for suicide.

F: And if you move from the domain of Orisa, as you said earlier on, the Yoruba believe in intensive living. The abiding atmosphere of the motor park, for example, is boisterous, comical, lively, but equally serious.

U: In Yoruba life tragedy and comedy are not separated. Look at Sango, the most tragic of Orisa, is also the greatest joker. Think of the entertaining performance of the Baba Elegun at the Sango festival, the delightful mixture of physical prowess and sleight of hand! Think of the Egungun masqueraders: the awe-inspiring ancestral masks, so holy that the public have to be protected from their touch by groups of young men who lash around wildly with whips. Yet these same Egungun produce the Alarinjo theatre which, sometimes during the same festival, lampoons all the village characters as well as other tribes and Europeans! They even make fun of Sango and don't stop short of the ancestral masks themselves! Tragedy and comedy live closely together in Yoruba land. They are seen as two sides of the same coin.

F: Absolutely, absolutely! The people to whom I would like to dedicate, and at the same time address this whole thing, if you permit me, are the younger generations of Africans, the Yoruba and other people whose experiences in life have never known a semblance of order! If our ultimate purpose is to use this as a sort of retrieval of all that appear irretrievably lost, the question that I would like to ask is that as a renowned education-ist, given the chance today—at the tail end of 20th century—what would you include and what would you leave out in the educational process of the average African child?

U: No culture has been more written about than Yoruba culture, and there is a vast body of knowledge that has been collected by Yoruba scholars. What we still need is a really comprehensive presentation of the world view, the philosophy and the religion. It is the religious aspect that many Yoruba scholars do not want to face squarely. They still have this hang up about "polytheism". There are exceptions of course, like Wole Soyinka. I remember a conference in Venice ... where the Nigerian writer, Ibrahim Tahir, said that Islam was about to become the religion of Nigeria... He got a very fierce response from Wole who said that both Christianity and Islam were in fact impediments to the development of Nigeria, whereas Yoruba religion and other traditional forms of worship were far more flexible and adaptable. Wole could see, already then, the tolerance and wisdom of the Yoruba religion. Perhaps it has been the weakness of Yoruba religion that it was too tolerant. The Yoruba welcomed Chris-tianity and Islam as other variants of the truth that could add another dimension to their life. They could not have imagined the viciousness with which they would be persecuted.

   What I would want to put across to a new generation of Yoruba, of Africans, or to any new generation—whether in Asia or Europe—is the tolerance of Yoruba religion, its understanding of human weakness, its way of creating harmony, and its respect for the individual. Above all, I would want to put across the notion that we become good members of a community not by obeying a set of abstract rules, but by developing and fulfilling our own potential and talents that are contained in the *ori* we have brought into the world. That is the core of Yoruba philosophy, and it is a wisdom that would benefit all mankind.

Ulli Beier talks to Olu Obafemi
"REFLECTIONS..."

O: It is widely acknowledged that you are one of the few individuals who made a tremendous impact on the development of African literature, art and culture in general. To clarify the nature of these contributions I would like to ask you a few questions. First of all, what do you consider your main contribution, and which achievement are you most fond of?

U: I can't really answer that because I did not go to Ibadan to make "a contribution". You should read my recent essay "In a Colonial University" (Iwalewa 1993). That essay describes in some detail how I came to Ibadan almost by accident, and how I got involved in various activities gradually, simply in response to certain situations.

Originally I had no other aim in mind except to teach English literature. But I soon found out that my students couldn't relate to much of what I said. It seemed like an alien subject. To make it more meaningful I tried to find out what African literature there was that I could refer to. My colleagues assured me that there was no such thing. I found their lack of curiosity difficult to understand. Of course, the great upsurge of Nigerian literature had not happened in 1950. But there were some great writers in the francophone countries, so I translated Senghor, Césaire, Rabéarivelo and Diop, and introduced them into my classes

One of the most exciting discoveries I made were S. A. Babalola's translations of *Ijala*, which opened up a whole new world for me. I suddenly realized what wealth of poetry was to be discovered in the Yoruba language with wit and wisdom and powerful images. Without knowing it at the time, my life had taken a decisive turn. Once you read *Ijala* you get drawn into a whole new life style.

As early as 1952 I held an Extra Mural Weekend School in Abeo-kuta called "African Poetry". It was a rather wild mixture of material that we looked at. It was not a highly organized course. But I think it made a point. It demonstrated the fact that literature was not some strange English invention or something one had to learn in order to pass ones school certificate or to become part of the new elite. It showed the students that they had their own tradition of classical literature which was as much as that of any nation, and it put English literature in its proper place. English literature was no longer the expression of a superior culture that was to be imposed on Nigerians in order to replace their own culture. It was merely another form of expression that could offer one a widening of the horizon, a further window onto the world.

I suppose I am still doing the same thing now—forty years later. When I put on an annual concert of African music in the Bayreuth Opera House I am trying to say to the German audience that "With due respect to Bach, Mozart and Beethoven, there are other classical music traditions; different, but as complex and intense and rewarding as your own. And you must listen to a *dundun* orchestra or to Igbo xylophones with as much concentration as you do to a Beethoven string quartet."

The wonderful thing about living in a new country, in a new culture, is that you make discoveries every day. My first years in Nigeria were full of surprises. Life could never become a routine. You develop a height-ened sense of awareness. Strangely enough, many of my colleagues at the University tried to shut themselves off from the experience; they created a ghetto around themselves. They saw their task as a civilizing mission. They had to create an elite group whom they could trust to rule Nigeria, and such an elite group had to absorb enough British values. The British recognized no other values in life than their own. I was lucky because after one frustrating year in the English Department I could switch over to the Department of Extra-Mural Studies which was headed by that dynamic and inspiring Ghanaian, Robert Gardner. There I had moti-vated colleagues like Gerald Moore and later, even Ezekiel Mphahlele. Above all I was independent of the London University syllabus. It was the students themselves, not the University of Ibadan (let alone the Uni-versity of London!) who determined what was to be studied. If I could also persuade them to study African Literature or African Art or even to found a Theatre Company, the University could not stop us.

Robert Gardiner gave me that freedom and he also gave me the inspiration. Gardiner used the Extra-Mural Department to raise all those issues that the University, in its ivory tower seclusion, always ignored. He saw literature not as an academic subject, not as a specialization in "Eng. Litt.", but as a way of understanding people, their problems, their philosophies and their cultures. He was a highly political man, and in many of our literature courses, we used literature to discuss political issues. My own contributions to the Extra-Mural Department were the cultural seminars. The pioneering venture was called "West African Culture". It was held on the University campus in the summer of 1953. We went on to launch in Ede in 1954 a course on Yoruba culture. This time we were on a much more solid ground, and the lecturers included three Oba— the Ooni of Ife, Timi Laoye and the Ogoga of Ikere. There were also S. A. Babalola, E. L. Lasebikan and the philosopher T.S. Sowande. All these people were not only highly knowledgeable about their culture, they were passionate about it! It was this course that inspired the creation of *Odu*, a literary journal. I dreamt in those days of the possibility of revising the entire structure of education in Yorubaland. That all these committed people could give an entirely new slant to the educational system the British had planted in Nigeria. But up till today Nigerian schools and universities still propagate, to a large extent, colonial ideas. Isn't that right?

O: Yes, it is, in a way.

U: I am sorry I have been rather long-winded in trying to explain how I got involved. The only real quality I brought to these experiences was, perhaps, flexibility.

O: Thank you very much. This is an aspect of your contribution about which not much has been recorded. Now, in an attempt to quantify your contribution you have been described in various ways as a border operator, a spokesman of African literature. And because of your organizational ability and your success in raising funds for various activities you were seen as a literary entrepreneur. An important area which I would like you to touch upon is the foundation of *Black Orpheus* which, I think, has done a lot to bring scholars and writers together. What was your motivation in starting *Black Orpheus*, and in what direction did you steer the magazine?

U: Well, it was quite simple really. I had been interested in African literature for a while and I was teaching it, but I had never thought of a magazine. Then in 1956 I attended the first Pan African Conference of African Writers and Artists organized by Presence Africaine. It was a very exciting conference, a high powered affair which was taken very seriously by the French media, and it was not treated like a fringe event. Picasso himself designed the poster. It was amazing for me to see how vital the literary movement was in the Caribbean and in the French African territories.

The highlight of the conference was the clash between Richard Wright and Aimé Cesaire. Richard Wright had been to Ghana at the invitation of Victor Pasmore, Nkrumah's West Indian adviser. He had gone with the illusion of "coming home" like so many other Afro-Americans. But Ghana bewildered him and he could not see any merit in the culture at all. In his book *Black Power* he describes Ghana as a place riddled with "superstition". So he stood up there on the rostrum and proclaimed: "Thank you white man for destroying our culture!" He felt that Africa had to be totally modernized, that it had to be "militarized" and that in the process of doing this it had to strip itself of its "dark" past.

It pained me deeply to hear him speak like that, because I had been an admirer of his writings for years, I had used books like *Black Boy* and *Native Son* in my classes. Césaire's response was passionate and inspiring. He had no difficulty in carrying the bulk of the audience with him. It was at this moment, that the idea of *Black Orpheus* was born. I wanted Nigerians to have access to this dynamic world. I wanted my students to share the excitement I had felt in Paris. I was also helped by meeting Janheinz Jahn for the first time. Of course we had corresponded for the last three years. He had published his anthology of African poetry in German as early as 1954 when African literature was virtually unknown in Germany. In the process of compiling his *Schwarzer Orpheus* he had corresponded for years with people all over Africa, including myself. I had helped him to get some material which included works by Mabel Imoukhuede, Dennis Osadebey and even some Ijala poems in S. A. Babalola's translations.

Jahn had, at the time, the largest existing archive on African literature, and he was a very useful and energetic partner. Once we had made up our mind to start a journal, we wasted no time. The Literature Bureau of the Ministry of Education in Ibadan was sympathetic. They were already publishing *Odu* and were happy with its success. So by September 1957 our first issue appeared with poems by S. A. Babalola, Leopold Sedar Senghor and Gabriel Okara, with an article on Amos Tutuola and a report on the Presence Africaine conference in Paris.

Black Orpheus was not a big commercial enterprise. The magazine was almost handmade. There was no staff, only voluntary workers. The covers were screen printed., and the edition did not exceed fifteen hundred. Yet, its influence was disproportionately high. In Germany Jahn found a friendly bookseller who took a hundred copies which found their way into the hands of writers and scholars. In Holland a passionate journalist called Van Brassem personally distributed another hundred copies. One of these reached the artist Ru van Rossem, who later became involved in the Mbari Clubs and ran graphic art workshops there. In South Africa the magazine had to be smuggled in and sold illegally—under the counter by Vanguard Bookshop in Johannesburg. The bookshop owner took considerable risk doing so!

Black Orpheus had no ideology. What we wanted to do was to provide a platform for writers, and our criterion was quality. We also wanted to acquaint West African English speaking writers with the literary activities that went on in French speaking Africa. At a later stage we even introduced North African Writers. We also kept the bridges open to the past. Each issue of *Black Orpheus* contained some translations of traditional poetry.

O: So the awareness that something existed before was there.

U: Of course. We wanted to remind people that all African cultures had lyrical, epical and dramatic forms, and that all this new literature was not happening in a vacuum. We were not literary archeologists! In the 1950s and 60s everything was happening at the same time! While some people were writing political poems for the *West African Pilot* and while Wole Soyinka was performing his first great plays, the hunters were still singing their *ijala,* the Sango priests were still chanting *Sango pipe* and the oracle priests were still reciting their *odu.* You did not have to go out of your way to find these things. Simply by sitting on my verandah on Ibokun Road in Osogbo I would hear the mother of twins improvising her songs in praise of *ibeji.* I would hear the *rara* chanting of the bride on her way to her husband's house. I would hear the *oriki* of all the major Orisa! It was all very much alive, and I felt it would be very wrong to pretend it was a thing of the past—with no relevance to the present. In those days even political campaigns were fought with the help of *dundun* drummers and *oriki* chanters!

O: Thank you. Thomas Benson wrote a book on the history of *Black Orpheus* and *Transition,* and he had very many things to say on *Black Orpheus* and your role in it.

U: Yes, but he never bothered to interview me. In fact, I never met him. But that's only by the way.

O: His contribution was good. It wasn't negative in any way, because he attributed *Black Orpheus* solely to you. But what interests me in his account is that he claims that aesthetically, you were leaning towards surrealism and that politically you loved the ideology of Negritude, though later on, you shifted your position.

U: No, no, that is completely incorrect. You can only publish the literature that exists. In 1957 there was no Wole Soyinka and there was no Christopher Okigbo. The first issue of *Black Orpheus* featured Gabriel Okara, hardly a Negritude writer. The first four issues may have had a predominance of French African, Caribbean and Afro American writing, but that was simply because Anglophone writing in Africa appeared on the scene slightly later. I met Wole Soyinka in London in 1958 after a Nigerian BBC producer had shown me three of his poems, "The Immigrant", "The Other Immigrant" and "My Next Door Neighbor". I was quite excited by these, and I rang him to make an appointment. He came to meet me at Gallery One in Soho where Susanne Wenger was holding her first London exhibition. I published the poems in our next issue, Nr. 5, which appeared in May 1959. But anyway, who published Wole's first plays?

O: It was you, I think. *The Three Plays.*

U: That's right. I created *Mbari Publications* and we published Wole's first three plays, J.P. Clark's *Song of a Goat*, Okigbo's first two volumes of poetry, J.P. Clark's first volume of poetry, Alex La Guma's novel, *A Walk in the Night*—which I had to smuggle out of South Africa. We published Mphalele's stories and Dennis Brutus' first volume of poetry (while he was in jail), Kofi Awoonor's first poems and Lenrie Peters from Sierra Leone. We published Ama Ata Aidoo's first short story in *Black Orpheus.*

So what do you mean by saying I was a Surrealist and a Negritude partisan? Where were Heinemann and Longmans in those days? Where were the American publishers? They wouldn't touch any of these works. As far as I can remember I only published one Surrealist story, "Because of the King of France", by Adrienne Cornell. She was an Afro American writer, married to a sociologist called Kennedy who was working in Ibadan. One day he came to me and said that his wife wrote stories, but was too shy to show them to anybody. Could I give her an opinion? I fell in love with that story and published it at once. And if I didn't publish any more Surrealist stories, it was because I didn't come across any others that I thought were good. That's all. Adrienne Cornell, also known as Adrienne Kennedy, by the way, went on to become a famous playwright in New York.

O: Thank you very much. I don't think Thomas Benson meant it negatively. But there is another thing people have been accusing you of. They said that you tried to dominate the critical voice of *Black Orpheus*, and that is why you used so many pseudonyms...

U: You seem to forget that there weren't any literary critics around in those days. Most creative writers don't really like to tear each other's work apart. And the Ireles and Nwogas appeared a little later on the scene. I used whom I could find, Gerald Moore contributed heavily, so did J.A. Ramsaran. Later on Ezekiel Mphalele and Ronald Dathorne shouldered much of the burden. I could persuade some people to contribute an occasional review—Cyprian Ekwensi for example or Dennis Duerden or Geombeyi Adali Mortty. As *Black Orpheus* became internationally known I could persuade famous people like Martin Esslin or Paul Theroux to write for it.

But in the early days I had to play the donkey. It became a similar issue when we started the Mbari Club in Ibadan. No Nigerian newspaper at the time had an arts page or a feuilleton. I went from editor to editor asking them to report on Mbari exhibitions and concerts and plays, but they kept saying that they had no one to do it, and they invited me to write for them myself. I did so for the first few weeks while I kept going around looking for people who eventually organized reviews columns or whole pages for local papers.

As for pseudonyms, Sangodare Akanji or Omidiji Aragbabalo are not my pseudonyms. They are my *oriki,* praise names, given to me by the Sango priests of Osogbo and the Erinle priests of Ilobu respectively. Maybe you didn't know it, but Wole also used a pseudonym in *Black Orpheus*, though he did not indulge in it as often as I did.

O: There was a feeling that *Black Orpheus* concentrated heavily on poetry and fiction but neglected the performing arts. Why so little drama?

U: A magazine can absorb a poem and a short story easily, but the reproduction of a complete play would burst its frame. That's why we published plays in Mbari Publications—Wole's plays, Duro's plays and J.P.'s plays.

O: There was this tremendous impact you had on artists like Twins Seven-Seven and Demas Nwoko. A lot has been said about the workshops you ran in Osogbo...

U: I am glad you mention this because there has been a lot of mythmaking around these workshops. But let's talk about Demas first. Demas Nwoko was trained in Zaria, at the Nigerian College of Arts Science and Technology. He was the leader in the revolt against the British art education system that was foisted on the students. Quite early on he evolved a very personal style of painting. Later he became a successful stage designer, and finally a brilliant, self trained architect. I think he is by far the most interesting architect operating in Nigeria. I had nothing to do with his brilliant career at all except that I have always admired his work. We were co-founders of Mbari in Ibadan and I exhibited his work. But that was all.

A lot of nonsense has been written about the Osogbo art workshops. I am not an artist. I have never painted a picture in my life, and I could not run an art workshop. Yet people who knew better because they were actually there—people like Michael Crowder and Frank Willett—have described me as running the Osogbo art workshops. This simply is not true. The first two workshops in 1962 and 1963 were run by Denis Williams, a West Indian painter and scholar whom I invited to Osogbo. His workshops created a lot of life and activity, but they did not produce any professional artists because they lasted only five days. Denis, being very busy in Ibadan on his research, could not do any follow up work as we had hoped. In 1963, however, Georgina Beier arrived in Osogbo and she opened a studio in which Rufus Ogundele and Jacob Afolabi could work. It was then only that these two artists developed the confidence and the skill to become professional artists. Then in 1964 Georgina ran the famous workshop from which Muraina Oyelami, Twins Seven-Seven, Bisi Fabunmi and Tijani Mayakiri emerged. Until we left Osogbo in December 1966 all these artists and some like Samuel Ojo, who joined the group later, were working in our house or in a studio we had opened for them in the Ataoja's palace. I arranged exhibitions for the artists. I created galleries for them. I wrote about them..., but I never taught them. But all this has been described in detail in the publication *Thirty Years of Oshogbo Art* which was published by Iwalewa-Haus in 1992. We don't really have to go into this again.

O: Thank you. This is the kind of clarification I thought was necessary for historical purposes. So you didn't teach art, but is it true that you taught creative writing in New Guinea?

U: Yes, I did run a creative writing class in Papua New Guinea, though at first rather reluctantly. I went to PNG because the newly founded University was looking for someone to teach "New Literature from Developing Nations". In other words, the kind of thing that I had been doing for the last fifteen years on the fringe of the University of Ibadan and almost against the University's wishes, I could now set up as the official literature course. I found that very tempting. The University of Papua New Guinea was, in those early years, the best university I have ever been in. It was independent of any Australian institution. It had a highly motivated staff—mostly Australians, and it had only 350 students at that time. I knew virtually every one of them.

I compiled a literature course consisting of a study of PNG oral traditions, African, Indian and Australian literature in English, Modern World Literature. English classics were merely brought in as optional subjects in the final year. The only problem was that literature was a "half unit" and it had to be combined with another language half unit. My best students hated the language courses and so I was in danger of losing them. The only way to keep them was to offer an alternative "half unit" and this is how I came to teach "Creative Writing"—with some trepidation, because basically I believed that it could not be done.

O: You're right. Nobody can teach the art of creativity.

U: I made the course a 'by invitation only'. During the first year students could submit their writing to me—stories, poetry, drama and whatever they wished. But at this stage they received no credit for it all. Out of these I would select about half a dozen with whom I thought I could work, and they could then drop the language part and take creative writing.

But it is a nerve wrecking experience for the teacher. When somebody submits to you a piece of writing, it's often very easy to improve it. But that's pointless unless you are quite sure what the student really wanted to do. Otherwise you are merely impeding his natural development. Teaching is not a matter of showing somebody some useful tricks, but of getting to know the student, of understanding him and giving him the confidence to be himself. It is a very delicate thing. The chemistry has to be right between the teacher and the student; you have to divest yourself of the image of authority. Georgina has this sensitivity in the highest degree, and that's why some of the greatest artists in New Guinea and in Nigeria emerged from her studio. But I think we are drifting...

O: Yes, we must talk about Duro Ladipo because people are intrigued about what kind of relationship you had with Duro Ladipo, to the effect that people think you have actually shaped his theatre. It was even said that the impact was so much that you were indispensible to him, and that he could hardly stand on his own feet after you left for New Guinea

U   Surely you know perfectly well, that this is nonsense. We left Osogbo in December 1966. My working association with Duro had lasted five years. But as you know, he went on producing new plays and performing round the world for another decade. He survived the years of the civil war when touring was difficult. He performed in Switzerland, in Yugoslavia, in France, Iran and Brazil. He made two tours of the United States. What more do you want a man to do, to prove that he can stand on his own feet?

Most of what was written about the relationship between Duro and myself was pure speculation. The authors never consulted either him or me. In fact with all the stuff that has been written about this, only one person ever came to interview me, and that was an Afro American who wrote a thesis on Duro for some American university. I never saw what he wrote though. About our relationship, there appeared to be two opinions—both equally absurd. Those who wanted to denigrate Duro (because they were partisans of Ogunde) claimed that Duro was no real artist at all because all his plays had been concocted by a white man.

Those who tried, as Yomi Ogunbiyi did, to rehabilitate Duro, then went on to say that I had nothing to do with it whatsoever.

The relationship between Duro and me is difficult to describe, like all human relationships. We were friends long before I knew he could compose music and long before he ever attempted to write a play. After he returned from the North in 1958 and opened the Popular Bar in Osogbo, we saw each other almost daily. We drank beer together, we talked, we argued. We went to the Osun festival together or we shared the ram with a Muslim friend during the *Ileya* festival. The most important thing I did for him was to stand by him during his confrontation with the Anglican Church. The church fathers had created a tremendous row because Duro had brought "pagan" drums into the church during his Easter Cantata in 1961. It was hard for him because his father was a catechist, and I think he never forgave Duro.

I opened a new circuit for Duro by taking him to Segun Olusola of WNTV and by arranging a performance of his Christmas Cantata at Mbari Ibadan. The Mbari Club in Ibadan inspired him and he was determined to have something like that in Osogbo too. It was not easy to raise money for this, but we managed to create Mbari Mbayo on a grant of £200. Of course I discussed his plays with him, just as he discussed other things with me—politics or family matters. It seems absurd but at that stage, I knew more about Yoruba history and religion than Duro did. But then he had been through an Anglican Mission school while I had had the benefit of the friendship of Timi Laoye of Ede who took great pains to open my eyes to the culture he loved so much. From him I first learned about the wisdom, the humor, the energy and above all, the tolerance of Yoruba culture. It is this tolerance, this openness of Yoruba culture that explains in the end my whole existence in Yorubaland. They made me part of everything. It took no time at all for me to start feeling much more at home with the Sango worshippers of Ede or Osogbo than with most of my colleagues at the university. I was no stranger in Osogbo or Ede or Ilobu. Let me tell you a little anecdote. In 1960 I took Langston Hughes, the Afro American poet around Osogbo, and everywhere we went the children shouted: "Oyinbo!" But they were referring to Hughes, and not to me! By then I was Sangodare Akanji to them.

To describe the relationship between Duro and me is the subject matter of a book I have just written. It's a book I wrote to pay homage to his genius. I think you will have to wait for it. Hopefully it will appear in Spring 1994. But one thing I might say is this. Remember what I said about teaching creative writing? There has to be this empathy, this wavelength between the teacher and the student. With Duro I had this wavelength as never before. And we were both students and teachers of each other. You might say we stimulated each other to the extent that I, who had never thought of myself as a playwright, began to write plays for his theatre.

O: What kind of plays? Obotunde Ijimere's plays?

U: Well, it started when Duro had to do a monthly TV play (at some stage even a weekly one) to keep alive. It is almost impossible for anybody to be that productive without wearing himself out. So I helped him out with ideas and sometimes sketched out a suggestion. These were bread-and-butter-plays, mind you, without any great artistic pretensions. One idea that came to me was to adapt an 18th century German play by Lessing about the competition of the three "great" religions, Christianity, Islam and Judaism. It was set in Jerusalem of the 13th century and it preached a spirit of tolerance and mutual respect. It was easy to adapt into an Osogbo setting. The competitors were Christianity, Islam and Osun worship, and the play pleaded for the recognition of Yoruba religion as a philosophy of life of equal value.

The Ijimere plays arose out of a translation exercise. Duro had never really written his plays down. The songs were memorized by the actors and the dialogue was improvised. But when a German TV team filmed a complete version of *Oba Koso* for ZDF, Second German Television, we had to produce a complete German text for the subtitles. It was only then that Duro made a complete written version of the play, and we sat down and produced an English version which was later turned into German. We enjoyed ourselves so much doing this that we went on to translate *Oba Moro* and *Oba Waja* as well. These three English versions were published by Mbari Publications. It was immediately after that that I wrote the first three Ijimere plays, *The Imprisonment of Obatala*, *Everyman* and *Woyengi*. Working with Duro had produced a certain mood. I enjoyed this game with language and I just carried on. *Everyman* and *Woyengi* were written very specifically for the theatre. I even had specific actors in my mind. *The Imprisonment of Obatala* was different. Here I got just carried away by language...

Now you want to know why I chose a pseudonym and why I chose such a crazy one. Ijimere really was a pseudonym, unlike Sangodare or

Omidiji. I chose a pseudonym because I felt that though I might have written some plays, this didn't turn me into a professional playwright. I didn't believe that I had any major contribution to make in this field. It is difficult to remember your feelings after so many years, but it is a little bit like this: You write some plays in a kind of daze; you realize it is working with Duro that has put you into that mood; you look at these manuscripts and you think: Have I really done this? So you invent some fictitious character. It's a joke you share with those to whom you offer the plays. It's also like a masquerade. Everybody knows there is a man underneath the cloth and the mask, but we also know that the man gets transformed into something else in the interim. Now it was not much of a secret at the time because Duro knew and so did the whole company in Osogbo. Wole knew, and so did all my friends at Ibadan.

O: You said Wole Soyinka knew. But Oyekan Owomoyela published a book in America and in this particular essay he said Soyinka gave *The Imprisonment of Obatala* the kind of perception which shows that it was a true self-apprehension of the Yoruba world view, because the writer was Yoruba.

U: Is Mr. Owomoyela trying to say that only a Yoruba can comprehend the Yoruba world view? And does he really think Wole is that narrow minded? Wole compared my play with the Brazilian play *Oxala* which deals with the same myth. But the myth and its interpretation had changed in the diaspora, acquiring new and different meanings. Whereas my own version was based on what I had learned in the very heart of Yorubaland. So quite naturally it was closer to the way Wole himself perceived it. The Yoruba world view is very flexible. After all nothing is written. There are no rigid commandments as in the Bible. The gods have to be re-interpreted all the time through their priests, and they have to be brought to life through the worshippers when they go into trance. So the image of the god changes, to the extent that the cult itself may split. This is particularly prominent in the Obatala cult, where you have Ogiyan, Ajagemo, Orisanla and so many variants of the basic concept. So my version, although quite a personal one, is legitimate. The Brazilian one is also legitimate. Wole Soyinka's Ogun is something quite different from the Ogun I have encountered in Ire Ekiti, but Yoruba religion is not dogmatic. That's its greatness. It is this flexibility also which made it possible for Susanne Wenger to play the role she did. She could not have done that in many other cultures. But I think we are deviating from the theme.

O: But why the choice of Obotunde Ijimere with all its bizarre connotations?

U: Well Ijimere is my favorite monkey. I knew these creatures well. They are dignified and wise. In Yoruba tradition they are sometimes referred to as *Babalawo*. I like the way they look you boldly in the face. The idea of Obotunde Ijimere is not as strange as you think. There are many such stories linked to *Egungun* and *Oro*. But I don't want to drift off into mythology again. The name was a joke. It was bandied around casually between Duro and me and some other friends, and then suddenly it stuck. It was also a way of signaling immediately that this was a pseudonym.

O: We will have to talk about Iwalewa-Haus because without this the story would not be complete. I know that it's attached to the University of Bayreuth. I know that it's a kind of multipurpose institute. But it also represents a kind of continuity for you, doesn't it?

U: That is correct. I was not at all interested in a job in Bayreuth. I had no desire to live in Europe again. I had been away for too long and I felt that if I couldn't live in Nigeria, Australia was far freer, far more relaxed than Europe. But this job, when the concept finally evolved after lengthy correspondences with the Vice Chancellor, was very tempting. I rejected the initial proposal of a museum outright. That's not my kind of job. It's too dead. But when they agreed that Iwalewa-Haus would not be just a museum of contemporary art from Africa and other non-Western countries, but that it would also be an art gallery with constantly changing exhibitions, that we could have artists-in-residence, and make African food, then I felt I had to take the job because here was an opportunity to combine all my past experiences from Nigeria, India, Papua New Guinea and Australia into one organic whole.

I saw lots of possibilities; the possibilities of providing new opportunities for my artist and musician friends from all those countries. People like Obiora Udechukwu, Muraina Oyelami, Middle Art, Rufus Ogundele from Nigeria or Kauage from Papua New Guinea—to mention a few could work here in peace—away from home pressures and everyday harassments. They could exhibit here, and mostly we had the opportunity to arrange further shows for them in other cities. So Iwalewa-Haus could open up new horizons for them in Europe while their prolonged presence in Bayreuth would give us the opportunity to work on their biographies or to have discussions with them on their aesthetic concepts.

Artists in residence would have the opportunity to meet German artists here, but they also have the opportunity to meet each other. Obiora Ude-chukwu for example first met Muraina Oyelami in Iwalewa-Haus! From a certain point of view I find our work in music even more important because an artist works in isolation. He can show his completed work to others and discuss it with them. But while he is creating he must lock himself in. On the other hand music is also a social art form. It's a joint effort of several people. Therefore it allows for all kinds of possibilities for intercultural experimentation. When I was working with Duro we brought the Agbor dancers to participate in the original performance of *Moremi*. So we had *dundun* and *bata* drummers as well as Igbo slit gongs and calabash horns. In the final scene Duro managed to combine all these instruments into one spectacular orchestral sound. I was hoping then, that this successful experiment would lead to a whole new development. Imagine the kind of orchestra a composer could create if he combined instruments from all over Nigeria—the trumpets of the North with the xylophones of the Plateau, the slit gongs of the East, the talking drums of the West and so on. But it never happened. Soon after the performance of *Moremi* the civil war came and made such interaction impossible, and later on no one seemed very interested. In Bayreuth I was able to pick up this idea again. Here we could bring together African or Indian musicians with great Jazz performers. More important still we could bring together musicians from say Africa, India and Indonesia to work together and create an entirely new music. I think I can say without exaggeration that in what is sometimes grandiloquently called "World Music" we at Iwalewa-Haus have played a leading part. We are a very small institution. I have only got one colleague, a half time secretary and a tiny vote. There are other institutions in this country with sufficient funds to fly in a xylophone orchestra of 18 Chopin musicians or the Kathakali Theatre with a cast of forty from Kerala. We could neither compete with that nor is it our priority. We are neither an ethnographic institute trying to show people the "authentic" cultures of other continents nor are we a concert agency. This is a place that likes to stimulate creativity. We are a new kind of Mbari, and I believe very strongly, like the Owerri Igbo who build the Mbari mud monuments, that without creativity a community is doomed. And there is another big lesson we learn from the builders of those Mbari houses in Igboland, It's the process of creation that is important, not the finished object... It is not the function of the artist to create museum pieces that last a thousand years. It is his function to constantly renew the creative process, to rethink the culture—to adapt, to modify, to transform. And so in this ever changing world African cultures must also transform themselves constantly by interacting with the other cultures of this world. This interaction takes place right here at Iwalewa-Haus, and we make such encounters possible. That is our major contribution. Groups like Okuta Percussion and Bassama were created here. It is also here that we created the concept of Karnatic Bach, and we got a jazz giant like Bill Cobham to play with an Alarinjo Masquerade from Erin-Osun!

O: I see. You feel we can't keep cultures separated and isolated.

U: How could we? Our politics and our economics are totally intertwined. Nobody can pretend to be independent. Shouldn't we then also explore the positive side of this situation? After all it depends on us how we handle this. If we remain passive, we shall become a global coca cola culture. But if we become aware and active, this meeting and confrontation and overlapping of cultures can lead to a tremendous enrichment. And there is also a very political element in what we do at Iwalewa-Haus. We are living here in a country—and in a continent—that sees a very strong resurgence of fascism and racism. Europeans feel more and more threatened by foreigners. Of course there have been speeches and marches and demonstrations against this hostility to foreigners. But when you stage concerts with a German, an Indian and an African musician playing harmoniously together; and when people see that the music they perform is greater than the sum of the individual parts that have gone into it, then you have made a very important point in the minds of people without having used any political rhetoric at all.

O: This is important—a syncretic development of the world.

U: Another thing we try to do is to break down peoples' compartmentalized thinking. In Germany people distinguish between E-Musik and U-Musik. E-Musik means *ernste Musik*, serious music, by which they mean "classical" European music. U-Musik is *Unterhaltungsmusik*, entertainment music. Radio and TV programs and concert programs and performance venues are all classified according to these categories. In practice this means that even the most complex African or Indian music is usually relegated to a Jazz club or even to a rock cellar.

I make a point of putting on an African or Indian concert in the Bayreuth Opera house once a year, if I can afford it. I need a lot of sponsorship to do this because the Opera House is tremendously expensive and it only seats 500 people. But it is the most beautiful theatre in Europe. Built in 1748, it is a very prestigious venue. And when someone goes there to listen to a Yoruba *dundun* orchestra he will realize that this is classical music in its own right and that you have to concentrate on it as much as you do on a Beethoven string quartet. Our first concert of this type in 1984 caused a scandal. It was considered a kind of sacrilege. We called it "Classical African and Indian Drum Music" and it featured, amongst others, Muraina Oyelami, Lamidi Ayankunle, Tunji Beier, T.A.S. Mani, Shashi Kumar and Ramamani. But today people have accepted these concerts as a normal annual event.

O: I gather that Iwalewa-Haus has had a great deal of success in Germany and beyond, and that you get a great deal of support from the City of Bayreuth itself. But what is your relationship to the University? How do you relate to the faculties and the research programs?

U: I have always existed on the fringe of universities. But I have come to realize that by and large universities are happy to have one department or institute that can do things that the university itself finds hard to do. At Ibadan the Extra-Mural Department played such a role. The University itself was a colonial ivory tower, but Robert Gardner's Extra-Mural Department stood in the midst of life! We were part of the culture and the politics of the country. Some people within the university resented this, but there were always those who were glad of having that extra dimension. Similarly the Institute of African Studies at the University of Ife could fulfill all kinds of cultural functions. We staged arts festivals, we ran a professional theatre company, we created a pottery museum, we ran a kind of Mbari club, Ori-Olokun, and of course, there we had a Vice Chancellor who gave us tremendous support, Dr. Oluwasanmi.

In Bayreuth we are in a similar position. Iwalewa-Haus is on the fringe of the University. But the University, by and large, is aware of the benefits it derives from the house. Iwalewa forms a link between the University and the town; it provides a stimulating setting for seminars and conferences. It establishes an international network for the University and it does all these wonderful things that a university cannot normally do—staging concerts, organizing exhibitions and so on. But while the university welcomes these activities it sometimes finds them difficult to handle, administratively. Also there are always those who think that what we are doing is not respectable or "academic", but I have lived with that kind of thing all my life. Those who opposed my early efforts on behalf of African literature in the University of Ibadan most strongly were those who later made their career as "experts" on African literature. Similarly, when Iwalewa-Haus opened in 1981 nobody in this country took contemporary African art seriously. Now museums and galleries are falling over backwards to promote African artists. The most prestigious German art magazine, *Kunst Forum*, published a special issue on contemporary African art called *Afrika-Iwalewa*.

O: This must be rather gratifying for you.

U: In a way it is. On the other hand, maybe it's time for me to leave and do something else.

O: What will you do when you leave Bayreuth?

U: I haven't got a clue. But if I get a chance, I'll sit down in a Yoruba village and write.

O: Just one more question. I find that both your first wife and your present wife and your children are all artists. Is this fortuitous or by design?

U: Nobody "designs" his life like that. You certainly can't design what your children may become. As for me, there is a cultural element here. I grew up with art. My father was a musician. He was a medical doctor, but like many physicians in Berlin in the twenties and thirties, he was also a musician, a highly gifted one at that. Chamber music was performed in our house once or twice a week, and I met many artists and musicians in our home So it became a normal condition of existence for me. Susanne Wenger was an established artist when she came to Nigeria. She was about thirty five years old at that time. The way in which Yoruba affected her life is another very big story, and it has been told many times. Georgina came to Nigeria when she was twenty one. She was already painting pictures, but she never referred to herself as an artist in those days. She hated the self-conscious association which the term carried in England. Like myself her life was formed by Yoruba; we both became what we are through the Yoruba experience because we laid ourselves open to it. Her contribution to the cultural development was more important than mine, but it has never been fully recognized either because she has never held big posts in academic institutions or because she does not write about what she does. Many young artists owe their career and their livelihood to her, and the process is still going on. For the last few years she has held an annual workshop at the Nike Centre with stunning success. Georgina is a very powerful artist in her own right, but she has always devoted more time to teaching and promoting others than to furthering her own career.

My older son, Tokunbo, lives in Sydney and he is an electronic engineer though with particular interest in sound recording. His personality was strongly influenced by his early years in Papua New Guinea. My younger son, Tunji, is a musician. I knew he was going to be a musician when he was 18 months old, and he saw the great *dundun* player, Ayansola, perform in our house in Ife. In a culture of musicians Ayansola towered like a giant above the rest. I could see then that the child would never forget this experience. But as we left Ife when he was only four years old, he had to wait until he was ten before his wish to learn Yoruba drumming would be fulfilled. Muraina Oyelami came to Sydney and taught him the *gudugudu*. After two weeks the two performed in public at the Festival of Sydney. When Muraina returned to Osogbo, Tunji followed him and stayed there for three months for further training. We had no hesitation to let him go by himself. Among his other teachers were Lamidi Ayankunle and Ademola Onibonokuta. By the time he was twelve he performed with the Oyelami Performing Group at the Singapore arts festival. Later he studied South Indian percussion in Bangalore. Since then he has formed several intercultural groups. The most established and successful among them is Okuta Percussion in which Rabiu Ayandokun from Erin-Osun, Ron Reeves from Australia and Tunji Beier created an entirely new music out of Yoruba, South Indian and Indonesian percussion. Here we have the kind of cross cultural interaction that I have always dreamed of, and in the success of Tunji I see a kind of fulfillment of my own life's work.

When people are trying to assess my "role" in Nigeria, they are forgetting that I did not go to "study" a culture. I was neither a historian nor an anthropologist. I just became part of it all because I responded to what I saw and to what I met, and because people treated me like another human being, not like a European or a colonialist or a scholar.

You said you wanted me to assess my "contribution" to African culture and particularly to Yoruba culture. I must have made some impact simply because I was there, because I was enthusiastic about their culture, and because I could see certain aspects of their life style with completely fresh eyes while they were simply taking it for granted. But let me tell you one thing. I took far more from Yoruba culture than I put back into it. What I learned from priests and kings and artists and friends about life and its meaning and ultimately also about myself—my limitations and my talents—was enormous. Whatever I have become in life, I owe to Africa, to Yoruba, to a myriad of people. People like Timi Laoye, Duro Ladipo, the Iya Sango in Ilobu—to name a few—had a lot to do with it.

Epilogue

ULLI RETURNED TO OBATALA, THE YORUBA
GOD OF CREATION ON 3rd APRIL 2011.

Memorial Card by Georgina Beier

The beautiful coffin in this card was designed and painted by Georgina Beier as a gift to Ulli.
—*Remi Omodele*

Index

100412-150-2-60W